The United States and the Regional Organization of Asia
and the Pacific, 1965–1985

Ideas and Action Series, No. 6

W. W. Rostow

The United States and the Regional Organization of Asia and the Pacific, 1965–1985

 University of Texas Press, Austin

First edition, 1986

Requests for permission to reproduce material from this work
should be sent to:
Permissions
University of Texas Press
Box 7819
Austin, Texas 78713

Library of Congress Cataloging in Publication Data

Rostow, W. W. (Walt Whitman), 1916–
   The United States and the regional organization of Asia and the
   Pacific, 1965–1985.
   (Ideas and action series; no. 6)
   Includes index.
   1. Asia—Economic integration.   2. Pacific area—Economic
integration.   3. Asia, Southeastern—Economic integration.
4. United States—Foreign relations—Asia.   5. Asia—Foreign
relations—United States.   6. Regionalism (International organization)   I. Title.   II. Series: Rostow, W. W. (Walt Whitman),
1916–   . Ideas and action series; no. 6.
HC412.R68   1986   337.1'5   85-9115
ISBN 0-292-78512-7

In memory of
Lyndon Baines Johnson

who shared a vision of the future with a pioneering
generation of statesmen in Asia and the Pacific

Contents

Tables

Preface

This is the sixth and final case study I plan to write in the Ideas and Action Series, although I hope others may decide to explore further this large theme.

Like its predecessors, the present volume starts with a decision; in this case, Lyndon Johnson's, in his Johns Hopkins speech of April 7, 1965, to throw his weight behind an already nascent Asian regionalism. As we shall see, this movement was led in the mid 1960s by a remarkable generation of Asian statesmen, among them Adam Malik of Indonesia, Thanat Khoman of Thailand, and Tunku Abdul Rahman of Malaysia. Strongly supportive from the wings were others like Tekeo Miki in Japan, Harold Holt, and a series of other Australian and New Zealand leaders who have brought their countrymen to the conclusion that their long-run destiny lies with the nations and peoples of Asia and the Pacific. This book is about their fears, hopes, and dreams, their successes and failures, and their interaction with forces at work in American political life as they affected the nation's performance in their region.

The book unfolds as follows: The operational setting in which Johnson's April 1965 decision was taken is outlined, and the intellectual concept it incorporated. The subsequent evolution of Asian regionalism is then traced down to the present. As becomes the telling of a still unfinished tale, the book includes a chapter that looks to the future. It reflects on how the economic organization of the Pacific Basin might begin in ways which mitigate or solve some of the problems that have thus far frustrated its initiation; and it includes some observations on the forces that might (or might not) yield in time a security organization for the Pacific Basin. The chapter also comments on the problems and prospects for generating effective subregional cooperation within South Asia, a serious if still fragile effort that acquired some substance with the agreement of the foreign ministers of South Asia of August 2, 1983. The book closes with a chapter reflecting on certain major issues posed by the analysis as a whole.

In addition to the usual solicitation of criticism from experts, I sent copies of an earlier draft to governments and nongovernmental experts in Asia and the Pacific. The role of the United States will not be irrelevant; but the organization of the region will, in the future as in the past, be determined primarily by its citizens and their governments. An American writing about Asian regionalism should, evidently, listen attentively to the views of those who live on the western side of the Pacific. And that is what I did in the course of a tour through the region undertaken with my wife in July–November 1983.

My first acknowledgment is, therefore, to the public officials along the way who took time from their urgent responsibilities to consider the line of argument developed in the earlier draft and offered comments, criticisms, and suggestions. A good many of their responses are reflected in the final draft; but they bear, of course, no responsibility for the text. They include officials in the governments of Australia, the People's Republic of China, Hong Kong, India, Indonesia, Japan, the Republic of Korea, Malaysia, New Zealand, the Philippines, Singapore, and Thailand. I am similarly indebted to the president of the Asian Development Bank in Manila and the executive secretary of the United Nations Economic and Social Commission for Asia and the Far East in Bangkok.

My perspective was further enlarged by discussions with a

great many scholars, businessmen, and other knowledgeable citizens in the forty or so cities of Asia and the Pacific we visited.

Among those in the United States and elsewhere who helped as academic colleagues or old friends, I should like to thank, in particular, William J. Beardsley, Richard E. Bissell, James L. Cochrane, John Crawford, Edward Fried, Paul F. Gardner, Ted Gittinger, L. K. Jha, Meheroo Jussawalla, Kook-Chin Kim, William Kintner, Hiroshi Kitamura, Kiyoshi Kojima, Hahn-Been Lee, Charles E. Morrison, C. V. Narasimhan, B. K. Nehru, Guy J. Pauker, Peter Polomka, Elspeth D. Rostow, Tarlow Singh, Hadi Soesastro, Sheldon W. Simon, Richard L. Sneider, Miyokei Shinohara, Thanat Khoman, Tun Tan Siew Sin, Rodney Tyers, Cyrus Vance, Kei Wakaizumi, Brian Waring, John Wong, Joseph Yager, and Chia Siowyue. The extensive and detailed critique of Mr. Morrison was particularly valuable.

I was also assisted by members of the East-West Center at Honolulu, led by Victor Li, whose hospitality and interest in our enterprise, at the very beginning of our journey, were memorable.

The staff of the Lyndon B. Johnson Library was, as always, extremely helpful and efficient in running down documentary materials; and, as in the other studies in which he served as research assistant, Dr. Ted Carpenter not only helped mobilize necessary primary and secondary source materials but was also a valued critic of drafts. Our work on this essay was supported by the National Endowment for the Humanities, whose help I wish, once again, warmly to acknowledge.

Special acknowledgments are required to those who made it possible for my wife and me to travel and, in the old phrase, to learn and to teach: the authorities of the University of Texas at Austin, who granted us a year's leave of absence; the Sloan Foundation, which helped so generously to finance the venture; the United States Educational Foundation in India, which appointed us in our individual capacities Distinguished

Visiting Fulbright Lecturers and then arranged visits to ten cities in three weeks, including meetings with a wide range of scholars and students, public servants, and leaders in the private sector; and officials of the Department of State and the United States Information Agency, in Washington and in fifteen missions in the Pacific and Asia. They helped support our enterprise, organized our schedules, got us in and out of airports, worked us hard, as they should have done, but looked after us with a kindness and consideration we shall always remember.

Finally, we thank the Rockefeller Foundation for taking us in for four weeks in November–December 1983 at the Study and Conference Center at Bellagio. There the insights generated in the Pacific and Asia were absorbed and this book completed in a setting of tranquility, beauty, and comfort, with unfailing support from the staff headed by Director Roberto Celli.

Lois Nivens, who shared during the 1960s in Washington some of the events and enterprises described, was an indispensable aide in multiple ways, including the not simple job of back-stopping a rather fast-moving two-person circus. Frances Knape typed the drafts and was otherwise helpful in this as in the other Ideas and Action ventures. The maps are the work of Molly M. Bankhead, who captured admirably the argument of the text.

I have noted in the other volumes of this series that the Ideas and Action project would not have been undertaken without the strong encouragement of my wife, Elspeth Davies Rostow, who believed I might usefully reflect on the large central question embedded in those periods of my professional life when I was diverted from strictly academic pursuits. In the case of this volume my debt to her goes further and is more specific. She shared—indeed, made possible—the trip through the Pacific and Asia. Day by day we discussed our perceptions, including those that bore on the present state and prospects for Asian regionalism. Out of those exchanges emerged the judgments which shaped this book in its final form.

W. W. Rostow

Veduta
Villa Serbelloni
Bellagio, Italy
December 1983

Maison des Sciences de l'Homme
Paris
May 1984

The University of Texas at Austin
February 1985

The United States and the Regional Organization of Asia and the Pacific, 1965–1985

1. U. S. Policy toward Asian Regionalism, 1965–1968

On the evening of April 7, 1965, in an address at Johns Hopkins University entitled "Peace without Conquest," President Lyndon Johnson threw the weight of U.S. policy strongly behind the organization of Asia on a regional basis for economic development purposes. As we shall see in Chapters 2 and 3, Johnson's initiative was by no means the beginning of Asian efforts at regional organization nor, even, the first occasion that Johnson had addressed himself to the theme. Nevertheless, the Johns Hopkins speech is a reasonable place to begin. It was an authentic benchmark both in U.S. policy and, to a degree, in the evolution of Asia.

Early April 1965 was a tense and difficult period in Washington as officials surveyed the panorama of Asia. The political and military situation in South Vietnam had been deteriorating since the beginning of the Buddhist protest against Diem in Hué on May 8, 1963. Deterioration continued after the military coup against Diem on November 1, 1963. Over the next nineteen months, there were eleven changes in government or attempted coups. The lack of unified, purposeful political leadership inevitably affected the South Vietnamese military effort. The situation moved palpably toward a definitive crisis in early 1965. Against the background of disarray in South Vietnam, four regular North Vietnamese regiments, infiltrated some months earlier, moved to cut South Vietnam in half along the line from Pleiku in the highlands to Qui Nhon on the coast. On January 27, 1965, Secretary of Defense Robert McNamara and Johnson's special assistant for national security affairs, McGeorge Bundy, addressed a joint memorandum to the president foreseeing "disastrous defeat" if present policies continued and asserting that hard choices would have to be made: essentially the choice between getting out or introducing substantial U.S. combat forces. McNamara and Bundy leaned to the latter option. By March 13, 1965, the regular bombing of North Vietnam had begun in response to the new role in the South of Hanoi's regular forces; and, starting in March, a limited number of U.S. Marine and Army airborne units were despatched to protect airfields in South Vietnam. Clearly, Johnson was moving toward the McNamara-Bundy recommendation, and further grave military decisions lay ahead.[1]

The situation inside Vietnam was framed by equally ominous prospects throughout Southeast Asia. Heartened by Hanoi's palpable progress in the takeover of South Vietnam, the People's Republic of China (PRC) was orchestrating an even larger plan for the expansion of Communist power. Two months after a visit to the PRC in November 1964, Sukarno withdrew Indonesia from the United Nations and joined a grouping that included Hanoi, Pnom-Penh, and Pyongyang as well as Beijing and Djakarta. Meanwhile, he conducted the confrontation with Malaysia aimed at both Borneo and the mainland, where Communist efforts to revive guerrilla warfare were undertaken. A substantial British and Commonwealth naval force was organized to inhibit these operations. At the Beijing New Year's Day diplomatic reception in 1965, the PRC foreign minister observed that "Thailand was next." It was palpable to every Asian leader, as well as to Johnson, that, if the United States permitted South Vietnam to be taken over, the whole of Southeast Asia would be promptly endangered. Writing in 1977, Sir Howard Beale, Australian ambassador in Washington (1958–1964), evoked in retrospect the reasons for the decision in Canberra to join the United States in introducing combat units into South Vietnam twelve years earlier:

> It is now [1977] said that there is no foreseeable threat to the security of Australia within the next fifteen years.
> . . . the scene was not at all like that when Australia gave assistance. What seemed much more likely at the time was that, had there been no intervention, South Vietnam would have collapsed and so would Laos and Cambodia (as they have now done), and the whole of Indo-China would have become communist; and, later still, Thailand, Malaysia and Singapore would also have been "liberated." There was no reason to suppose that the communists would be content to stop in Indo-China for that was not what they had proclaimed or done elsewhere. This is what Lee Kuan Yew meant when he said, "We may all go through the mincing machine."
> The most important problem for Australia was what might happen in Indonesia. . . . Sukarno was already trying to perform a precarious balancing trick between the army and the P.K.I. (Communist party of Indonesia), and it seemed likely that, surrounded by regimes under communist control or influence, and with the United States no longer near at hand, the powerful P.K.I. would have prevailed and Indonesia would have become a communist state. . . . Such a regime in Djakarta could have made Australia's life very uncomfortable, indeed, with the strong possibility that, sooner or later, upon some issue or other, we would have had either to give way or fight.
> Not all of this might have happened (although some of it has), but Australia went into Vietnam with the Americans so that it might be less likely to happen.[2]

In the late winter and spring of 1965 there were not many among the Communist as well as non-Communist leaders of the region who did not believe in the domino theory on the basis of rather vivid evidence.

Johnson confronted still another problem at that time. The regular bombing of North Vietnam begun in March 1965 had focused the minds of a good many political leaders on the possibility that the struggle in Indochina was likely to become more intense, risking the engagement of larger states. Among those anxious leaders were the chiefs of seventeen nonaligned governments who met in Belgrade in mid-March. Their declaration of March 15 called for the beginning of peace talks among interested parties "without preconditions." A positive reply from the United States was, evidently, called for, and it was given at Johns Hopkins.

Finally, and most important of all, Johnson, after some uncertainty, concluded that, as tensions heightened across the Pacific, a general statement of policy toward Vietnam and Asia was required for the American people.

The Johns Hopkins speech was, therefore, addressed to multiple audiences: the American people, the leaders in the Communist capitals and those associated with them, the nonaligned nations of the Belgrade conference, the anxious peoples of non-Communist Asia, including the South Vietnamese, and America's non-Asian allies.

What concerns us here is only one component of the speech: its passages relating to cooperative efforts in Asia for economic and social development. Here are the relevant portions of the text:

> These countries of Southeast Asia are homes for millions of impoverished people. Each day these people rise at dawn and struggle through until the night to wrestle existence from the soil. They are often wracked by disease, plagued by hunger, and death comes at the early age of 40.
>
> Stability and peace do not come easily in such a land. Neither independence nor human dignity will ever be won, though, by arms alone. It also requires the work of peace. The American people have helped generously in times past in these works. Now there must be a much more massive

effort to improve the life of man in that conflict-torn corner of our world.

The first step is for the countries of southeast Asia to associate themselves in a greatly expanded cooperative effort for development. We would hope that North Viet-Nam would take its place in the common effort just as soon as peaceful cooperation is possible.

The United Nations is already actively engaged in development in this area. As far back as 1961 I conferred with our authorities in Viet-Nam in connection with their work there. And I would hope tonight that the Secretary General of the United Nations could use the prestige of his great office, and his deep knowledge of Asia, to initiate, as soon as possible, with the countries of that area, a plan for cooperation in increased development.

For our part I will ask the Congress to join in a billion dollar American investment in this effort as soon as it is underway.

And I would hope that all other industrialized countries, including the Soviet Union, will join in this effort to replace despair with hope, and terror with progress.

The task is nothing less than to enrich the hopes and the existence of more than a hundred million people. And there is much to be done.

The vast Mekong River can provide food and water and power on a scale to dwarf even our own TVA.

The wonders of modern medicine can be spread through villages where thousands die every year from lack of care.

Schools can be established to train people in the skills that are needed to manage the process of development.

And these objectives, and more, are within the reach of a cooperative and determined effort.

I also intend to expand and speed up a program to make available our farm surpluses to assist in feeding and clothing the needy in Asia. We should not allow people to go hungry and wear rags while our own warehouses overflow with an abundance of wheat and corn, rice and cotton.

So I will very shortly name a special team of outstanding,

patriotic, distinguished Americans to inaugurate our participation in these programs. This team will be headed by Mr. Eugene Black, the very able former President of the World Bank.

In areas that are still ripped by conflict, of course development will not be easy. Peace will be necessary for final success. But we cannot and must not wait for peace to begin this job.[3]

We shall explore in Chapter 3 the origins of this strand in the Johns Hopkins speech.

The first clear operational result of Johnson's address was to alter U.S. policy toward the concept of an Asian Development Bank (ADB); although it was primarily the Mekong Valley that Johnson had in mind when the speech was delivered. Formal discussions had begun on the ADB as early as August 1963 within the secretariat and among the governments of the United Nations Economic Commission for Asia and the Far East (ECAFE).[4] The leader in this early stage was the executive secretary of ECAFE, U Nyun. The creation of the bank was initially opposed by both the U.S. government and the World Bank. The U.S. Treasury led the opposition in the executive branch. The Treasury instinctively resists expansion of foreign aid because of its budgetary implications and resists even more strongly the expansion of development assistance in multilateral forms because it dilutes the Treasury's voice in the disposition of aid resources. The World Bank regarded the creation of an ADB as a dilution of its responsibilities and authority in the field of development lending. As late as March 1965, at an ECAFE meeting in Wellington, New Zealand, the U.S. delegate took a distinctly reserved position: the United States would cooperate with such a regional bank (which Japan was already prepared to help finance); but it probably would not join. Within a month Johnson had recruited Eugene Black to lead the charge in creating the bank. Black, who had opposed the idea as president of the World Bank, threw himself into the task with verve and skill. Agreement was reached in principle on December 4, 1965; and it entered into force on August 22, 1966, with thirty Asian and non-Asian founding members, soon joined by Indonesia.

Like a good many other creative acts of post-1945 U.S. diplomacy, the switch of policy to support for the ADB was the result of crisis. The Inter-American Development Bank (IADB) was, for example, the product of a sense of crisis in U.S. relations with Latin America in 1958. The ADB emerged from the 1965 crisis in Southeast Asia and Johnson's vision of what a total policy toward the region should be. In both cases the shift in U.S. policy was a catalyst that brought to life institutions which had already generated wide regional support in principle.

In addition to spearheading the creation of ADB, Black, acting on Johnson's instructions, accelerated work already under way on the development of the Mekong Basin. A Mekong Committee, under U.N. auspices, had been set up in 1957 to begin to fulfill the grand vision of harnessing the potential power of the 2,600-mile river which winds its way from Tibet to the delta in South Vietnam. The task, if ever complete, will require several generations of large-scale investment in an environment of peace and international concert. Again, Johnson's support for Asian regionalism intensified efforts which already commanded widespread international support, notably work on the dams at Nam Ngum in Laos and Prek Thnot in Cambodia.

As the United States moved to increase its military commitment to the defense of Vietnam, there were five substantial political events in Asia:

—In June 1965 Japan and South Korea, after much controversy in the latter, normalized their relations.

—Following immediately upon normalization of relations with Japan, the Asian and Pacific Council (ASPAC), a consultative body of nine nations designed to foster economic and political harmony in the region outside the framework of military pacts, was launched at South Korean instigation.

—In Indonesia, the Communist coup, mounted against the General Staff with Sukarno's connivance on September 30, 1965, was launched and barely failed. After much bloodshed a non-Communist military government emerged prepared to rejoin the United Nations and participate in the constructive enterprises of Asia.

—In November 1965, a few weeks after the failure of the Communist coup in Indonesia, the Cultural Revolution began in the PRC, shattering the image of a nation tightly unified under Mao's leadership.

—In January 1966, peaceful relations were reestablished between India and Pakistan after the disruptive war of August–September 1965.

Johnson seized the occasion of a talk to the American Alumni Council on July 12, 1966, to take stock of these and other developments. It was his first major review of the Asian scene as a whole since his Johns Hopkins speech. It was structured around four explicit propositions: the abiding need for the United States to meet its obligations in Asia as well as Europe, as a Pacific as well as an Atlantic power; the need to frustrate aggression; the need to build political and economic strength by cooperation among the Asian nations; and the need for reconciliation among "nations that now call themselves enemies," a passage in which he addressed himself, in constructive terms, to the PRC in particular.

Here is Johnson's statement on cooperation in Asia:

> . . . the untold story of 1966 is the story of what free Asians have done for themselves, and with the help of others, while South Vietnam and her allies have been busy holding aggression at bay.
>
> Many of you can recall our faith in the future of Europe at the end of World War II when we began the Marshall Plan. We backed that faith with all the aid and compassion we could muster.
>
> Well, our faith in Asia tonight is just as great. And that faith is backed by judgment and by reason. For if we stand firm in

Vietnam against military conquest, we truly believe that the emerging order of hope and progress in Asia will continue to grow and to grow. . . .

In the last year:

—Japan and Korea have settled their longstanding disputes and established normal relations with promise for a closer cooperation;

—One country after another has achieved rates of economic growth that are far beyond the most optimistic hopes we had a few years ago;

—Indonesia and its more than 100 million people have already pulled back from the brink of communism and economic collapse;

—Our friends in India and Pakistan—600 million strong—have ended a tragic conflict and have returned to the immense work of peace;

—Japan has become a dramatic example of economic progress through political and social freedom and has begun to help others;

—Communist China's policy of aggression by proxy is failing;

—Nine Pacific nations—allies and neutrals, white and colored—came together on their own initiative to form an Asian and Pacific Council;

—New and constructive groupings for economic cooperation are under discussion in Southeast Asia;

—The billion dollar Asian Development Bank which I first mentioned in Baltimore in my televised speech a few months ago is already moving forward in Manila with the participation of more than 31 nations;

—And the development of the Lower Mekong River Basin is going forward despite the war.

Throughout free Asia you can hear the echo of progress. As one Malaysian leader said: "Whatever our ethical, cultural, or religious backgrounds, the nations and peoples of Southeast Asia must pull together in the same broad sweep of history. We must create with our own hands and minds a new perspective and a new framework. And we must do it ourselves."

11

For this is the new Asia, and this is the new spirit we see taking shape behind our defense of South Vietnam. Because we have been firm—because we have committed ourselves to the defense of one small country—other countries have taken new heart.[5]

In the midst of this cooperative ferment, encouraged and strengthened but not created by Johnson, President Park of South Korea proposed a conference of the chiefs of governments which had forces engaged in Vietnam; that is, the governments of Australia, the Republic of Korea (ROK), New Zealand, the Philippines, Thailand, the United States, and Vietnam (GVN). After much intergovernmental communication, it was agreed to hold the conference in Manila on October 24–25, 1966. Although there was a good deal of strictly Vietnam business to contract among the seven governments, Johnson decided to use the occasion to travel widely in Asia and to dramatize the larger Asian perspective which framed his policy in the region. He left Washington on October 17 and returned via Alaska on November 2, having traveled 31,500 miles.

The Manila Declaration of October 25, 1966, followed closely the headings of the Alumni Council speech:

Goals of Freedom
We, the seven nations gathered in Manila, declare our unity, our resolve, and our purpose in seeking together the goals of freedom in Viet-Nam and in the Asian and Pacific areas. They are:
1. To be free from aggression.
2. To conquer hunger, illiteracy, and disease.
3. To build a region of security, order, and progress.
4. To seek reconciliation and peace throughout Asia and the Pacific.[6]

Johnson exploited his travels to drive home at virtually every stop the theme of Asian regional cooperation, notably, in his speeches at the East-West Center in Honolulu; at a Parliamentary luncheon in Wellington, New Zealand; at a similar occasion in Canberra; at the Manila Conference; at a state dinner in Kuala Lumpur; in his joint statement after discussions with President Park in Seoul; and in the rain at Dulles Airport on the night of November 2. The emphasis was uniformly on his faith that, in the end, Asia and Asians would shape their own destiny and that the role of the United States and others willing to help was to assist in a critical transitional period, "when needed and when invited." For example, in Wellington on October 20, 1966, Johnson stated:

> The key to Asian peace in coming generations is in Asian hands.
> For it is Asia's initiative that will found the institution of progress.
> It is Asia's example that will inspire its people to build on the bedrock of social justice.
> It is Asia's dream that will determine the future for three of every five human beings on earth.
> And I know that your nation and my nation will respond to that dream and will respond willingly and will respond generously.[7]

As nearly as one can make out in retrospect, Johnson's emphasis during this trip on the future organization of Asia had little resonance in the United States. The Johns Hopkins speech had been widely reported and supported. But this was a year and a half later and the United States was now directly engaged in a difficult war. Approval for Johnson's handling of the war had dropped in the polls from its peak (57 percent) in January 1966 to 43 percent in October. A substantial part of that decline consisted of self-designated "hawks," who remained a majority in the polls until the spring of 1968. They felt Johnson was not pursuing a sufficiently decisive military strategy. In this setting press coverage of the Manila Conference concentrated on the continuing struggle in Vietnam, including especially a formula agreed to at Manila for the withdrawal of all foreign troops within six months of a North Vietnamese withdrawal from South Vietnam. The major exceptions were an article in the *U.S. News and World Report* of October 31, 1966, headed, "Asia: World's New Frontier," and a piece in *Fortune* (December 1966) entitled "New Building Blocs for Asia," which began as follows:

> It's too bad that the news reporting of the Manila Conference left the impression that it was principally concerned with cooking up a political formula for inducing Hanoi to negotiate the Vietnam war. The deepening American involvement in that war unavoidably overshadowed all other considerations at Manila, but war-waging did not dominate the agenda by any means.
>
> The principal discussions concerned the future shape of the Pacific Asian world. In a quiet way, there was a good deal of talking back and forth about economic and social development, and about how various difficulties might be overcome on a collective basis. In these matters, President Johnson and Secretary Rusk deliberately retired into the background. The Asian and Pacific statesmen did most of the talking, and it was clear that they had their own ideas about how they and their neighbors might best begin to work together on affairs of common value. This preliminary search for common ground is what made the Manila meeting a genuine turning point in the relations of East and West.[8]

Although thought in the United States about Asia continued understandably to focus on a protracted, slow-moving war, in which Americans died and were wounded every day, Asians continued to act in 1967–1968 as if they shared Singapore Prime Minister Lee Kuan Yew's judgment of the American role in Vietnam. On June 15, 1966, Lee said the United States was "buying time" for the nations of Asia and ". . . if we [in Asia] just sit down and believe people are going to buy time for ever after for us, then we deserve to perish."[9]

The most important institutional development of these two years was the emergence of the Association of Southeast Asian Nations (ASEAN) on August 8, 1967. The text of the ASEAN Declaration at Bangkok is given in Appendix A. ASEAN's origins reached back to the Association of Southeast Asia (ASA) established on July 31, 1961, by Malaya, the Philippines, and Thailand, whose impulse to move toward association had been still earlier foreshadowed in the diplomatic initiatives referred to as Maphilindo. ASA's activities were confined to economic, social, and technical fields; but its creation reflected an uneasiness about the security of the region. Specifically, there was dissatisfaction with the weakness of SEATO in the face of the Communist incursions into Laos, notably the ambivalent policies of Britain and France. This was compounded by the pursuit of a neutral Laos in U.S. negotiations with the U.S.S.R. and uncertainty about what stance the United States would ultimately take toward the gathering Communist pressure on South Vietnam. In addition, ASA responded to a shared desire of these intensely nationalistic but vulnerable states, freshly emerged from colonialism, to begin, at least, to reduce their dependence on external powers and to take more of their destiny into their own hands. Thus, the major themes of ASEAN as of 1985, including a common preoccupation with the independence of the Indochinese states, were present in ASA more than twenty years earlier.

The emergence of post-Sukarno Indonesia provided a practical basis for the creation of ASEAN. The discussions between the Indonesian foreign minister Adam Malik and the Malaysian deputy prime minister Tun Abdul Razak, which ended the confrontation and normalized relations, led directly to the notion of establishing a grouping wider than ASA. A series of meetings at the Thai seaside resort Bangraen yielded ASEAN, in which Singapore as well as Indonesia joined the original ASA members; but the settlement between Djakarta and Kuala Lumpur was a necessary prior condition.[10] Most of the work going forward in ASA was taken up by the new organization, which called for collaboration and mutual assistance in economic, cultural, technical, scientific, and social fields. The first operating tasks referred to the ASEAN Standing Committee, located in Djakarta, were: tourism, shipping, fishing, and intraregional trade. But beneath the surface were the security concerns of the region reflected in this statement of the founding declaration: "Considering that the countries of South-East Asia . . . are determined to ensure their stability and security from external interference in any form or manifestation in order to preserve their national identities in accordance with the ideals and aspirations of their peoples."

Meanwhile, the ADB opened its doors on December 19, 1966, made its first loan agreement on January 25, 1968, and added six others as well as eleven technical assistance agreements by the end of the year.

In the late 1960s another process was under way. Ideas for functional cooperation in Asia, often initially sponsored by ECAFE, began to move toward operational form or, in some cases, into operation. The major such fields were transport, communications, and education. A coordinating committee of Southeast Asia Senior Officials on Transport and Communications emerged to establish priorities among regional projects and to arrange for feasibility studies, and the ministers of education in Southeast Asia formed a council (SEAMEC) to economize resources and elevate the quality of education through the creation of regional institutions. Among the latter were the Regional English Language Center in Singapore and the Asian Institute of Technology in Bangkok.

As these ventures went forward, primarily on their own momentum, Johnson made sure that the U.S. share in the ADB was supported by the Congress and that U.S. assistance was available, when requested, for other regional ventures in Asia. In his State of the Union Message of January 10, 1967, he said:

> This forward movement is rooted in the ambitions and the interests of Asian nations themselves. It was precisely this movement that we hoped to accelerate when I spoke at

Johns Hopkins in Baltimore in April 1965, and I pledged "a much more massive effort to improve the life of man" in that part of the world, in the hope that we could take some of the funds that we were spending on bullets and bombs and spend it on schools and production.

Twenty months later our efforts have produced a new reality: The doors of the billion dollar Asian Development Bank that I recommended to the Congress, and you endorsed almost unanimously, I am proud to tell you are already open. Asians are engaged tonight in regional efforts in a dozen new directions. Their hopes are high. Their faith is strong. Their confidence is deep.[11]

And a year later, on the same occasion: "In Asia, the nations from Korea and Japan to Indonesia and Singapore worked behind America's shield to strengthen their economies and to broaden their political cooperation."[12] And, then finally, in his last appearance before the Congress, a more terse and more general reference: "I think we must continue to support efforts in regional cooperation"; for, as we shall see in Chapter 3, Johnson's stance toward Asian regionalism was not merely the product of the acute crisis in Asia he confronted throughout his presidency, it was also part of a wider policy he pursued systematically in Latin America, Africa, and Europe, as well.[13]

So much for the essential facts about U.S. policy toward Asian regionalism in the period 1965–1968. We turn now to a deeper look at the extraordinary problems that had (and have) to be overcome for Asians to move forward in regional cooperation and at the impulses that permitted some limited progress to be made in the late 1960s.

2. Asian Regional Cooperation: "Absurd or Inevitable?"

In his book *Alternative in Southeast Asia* (1969) Eugene Black poses the question included in the title to this chapter. At first sight, the effective regional organization of Asia seems much more absurd than inevitable. After all, putting the Soviet Union aside, almost 60 percent of the population of the world lives in Asia. It contains the two largest nations in the world, China and India, and the inherent complexities of their relations with their neighbors and with each other. Geographically, we are talking about the majestic arc stretching from Afghanistan to Japan. Taken literally, the task of organizing Asia on a regional basis would be just about as elusive as that attempted by the United Nations.

Aside from Japan, Australia, New Zealand, Hong Kong, and Singapore, all the countries of Asia are in one stage or another of development short of advanced industrial status. In terms of real product per capita, the nations of developing Asia themselves vary over a range of 1 to 15: from Bangladesh at $118 (1979) to Taiwan at $1,748 (1979). Although trade among the developing countries of Asia is rising, their major economic ties have been to advanced industrial countries. For example, while trade among the ASEAN countries rose from less than $1 billion in 1967 to almost $9 billion in 1979, its proportion to total ASEAN trade fell from about 19 percent to 17 percent. Like other developing countries, those of

Asia confront difficult domestic challenges which absorb most of their political energies. Their forms of political organization constitute a spectrum from western-style democracy to military or Communist party dictatorship. They differ in racial, religious, and cultural heritage; and history has burdened some with deeply rooted antagonisms toward neighboring states.

A region with those characteristics is not, on the face of it, a logical prospect for organization on a reasonably harmonious, cooperative basis. Nevertheless, one organization exists embracing all of Asia (now excepting Taiwan): the United Nations Economic and Social Commission for Asia and the Pacific (ESCAP), initially called the Economic Commission for Asia and the Far East (ECAFE). ECAFE was created on March 28, 1947, by a resolution of the United Nations Economic and Social Council (ECOSOC) that also created the Economic Commission for Europe.[14] No doubt the impulse to set up ECAFE arose, in part, from a desire to assure that Asia was not denied a United Nations institution of the kind Europe was about to acquire. (A regional economic commission for Latin America was created as early as February 1948, an African commission in April 1958.) The problems of economic development did, of course, provide an important strand of common interest, as it did for the Latin American and African commissions. But John White notes the peculiar difficulties of ECAFE stemming from the scale as well as the political and cultural heterogeneity of the region.

> Of the regional economic commissions of the United Nations, the Economic Commission for Asia and the Far East (ECAFE) is the most disadvantageously placed in political terms, for either it removes itself from reality by trying to apply a single prescription to the whole of the region it serves, or it fragments its own identity by speaking with different voices in different places. . . .
> The divisions of Asia are different in kind from the nor-

mal subdivisions of other continents. The Latin and Nordic peoples of Europe; the peoples of East and West Africa; the Atlantic and Andean states of Latin America: each pair falls recognizably within a single cultural framework. But the division between the Indic and Sinic peoples of Asia, for a start, is a division on a continental scale.

. . . The category of Asian nations is purely a nominal one: the concept has no content.[15]

White's contrast between the schisms of Asia and those of other regions is sharper than reality justifies. But the scale, cultural diversity, and political divisions of Asia are clearly formidable.

In the face of these obstacles, ECAFE found a mission not merely in systematic collection of data and the conduct of research on regional economic problems but also as the midwife for subregional cooperative ventures. These ultimately emerged with independent institutional identities and did not attempt to include all ECAFE members. Black pays tribute to ECAFE's role, beyond its important part in the creation of the ADB:

. . . There are a vast number of commissions, committees, working groups, and so on in existence today for the purpose of promoting development cooperation in the area.

Most of these organizations can trace their origin to one of the many conferences of the U.N.'s Economic Commission for Asia and the Far East. A few names of ECAFE-sponsored activities suggest the range of subjects: The Asian Coconut Community; The Committee for Coordination of Prospecting for Mineral Resources in Asian Off-shore Areas; The Meeting of Government Experts on Trade Expansion; The Working Group of Planning Experts on Regional Harmonization of Development Plans. Although all of these activities suggest a serious purpose, obviously not all of them can be taken seriously. U.N. activities are, if anything, more susceptible to Parkinson's Law of bureaucratic proliferation than are national organizations. . . . But with all its inefficiencies, ECAFE does deserve credit for having stimulated most of what is truly useful in activities designed to promote regional development cooperation.

ECAFE is also largely responsible for the most useful studies and investigations into the possibilities of regional trade cooperation.[16]

As ESCAP, ECAFE has survived, and its splendid quarters in Bangkok are busy with meetings, staff studies, the mounting of expert groups on problems in every region of Asia. In its annual report of April 1983, the ESCAP secretariat was able to report that its seven major standing committees had mounted some 187 meetings over the previous year. There is in all this an element of Parkinson's Law, as Black observed. But undoubtedly, the fragile beginnings of South Asian subregional cooperation in the early 1980s (briefly described in Chapter 6) owes something to the ethos created and stubbornly fostered by ESCAP, as do a good many earlier subregional efforts. The cost of an organization like ESCAP is real and its benefits not easy to measure; but in a world caught up in all manner of explosive tensions and expensive arms races, it clearly pays its way.

Another venture in economic cooperation of wide scope is the Colombo Plan. It was generated at a Commonwealth ministerial meeting in Ceylon in 1950 and went into effect the following year. Like ECAFE, it responded to the one available unifying strand in Asia; that is, a common concern with economic development. Its political base, however, was quite different. It represented an important component of the conception of the British Commonwealth which emerged in the wake of independence for India, Pakistan, and the other former British imperial holdings. Operationally, it derived from a formulation by the Australian foreign minister, P. C. Spender, who had already articulated what was to become a central theme of Australian foreign policy:

Geographically Australia is next door to Asia and our destiny as a nation is irrevocably conditioned by what takes place in

Asia. This means that our future to an ever-increasing degree depends upon the political stability of our Asian neighbors; upon the economic well being of Asian peoples and upon understanding and friendly relations between Australia and Asia.[17]

Britain could, in time, withdraw substantially from east of Suez: Australia could not. Provided with reasonable security by the ANZUS Treaty (1951), it has continued steadily to play a quiet but active and generally constructive role in the regional affairs of Asia.

The Colombo Plan, as it emerged, is a curious kind of international organization. Writing in 1955, one analyst noted:

> It is not, as some observers believed when the program was first announced in the fall of 1950, comparable to the Marshall Plan. It is not a blueprint for the development of south and southeast Asia. It does not have a central organization such as the Organization for European Economic Cooperation. Finally, it was not initially backed by substantial external financial assistance granted by one nation to the area.[18]

Nevertheless, it expanded to embrace twenty-five members, including the United States, with its annual consultative meetings attended by many observers including the major international economic organizations. It has remained a North-South forum where development issues are discussed "in a constructive spirit free from acrimony and controversy."[19] It has generated technical assistance and training programs, including the Colombo Plan Staff College for Technician Training and a program for mutual technical assistance among the developing countries within its membership. Its meetings focus on special topics; for example, in 1980, the development of renewable energy resources appropriate for use in rural areas. It takes pride in the small size of the permanent staff. This low-key venture has maintained its viability for more than thirty years.

In the wake of the Korean War and, then, the Geneva Conference of 1954, dividing Vietnam into Communist and non-Communist states at the 17th Parallel, a quite different kind of cooperative organization (SEATO) was created on the basis of the Southeast Asian Treaty. The concept of such an organization was recommended by Winston Churchill to Dwight Eisenhower on January 12, 1953, shortly before the latter's inauguration as president. The Southeast Asia defense treaty was signed in Manila on September 8, 1954, and went into effect on February 9, 1955. The members of SEATO were: the United States, the United Kingdom, France, Australia, New Zealand, the Philippines, Thailand, and Pakistan; but, in a protocol, the protective mantle of SEATO was also thrown across the three non-Communist states which succeeded French colonialism in Indochina: South Vietnam, Laos, and Cambodia.

Evidently, the central concern here was for the future independence and security of the weak and fragmented states which, together, occupied this strategically sensitive region. Up to this time the United States had entered into bilateral security agreements with South Korea, Taiwan, Japan, the Philippines, Australia, and New Zealand. SEATO embraced, in effect, five states in the region with the possibility of support from six states outside, each of which, in case of aggression in the region, accepted the commitment to "act to meet the common danger in accordance with its constitutional processes."

ASPAC (see above, p. 9) arose, essentially, from a political rather than economic or military problem in Asia. As South Korea normalized its relations with Japan against a background of opposition and anxiety, the leaders in Seoul felt it important, in fact as well as in image, to demonstrate that their country was not about to be locked into a neocolonial relationship with its larger former imperial master. Positively, they wished to define South Korea as part of the Asian and Pacific community quite apart from its special security link to the United States. And there was, at the time, an answering response from other governments in the region, to which the emergence of the PRC as a nuclear-weapons power late in 1964 contributed. The result was an organization of nine nations (with Laos participating as an observer) whose broad purpose was to consult at the ministerial level and try to harmonize political and economic policy in the region. Some Australian and Japanese foreign aid flowed through ASPAC; but it lacked a lucid operational objective. It survived until 1973, when recognition of the PRC led certain members of ASPAC to withdraw because of the participation of Taiwan and the GVN in Saigon.

Putting aside the ADB, which translated a virtually universal Asian concern with economic development into a useful operational instrument, what one observes in the 1960s is a widespread impulse for the non-Communist countries of East Asia and the Western Pacific to draw together, confronting considerable difficulty in converting that impulse into strong institutions with clear agreed purposes and serious working agendas.

Three forces made Asian regional cooperation in the 1960s not absurd—but certainly not inevitable.

First, each major government had a quite specific local rationale for turning increasingly to others of the region in mutual support. Korea, for example, had lived its troubled life caught among three contending giants: Japan, Russia, and China. American strength had, from 1950, protected it against external pressures. But as South Korea looked to a future in which the American role was likely to diminish, it made sense in Seoul to help build a larger grouping in which South Korea's relations with Japan would be intimate but Japan would not be overbearing, and within which it could find a wider political base than in the past in confronting Russia and China as well as North Korea. For Japan, Asian regionalism was a way of moving out from the home islands in a nonthreatening manner through multilateral institutions which dimmed painful memories of the days of Japanese imperialism. The Japanese found regional institutions congenial for reasons similar to those of the Federal Republic of Germany after World War II. For the Philippines and Thailand, Asian regionalism was a way of finding local strength and support and diluting the image of American tutelage without wholly losing the advantages of ultimate American security guarantees. For Malaysia and Singapore—and indeed, Australia and New Zealand—Asian regionalism promised a partial substitute for the British withdrawal as well as closer political association with Japan, which was becoming rapidly the dominant trading partner of virtually all the nations of the area. For Taiwan, a member of the ADB and ASPAC, regionalism offered not only a widened base of support in its political confrontation with Beijing, but also a long-run hedge against the possibility of the PRC's entrance into the United Nations and enlarged participation in the affairs of Asia. For Indonesia, after the failure of the Communist coup in October 1965, regionalism provided a base for dealing with its somewhat sensitive, smaller neighbors in an atmosphere of mutual confidence, while exercising a degree of constructive leadership. For Australia and New Zealand, regionalism was a route for cultivating constructively and contributing to the stability of the dynamic Asia with which they would increasingly be associated.

As we shall see again when we explore the prospects for the Pacific Basin in Chapter 6, nations apply a hard-headed, self-centered test of national interest to the question of whether or not they join an international organization. And it is on the reality and continuity of that collection of national interests that an international organization must depend for viability and survival.

The second reason for the impulse for Asian regionalism in the 1960s was more general: the problem of China. Mass and geography made China the central problem of Asia, once its unity was achieved in 1949, as Germany became the central problem of Europe once it was unified in 1871. That fact did not decree relations of permanent hostility, but it did mean there was a sensitive and abiding set of problems to be solved: How should the fragmented smaller countries of the region deal with the largest nation in the world making its way haltingly but inevitably to full industrialized status? In 1965, as detailed in my *Diffusion of Power*, the question was not one for leisurely speculation, but urgent and direct: Beijing, already over the nuclear-weapons threshold, working overtly with Djakarta and Hanoi, was actively leading an explicit effort to take over Southeast Asia in a nutcracker movement, of which Hanoi's attack on South Vietnam was one arm and Sukarno's Malaysian confrontation the other. But regionalism, as it emerged in Asia in this period, was not primarily addressed to the immediate threat. The institutions being set up for the long haul in 1966 looked beyond the wars in Southeast Asia to a regional cohesion that would permit, in time, relations of dignity and balance with a mainland China which might emerge more rational and temperate than the nation caught up in the Cultural Revolution. Lyndon Johnson regularly and explicitly encouraged that patient long-run stance toward China (see below, pp. 39–44).

The third reason for the impulse of the Asian and Pacific states to come together was the feeling, sensed clearly in Asia from 1966, that the American effort in Vietnam was likely to be transient and the United States could only buy time for Asia to organize itself. This mood was reinforced by both the antiwar movement in the United States and Johnson's urging, on his 1966 tour, that Asia organize so that it could increasingly shape its own destiny.

The part of Asia which has felt most strongly and consistently the need for cohesion has, evidently, been Southeast Asia. The major reason is that the area has been the scene of chronic armed violence since the end of the Second World War. The struggle in Indochina began as early as November 1946 and has continued through many stages into the 1980s, with only a transient respite in the period 1954–1958. Guerrilla warfare began in Burma in April 1948, in Malaya in June of that year, in Indonesia and the Philippines in the autumn. Thailand experienced chronic problems of insurgency along both its Indochinese and Malayan frontiers. In addition, of course, there was the Indonesian confrontation with Malaysia and the shock of the Communist victory of 1975 in Indochina, followed by the complex struggle in Cambodia creating acute tension on the Thai border, a brief clash on the China-Vietnam frontier, and considerable anxiety throughout the region.

Chronic military conflict in Southeast Asia reflected a convergence of three distinct kinds of problems: first, the normal tension and domestic schisms of former colonies taking their first, early steps toward national unity and a sense of nationhood, in the face of regional, tribal, and racial differences within their borders; second, systematic (but sometimes conflicting) Communist efforts to exploit these vulnerabilities by support for insurrectional groups; third, as in so many other parts of the world, arbitrary colonial boundaries left a heritage of conflicting territorial claims to successor states that threatened to set the new nations at each others' throats. This was the case not only between Indonesia and Malaysia but also between Malaysia and the Philippines.

These multiple sources of insecurity were heightened by the fact that the nations of Southeast Asia were located in a region of palpable strategic interest to the major powers. (Appendix B analyzes at greater length the character of the strategic interests of the major powers in Southeast Asia and the evolution of the strategic balance since 1940.) None forgot—or was likely to forget—the thrust of Japan that had engulfed the whole region down to Singapore, Indonesia, and the Burmese frontier with the Indian subcontinent in 1941–1942. India and China, the Soviet Union and the United States all exhibited anxieties, ambitions, or both, as they contemplated Southeast Asia. India, for example, regarded the independence of Burma from control of any other major power as essential to its security. On this ground, it aided the Burmese in their effort to deal with guerrilla warfare, and viewed with concern any threat to the independence of Thailand and Malaysia. China, down to 1965, viewed the whole region as an arena for possible expansion of its authority, but subsequently observed with apprehension the rise of Soviet influence in Hanoi, the emplacement of Soviet air and naval units in Vietnam, and the construction of a major Soviet naval base in Kampuchea, at a time when Soviet forces were massively mobilized on China's inner frontiers. China's view of the United States in Southeast Asia was ambivalent: it is hard to know if the authorities in Beijing were more concerned when the United States asserted a strong position in Southeast Asia in the second half of the 1960s or when it withdrew in 1975, leaving a vacuum the Soviet Union sought to fill. On the whole, the latter circumstance was probably judged more dangerous to Chinese interests.

As for the United States, it has, since 1941, exhibited a systematic tendency to react if Southeast Asia appeared threatened with take-over by a potentially hostile major power; but its ability and will to hold a position in the region has been under question since 1966, if not earlier.

In addition to these particular geopolitical perspectives of major powers, there is the universally relevant fact that Southeast Asia surrounds a critically important sea route including the narrow Malacca straits, which separate the Indian Ocean from the South China Sea. Japan, as a great industrial nation mortally dependent on foreign trade, is particularly sensitive to the need for the straits to remain reliably open.

A third question was posed for the countries of Southeast Asia by their common commitment to accelerated economic development: to what extent could their national efforts be reinforced by intensified cooperation within the region? As always, the primary tasks of development were domestic; a great deal of their trade was with countries outside Southeast Asia, especially with Japan; and their sources of external financing were also preponderantly from outside the region, excepting the ADB. Nevertheless, there was an impulse to search for concrete areas of mutual support.

All these elements can be discerned in the coming together of ASEAN in 1966–1967 and in its subsequent evolution, which will be considered in Chapter 4.

In South Asia in the mid-1960s the scene was much less hopeful. The governments of both India and Pakistan were aware that large economic stakes depended on peace, expanding trade, and economic cooperation within the subcontinent. If they forgot, their friends in the World Bank consortia, which supported development in both countries, reminded them every day. But they simply could not generate leadership with the will and capacity to make stable peace. Only in the early 1980s can one detect the beginnings of a movement which, with luck, statesmanship, and time, might conceivably reverse the first three tragic decades of independence in South Asia (see below, pp. 130–139).

This brief survey of organizational initiatives in Asia since the Second World War suggests a few general observations. First, Asia is so vast and its nations so variegated that only ESCAP and the ADB embrace the region as a whole. Second, strong political and strategic interests are at work, tending to bring together subregional groupings in Asia. This is true, for example, for Southeast and South Asia and, as we shall see, for the Pacific Basin as a whole. The political and strategic common interests appear paramount even when the working agenda is wholly or substantially economic. Third, in no case do these conventional subregional geographic designations define precisely the countries that might fall within them. At the margin, membership in the clubs that have emerged has depended on arbitrary political decisions to invite or not invite particular states to join or on decisions by particular states to join or not to join. This is a familiar process in regional groupings. It can be observed, for example, in the expansion of the Organization of American States (OAS) to include the states of the Caribbean and the progressive extension of membership of the European Economic Community (EEC) and the Organziation for Economic Co-operation and Development (OECD). If the July 1984 tentative intergovernmental initiative toward the organization of the Pacific Basin succeeds (see below, pp.117–118), we will certainly see an example of the group which met initially in Djakarta.

In response, then, to the question posed at the head of this chapter, one can conclude that, from an Asian point of view, regional and subregional cooperation in the second half of the 1960s was neither absurd nor inevitable; that the most compelling forces making for cooperation came to rest on the countries in Southeast Asia; but that effective cooperation there—and throughout Asia—required that quite formidable forces making for separatism or even hostility be overcome.

We turn now to the question of why Lyndon Johnson threw his weight behind the difficult but not necessarily hopeless cause of regional cooperation in Asia.

3. LBJ and Regionalism: Asia and Elsewhere

It is difficult to trace out with confidence exactly how ideas take root in the mind of another individual. Indeed, it is not easy to do this for oneself. Johnson provided, however, some clues with respect to his view of Asia. Clearly, his brief 1942 trip to embattled Australia left strong and warm memories of that country and its people. As a senator he shared the political vicissitudes and crises of the Korean War. But, by his own account, the debates on Hawaiian statehood were a turning point in his perception of Asia.

Opposition to Hawaii's entrance into the Union had strong racial overtones—an opposition Johnson initially shared. Here is a passage from a speech by Johnson delivered on October 18, 1966, at the East-West Center at the University of Hawaii, which, I can attest, he dictated on Air Force One for insertion into the text:

> My forebears came from Britain, Ireland, and Germany. People in my section of the country regarded Asia as totally alien in spirit as well as nationality. East and West meant to us that Texas was west of where Sam Gilstrap lived— Oklahoma.*

*Gilstrap was an old friend of Johnson from his NYA days who moved to Oklahoma and was, in October 1966, deputy chancellor of the East-West Center in Honolulu.

We, therefore, looked away from the Pacific, away from its hopes as well as away from its great crises.

Even the wars that many of us fought here were often with leftovers of preparedness, and they did not heal our blindness.

I remember we felt we would get some planes out here after they had all they needed in Europe in the early forties.

One consequence of that blindness was that Hawaii was denied its rightful part in our Union of States for many, many years.

Frankly, for two decades I opposed its admission as a State, until at last the undeniable evidence of history, as well as the irresistible persuasiveness of Jack Burns, removed the scales from my eyes.

Then I began to work and fight for Hawaiian statehood. And I hold that to be one of the proudest achievements of my 25 years in the Congress.[20]

Later in the speech he referred to Hawaii as "a model of how men and women of different races and different cultures can come and live and work together; to respect each other in freedom and in hope." There is no doubt that John Burns had a considerable impact on Johnson. Burns was the Hawaiian delegate (without voting rights) to the Congress in the late 1950s, and later governor of the state. The period of intense and ultimately successful struggle for Hawaiian statehood (achieved in 1959) coincided with the emergence of Johnson as an effective civil-rights leader in the Senate; notably, his critical role in the passage of the 1957 legislation, the first formal civil-rights action by the Congress since the Civil War. The link in his mind between his positions on civil rights and on Asia remained throughout his life.

In May 1961 Johnson, as vice president, was plunged deeply into the Asian scene. At Kennedy's request he visited South Vietnam, Thailand, the Philippines, Taiwan, India, and Pakistan. His report to Kennedy of May 23, 1961, is reproduced as Appendix C. For our narrow purposes, the following passages are particularly relevant, foreshadowing themes Johnson would pursue as president:

> We should consider an alliance of all the free nations of the Pacific and Asia who are willing to join forces in defense of their freedom. Such an organization should:
>
> a) have a clear-cut command authority;
>
> b) also devote attention to measures and programs of social justice, housing, land reform, etc. . . .
>
> . . . the greatest danger Southeast Asia offers to nations like the United States is not the momentary threat of Communism itself, rather that danger stems from hunger, ignorance, poverty, and disease. We must—whatever strategies we evolve—keep these enemies the point of our attack, and make imaginative use of our scientific and technological capability in such enterprises. . . .
>
> What we do in Southeast Asia should be part of a rational program to meet the threat we face in the region as a whole. It should include a clear-cut pattern of specific contributions to be expected by each partner according to his ability and resources. I recommend we proceed with a clear-cut and strong program of action.

The impact of Johnson's trip was reflected in a vivid talk of June 6 to the Advertising Council. I happened to have been assigned by Kennedy to chair the session, which was an annual briefing on the policies of the incumbent administration. It was the first time I observed Johnson in action, aside from official meetings and formal social occasions. As something of a connoisseur of speeches in favor of foreign aid, I found Johnson's as effective a case as I had ever heard.[21]

During the 1950s Johnson had been a steady and reliable supporter of development assistance in Congress. But what he saw and felt in Asia in May 1961 appears to have rendered the drama of modernization more real and human to him than ever before.[22] Asia was no longer an abstraction. It was a region teeming with poor, aspiring people led by highly nationalistic, hard-pressed politicians sceptical of the United States but, for the time being, dependent, in differing degrees, on it. Moreover, with Japan leading the way in growth among advanced industrial countries, Taiwan clearly finding its feet, and the others determined to move forward, it did not require much imagination or a computer to conclude that a modernized Asia would in time emerge, embracing about 60 percent of the world's population, which the United States would have to take very seriously indeed. This insight was, for example, the basis for Johnson's personal leadership in launching in 1959 the legislation creating the East-West Center in Honolulu, seeing it through the Congress, and continuing, even as vice president, to assure adequate funding for it.

While Johnson, against this background, was sharing in the formulation of policy toward Asia during the Kennedy administration, a related but broader line of thought was developing in the Policy Planning Council of the State Department, of which I was chairman from December 1961 to the end of March 1966.

One of my first two assignments to the council was to explore the possibilities of intensified regional economic cooperation in Asia, a subject which interested me but which I had not been able to pursue in the midst of my more operational White House responsibilities of January–December 1961. (The other assignment was to formulate a plan to assure the continued viability of West Berlin, recently walled off from the East.) As detailed in *The Division of Europe: 1946*, the second volume in this series, regional cooperation and institutions had first engaged my attention in Europe in 1945–1946 when working on German-Austrian economic problems and then in Geneva (1947–1949) when a member of the secretariat of the Economic Commission for Europe (ECE). Regional cooperation seemed to be a method which not only exploited certain economic opportunities but which also might mitigate tensions and provide a stronger and more dignified stance for Europe vis-à-vis both the Soviet Union and the United States. Similar considerations argued for regionalism in the developing continents; but the road there was, evidently, bound to be longer and more difficult, a fact impressed upon those of us working in the ECE by our colleagues in ECAFE and ECLA (the Economic Commission for Latin America).

Those who worked on Asian affairs in the State Department Planning Council in early 1962 were sceptical about Asian economic cooperation but obliging. Nothing dramatic emerged in the short run, although our interest led to some useful exchanges with Australian representatives in Washington; and we were quite knowledgeable about Asian thought on regionalism and regional institutions when, in 1964, the formulation of policy in Asia rose in priority under pressure of the gathering political and military crisis in Southeast Asia.

But it was a wider review of the world scene in the period after the Cuba missile crisis that forced me to come to grips more urgently with the whole issue of regionalism in the developing regions. This protracted global assessment yielded a formal paper of the Policy Planning Council entitled "Some Reflections on National Security Policy," April 1965 (extracted in Appendix D). Its central theme had been discussed in the State Department and elsewhere in Washington for some months prior to publication, and it was widely circulated in Washington and to U.S. embassies abroad. Its introductory statement was the following:

> This paper was generated in the early months of 1965 as an attempt to take stock of our position on the world scene as it has unfolded since the Cuba missile crisis: a scene marked by some decline in the pressure being exerted from Moscow on the outside world; a heightening in various Communist efforts in subversion and guerrilla warfare; and a marked rise in assertive nationalism within both the Communist and non-Communist worlds.
>
> The principal operational theme is the possible role of re-

gionalism in the resolution of the triangular dilemma observable in many parts of the Free World; that is, the clash between simple nationalism, on the one hand, and, on the other, collective security and the requirements for collective action in the solution of welfare problems.

To the triangular dilemma abroad was added an observation about affairs at home: "Although the proportion of U.S. resources devoted to national security purposes (including foreign aid) has been declining, there is much talk of U.S. overextension on the world scene."

We thought we perceived in 1963–1965 some short-term reduction in the direct Soviet threat as a result of the outcome of the Cuba missile crisis. In consequence we also perceived a world in which peoples and governments felt more free to indulge their nationalist impulses. These were times when tensions between India and Pakistan over Kashmir and between Greece and Turkey over Cyprus were rising. There was acute tension between Ethiopia and Somalia, Algeria and Morocco. Nasser and Sukarno assumed assertive postures in their respective regions. Some of this rising nationalist sentiment assumed anti-American forms, and a few USIA buildings were attacked. Confronted with this phenomenon and less fearful after the outcome of the Berlin and Cuban missile crises of 1961–1962, public opinion in the United States tended to turn inward after some twenty years of intense involvement in foreign affairs, including two bloody wars. There was a popular feeling that if the developing nations wished to reduce their ties with the United States and go it alone, that was just fine. But, in fact, neither the security nor the economic problems confronted in the developing regions were susceptible of solution on a simple national or bilateral basis. Moreover, unrestrained nationalism could create situations dangerous to U.S. interests, as the Cyprus and Middle East crises of the 1960s demonstrated.

We concluded that regional cohesion might bring into play

local forces for moderation in the settlement of regional quarrels; for example, the role of the Organization of African Unity (OAU) in the Algeria-Morocco and Ethiopia-Somalia disputes. Regional cohesion might also render Communist political or military penetration more difficult. It would also provide mutual reinforcement in economic-development efforts. And, to the extent that regional cooperation actually occurred and produced these results, it would permit the United States to draw back in degree, assuming a secondary role in the affairs of the developing regions. In general, we concluded, regionalism offered developing nations a way of dealing with the United States and other industrial powers "on a basis of greater dignity (i.e., bargaining power) than bilateralism permitted."

In surveying the realistic possibilities for moving forward along those lines in each region, our paper was reasonably hopeful about Latin America, much less so with respect to Africa, the Middle East, and Asia. Nevertheless, we urged that the United States quietly and steadily support impulses toward regional cohesion as a long-run policy, and, in doing so, it should bear in mind that "either dramatic U.S. pressure or U.S. passivity is apt to be counter-productive."

On Asia the paper had this to say:

> With respect to Asia, no satisfactory single organizational framework exists equivalent to our elaborate Inter-American and Atlantic structures; and none is yet in sight. In a series of essentially bilateral moves, we have filled since the war the power vacuums in South Korea, Taiwan, Japan, and Indochina. Important elements of collective organization exist in SEATO, ANZUS, the Colombo Plan, and the India and Pakistan consortium arrangements. Nevertheless, we are in a position where Japan is groping to move out in a more responsible way on the Asian and world scene; there are impulses in the Philippines, Korea, Thailand, Malaya, and even Indonesia to find additional means for regional cooperation. But the possible shape of an Asian regional organization evidently awaits

the outcome of the confrontation in Southeast Asia and an answer to the question of the relative power in Asia of China and the United States. Until the relevance of U.S. military power on the Asian mainland is firmly established, in the face of Communist techniques of insurrection and guerrilla warfare, the political character of Asia and its vision of long-run U.S. relations cannot be determined. In these circumstances, we must evidently move piecemeal where we can: to settle the Japanese-Korean dispute and to handle our relations with Korea in such a way as to strengthen their sense of independence and of their participation in a community which transcends the Japan-Korea relation; to encourage Japan to formulate and share with us a responsible vision of its interests and willingness to undertake commitments in Asia, beyond our narrow bilateral agenda; to cope as best we can with the surge of nationalism in Southeast Asia and elsewhere through *ad hoc* partnership arrangements in specific fields; and to work in the Indian subcontinent in ways which damp the Kashmir dispute, avoid an Indian national nuclear capability, and accelerate the critically important economic development of those vast but impoverished countries. Nevertheless, as we come to deal with and finally to settle the struggle in Viet Nam and Laos, we should begin to explore in our own minds the kinds of more substantial and extensive regional relations that might be built up among the Asians themselves and in their relations to the U.S.

The Policy Planning Council in the State Department is usually quite a long way, bureaucratically speaking, from the White House. Kennedy, however, established a direct channel of communication which permitted me to send him any papers I wished to or to arrange an appointment to talk directly with him if I was so minded. (The Secretary of State fully supported this somewhat unorthodox arrangement. He simultaneously received copies of what I sent to the White House; and I reported to him promptly the substance of any conversations with Kennedy.)

Johnson habitually solicited ideas from a wide spectrum of

people, in and out of government, on a personal rather than bureaucratic basis. In early June 1964 Johnson for the first time asked me to set down my views for him on Southeast Asia; and he subsequently instructed me to send directly to him ideas I judged might be useful. (Jack Valenti was the usual channel, with copies sent to McGeorge Bundy as well as to Dean Rusk.) Sometimes the channel operated in reverse. On Tuesday, October 27, 1964, I was instructed to produce by Friday two ideas for use by the president. I forwarded three, of no great brilliance, on Thursday afternoon.

It was out of this kind of lively, informal, two-way communication between the Planning Council and the White House that our ideas about regionalism in general and with respect to Asia came to Johnson's attention. In a draft speech for the president on Southeast Asia of June 7, 1964, I had included this passage:

> If, at this fateful crossroads, we turn towards peace, not war, new opportunities will open for us.
> The Mekong Valley, now the scene of bloody struggle, could be turned by a great international effort into a mighty engine of peace and progress. We in the United States stand ready to help in these and other adventures of construction.

In a memorandum to Secretary Rusk of November 23, 1964, I broadened the notion beyond the Mekong.

> In the President's public exposition of his policy, I would now add something to the draft I did to accompany the June 6 memorandum to the President. I believe he should hold up a vision of an Asian community that goes beyond the Mekong passage in that draft. The vision, essentially, should hold out the hope that if the 1954 and 1962 Accords are reinstalled, these things are possible:
> a. peace;
> b. accelerated economic development;
> c. Asians taking a larger hand in their own destiny;
> d. as much peaceful coexistence between Asian Communists and non-Communists as the Communists wish.[23]

I elaborated this theme further in a memorandum to Mc-George Bundy of January 9, 1965.

But it was in March that the concept of regionalism, in general, was brought to the attention of the White House when I sent over a draft of the long Planning Council paper on regionalism. I was urged by Rusk and Bill Moyers to isolate briefly its implications for policy, which I did in a memorandum of March 29, 1965, which sought to define and articulate a Johnson Doctrine (see Appendix E). Its central theme and the key passages bearing on Asian regionalism were as follows:

> To anticipate a major conclusion, what emerges is this: It is our interest in each of the regions of the Free World to assist in the development of local arrangements which, while reducing their direct dependence on the United States, would leave the regions open to cooperative military, economic, and political arrangements with the U.S. . . . .
>
> This is the appropriate central theme of U.S. policy, transcending the distinction between developed and under-developed areas. . . .
>
> In Asia, security relations with the U.S. have been, essentially, bilateral as we sought to fill the vacuums created by the Second World War and its aftermath in Korea, Japan, Formosa, Indochina, India, and Pakistan. Regional economic organizations exist but have been weak; that is, the Colombo Plan and ECAFE. A new impulse toward economic regionalism centers around the Asian Development Bank. The Mekong development scheme is largely in abeyance due to the Laos—Viet Nam crisis. Nevertheless, there are potentialities for developing Asian regionalism in the face of the spreading desire of the Asians to take a larger hand in their fate and in the face of the common threat to Free Asia, represented by the Communist China nuclear capability. . . .
>
> . . . Here is a possible passage for a speech by the President.
>
> ". . . But there are other forces moving in this world of ours. On every continent men and women, having gathered

confidence and strength in this first postwar generation, seek to take a larger hand in their own destiny.

"They recognize that this is a highly interdependent world.

"They recognize that we all need each other.

"But they want to be less dependent on the United States and on other external powers.

"We recognize, we understand, and we support this sentiment. . . .

"This was why we supported, and we still support, a policy of European unity.

"This was why we have supported, and shall continue to support, movement toward Latin American economic unity. This is why we support the Inter-American Committee on the Alliance for Progress, in which Latin Americans have assumed a major responsibility for leadership in the Alliance.

"In other areas as well—in Africa, Asia, and the Middle East—we are the friends of those who wish to organize their affairs together; who wish to settle their own problems to the extent that they can; who wish to take the leadership in developing their own economies, in their own ways. . . .

"It is in this federalist spirit that we are prepared to play our part in constructing a new world order." [24]

Operationally, this flow of material from the Policy Planning Council forms one part of the background for the Johns Hopkins speech. I would underline that many others had a hand in contributing to its contours, content, and phrasing.[25] The speech file at the LBJ Library indicates that the following, at least, were actively engaged in the enterprise or solicited for ideas by Johnson: McGeorge Bundy, Horace Busby, Arthur (Tex) Goldschmidt, Richard Goodwin, Jack Horner, Bill Moyers, Philip Potter, and Jack Valenti.[26] A number of anonymous State Department officials also had the opportunity to contribute. Quite typical of Johnson's method of casting his net wide is the fact that two members of the press and an international civil servant are on the list. Johnson read drafts of the speech and solicited comments from a group from Americans for Democratic Action (ADA) and assorted members of the press corps.

Even more important than its role in the staff work leading to the Johns Hopkins speech, the Planning Council's doctrine converged with and systematically elaborated ideas on the future of Asia at which Johnson had already arrived quite independently, as the earlier part of this chapter demonstrates.

In holding up a large constructive vision of American purposes in Asia on April 7, 1965, in Baltimore, Johnson was responding to a deep American instinct and pattern of behavior. When confronted with the ugly reality of war or its likelihood—as Johnson was in the spring of 1965—Americans have instinctively reached out to give active expression to the large ideals in which our sense of nationhood is rooted. Thus, for example, the transcendent terms of the Declaration of Independence and the Gettysburg Address, of Wilson's Fourteen Points and the Atlantic Charter. A similar impulse underlay the balancing of the Truman Doctrine with the Marshall Plan, the confrontation with Cuba and support for Latin American economic and social development in both the late Eisenhower and Kennedy periods. And so it was with the image of Asia's future evoked by Johnson as he came to his critical decision on Southeast Asia.

The great positive purposes articulated on these occasions were, in each case, both a reflection of our operating style and a legitimate part of the struggle under way. Their evocation not only widened the basis for public support in the United States but, to the extent that they were judged credible by those engaged outside the United States, they also rallied support abroad.[27]

In any case, this was the conceptual, and operational, setting in which Johnson as president proceeded in April 1965 with the "clear-cut and strong program of action" in support of Asian regionalism which he had defined in his memorandum to Kennedy of May 1961.

In *The Vantage Point* Johnson devotes a chapter to "The

New Age of Regionalism." He begins by explaining the background to the passage in his January 12, 1966, State of the Union Message, asserting: "We will take new steps this year to help strengthen the Alliance for Progress, the unity of Europe, the Community of the Atlantic, the regional organizations of developing continents. . . ." He notes a passage from a State Department contribution to the State of the Union Message, in which the Planning Council had a hand.[28] He then explains his own perspectives:

> I believed that we had reached a turning point in our relations with the rest of the world. After twenty years of sacrifice, generosity, and often lonely responsibility, the American people felt that other nations should do more for themselves. What worried me most was that we might be tempted to pull away from the world too quickly, before solid foundations could be built to support the desire of other nations for self-reliance. I knew that there was a deep current of isolationism in our country that two world wars had not eliminated. . . .
>
> But most Americans had learned that the world *was* our business. Our security depended on collective strength and a reasonably stable world order. Millions of American jobs depended on expanding world trade. If we suddenly pulled away from the world society we had helped to create, we would find ourselves neither safe nor prosperous. It seemed to me there was a sensible middle course: to pull back, but not too far; to reduce our share of the burden, but not too fast; and to urge others to take a larger hand in their own destiny, but not more quickly than they could manage.
>
> The world was not ready for a global solution. The United Nations had proved its worth in many situations, but it did not have the peacekeeping machinery needed for universal order. The Iron Curtain had rusted through in many places, but it was still there, separating men and nations. A veto in the UN Security Council would still frustrate effective action in crucial situations.
>
> At the other end of the spectrum, individual nations could

never solve all their problems alone. This was especially true of rich nations and even of great powers. The answer was somewhere between a world community and a system based on narrow nationalism. . . . Thus the concept of regionalism in areas outside Europe emerged as one of my administration's most serious commitments in its efforts to build a stable world order.[29]

It is not difficult to understand, therefore, that when I moved on April 1, 1966, from the State Department to the post of special assistant to the president for national security affairs there was little difficulty in persuading Johnson to see how far forward we could move the process of regionalism. The opportunity arose from an instruction he delivered immediately on my arrival. Johnson said that he had made his commitment at home to the Great Society and abroad to the defense of Southeast Asia. But the world would not stand still and wait. Therefore, he wanted me, in addition to the regular duties of the post, to propose new foreign-policy initiatives to meet or anticipate problems in other parts of the world. (Rusk supported this instruction, requesting only that I inform him promptly of any new policies suggested to the president so that he would be in a position to express his views.) Thus, in addition to urging that the trip to Asia in the autumn of 1966 focus substantially on potentialities for regional cooperation (see above, pp. 37–40), I was able to contribute, along with my colleagues on the NSC staff and elsewhere in the government, to proposals for increased cohesion in both Latin America and Africa, as well as to an effort to reconcile continuity in NATO with an amelioration of relations with the East. It may be useful, briefly, to review these Johnson efforts, for they suggest more concretely the broad matrix of thought and aspiration which also informed Johnson's approach to Asia.

In Latin America, of course, regionalism was an older story than in the other developing nations. The old idea of cooperation in the western hemisphere, rooted in concepts as different as Bolivar's vision of a unified Spanish America and the Monroe Doctrine, acquired institutional expression in 1890 with the creation of the Pan-American Union. From this base the OAS emerged after the Second World War (1948), based initially on two Latin American objectives: to prevent the military intrusion of extra-hemispheric powers into the region; and to inhibit the United States in conducting the kind of interventions into the life of Latin American nations that had marked earlier years in the century. To these interests was added the hope that the United States, initially focused in the postwar years on the recovery of Western Europe, would turn its attention and resources to the economic and social development of Latin America. Thus, initially, the OAS was a focal point for relations between Latin America and the United States: American military strength and economic resources were to be sought; American impulses to intervention were to be discouraged. Despite many common strands in their complex cultural heritage, there was little initial impulse to cooperation among the Latin American nations themselves, except for the highly civilized OAS commitment to settle intraregional disputes peacefully.

As of 1961 economic life in Latin America tended still to be focused on the great coastal cities built up to mobilize exports and to receive imports from Europe and the United States rather than to support intraregional trade. Most telephonic communications between Latin American countries had to pass through the United States. The development of the interior of most Latin American nations was neglected.

As the Alliance for Progress moved forward, this situation began to change. Most of the population in Latin America lived in countries whose economies were shifting from light consumer-goods industries to metals fabrication, chemicals, light electronics, and other reasonably sophisticated industries. The high tariff barriers, small markets, and inefficiency which had marked the first stage of Latin American industrialization slowed down expansion in the newer sectors on which Latin American growth depended. It is one thing to have an inefficient textile plant; it is a quite different matter to have a white elephant steel mill or chemical fertilizer plant, where much greater amounts of capital are required. Thus, Latin American leaders began to look to a widening of regional markets as a way of inducing the competitive efficiency the new technologies required.

At the same time, they turned to the long-neglected development of the Latin American interior: to exploit natural resources and to open new areas for agricultural settlement. As they moved to develop their inner frontiers, the Latin American nations began, as it were, to run into each other. To build the Carretera Marginal along the eastern slopes of the Andes required, for example, cooperation between Peru and Bolivia, Ecuador and Colombia.

Johnson threw his weight behind the Latin American movement toward both trade and physical integration. On April 15, 1966, on a long-scheduled visit to Mexico, he rallied behind a proposal of President Illia of Argentina that the presidents of the American republics meet. A year of rather careful diplomatic and political preparation preceded the gathering of the dignitaries, with Lincoln Gordon, then assistant secretary for Latin American affairs, playing a central role.

The proposals explored with the Congress before the Punta del Este meeting of April 1967 included an American contribution of $250–500 million to a fund designed to cushion strains that might arise from movement toward a Latin American common market. A second proposition was for the United States to put into the Inter-American Bank (IAB) an additional $150 million earmarked for multinational projects which would more closely link the Latin American nations.

In the end, Congress balked at granting Johnson, before the event, the specific commitments he wanted. The funds to encourage and ease the transition to a common market still remain to be created; but the IAB was granted, in time, additional funds which have been used to expand resources allocated to multinational projects.

In fact, however, in the wake of the Punta del Este summit conference, the Latin Americans made little serious progress in overcoming the nationalist barriers to achieving the goal commonly agreed on. The most promising limited step forward, the building of an Andean common market (including Colombia, Venezuela, Ecuador, Bolivia, Peru, and Chile), foundered initially on Venezuelan unwillingness to risk its high-wage, high-cost industrial establishment in competition with neighbors technologically advanced but lacking the bounty of large oil resources. Johnson did succeed, however, in dramatizing an authentic concern for Latin American problems, the inescapable need for Latin Americans to solve among themselves the problems of economic cooperation and unity, and the transition of the United States to a reduced role in the hemisphere.

Johnson's last major act in Latin American policy was to visit the presidents of the members of the Central American Common Market in July 1968 to encourage them to go forward with their enterprise, which had accomplished far more in the 1960s than most had initially predicted, but which was beginning to confront severe difficulties as the easier gains of trade integration were accomplished and harder problems of industrial location were confronted. It was not a major diplomatic venture; but the depth and authenticity of his concern with Latin America never shone through more clearly than on his visit to a small elementary school named for him in San Salvador, and at his opening of a television facility for secondary education in a normal school at San Andrés. And it was on this valedictory trip abroad that he summarized most fully his view of regionalism in Latin America, Africa, and Asia and expressed for the first time his "hope that as the nations and peoples of the Middle East find their way to stable peace, they, too, will find dignity and hope in working together on a regional basis. . . . [The] resources available to them also offer unique possibilities." [30]

In Africa, regionalism had a somewhat different meaning than in Europe, Asia, and Latin America. Unlike the other continents, Africa did not in the 1960s confront the kind of balance-of-power problem posed by Germany and Russia in Europe, Japan and China in Asia, and the United States in the western hemisphere. There was the hope, at least, that geography might permit a postcolonial Africa to work out its destiny without the threat of major-power intrusion or efforts to achieve hegemony. To assure that result was a major political purpose of the OAU. If that purpose were achieved, the role of the United States in the evolution of postcolonial Africa might remain, as it had mainly been, subsidiary.

Johnson supported this impulse among the African states, but also perceived the possibility, even necessity, of economic regionalism and subregionalism in a continent many of whose nation-states emerged from colonial history too small for the effective exploitation of much modern technology. The American interest would be satisfied in Africa, as elsewhere, if no single power threatened to dominate the area and if the problems of modernization and racial tension could be solved in ways that avoided chaos or major violence threatening the international order.

Out of these perceptions Johnson made the only speech by an American president wholly devoted to Africa, on May 26, 1966. [31] It was the product of many prior months of prodding the bureaucracy to produce a coherent approach to African problems.

On the basis of the doctrine of regionalism stated on that occasion, Johnson instructed Ambassador Edward Korry, then assigned to Ethiopia, to recommend new proposals for the support of African economic and social development. American aid programs and those Washington could influence (for example, through the World Bank) began, in fact, to be reshaped to support regional and subregional ventures in Africa.

Like Kennedy's vision of a Grand Design for Europe and the Atlantic on July 4, 1962, and Johnson's visions of Asian and Latin American regional cohesion of 1966 and 1967, the road to African regional cooperation was obviously going to be long and erratic, full of frustrations and setbacks. In Europe and Japan economic modernization occurred against a historical background which had already yielded strong, experienced nation-states. This was not true for Latin America, nor for most of the independent states which emerged from colonialism in the twentieth century. The problem has been particularly acute in Africa. The central postcolonial problem of most African nations was, in fact, the tension between central government and more deeply rooted tribal and regional loyalties. In some cases, statehood, let alone a pervasive sense of nationhood, was fragile. Regional and subregional economic cooperation was distinctly second-order business as compared to urgent and inescapable domestic political problems. Moreover, many of the initial tasks of modernization did not require much regional or subregional cooperation; for example, elementary education, road building, improvements in agricultural productivity, basic measures of public health. African regionalism made slow progress at best; but no thoughtful African or sympathetic observer of Africa failed to perceive that, in the end, regionalism and subregionalism would have to play a large role if Africa was to maintain its freedom from foreign intrusion and produce in time modern societies which, while maintaining loyalty to their old cultures, successfully absorbed what modern science and technology could offer.

One of my earliest proposals to Johnson in April 1966 was that he generate from the bureaucracy new proposals that would increase the cohesion of NATO and the North Atlantic Community, while moving toward détente with the East.

Knowing from fresh experience as State Department planner the schisms and lacerations in the bureaucracy over NATO nuclear policy, I suggested that we clearly separate the nuclear issue from other less contentious matters. On these nonnuclear matters, I knew a number of ideas had been generated in the Policy Planning Council and elsewhere. As I said in a memo to the president of April 21, 1966: "One purpose of this NSAM [National Security Action Memorandum] is to make sure that what we all agree about in the U.S. Government is staffed out and made as effective an item in our policy as can be done. . . . [that we] set the framework for constructive work which would unite not divide the town."

A NSAM of April 22, 1966, incorporated this perspective. It was the framework within which work went forward on McNamara's nuclear-planning group, trade and monetary matters, the handling of the shift of NATO headquarters to Brussels, and the effort to balance and reconcile a strengthening of ties within the West and movement toward détente with the East. Proximately, it also gave impetus to a task force on NATO policy, headed by Dean Acheson, which had been at work for some time.

One of its papers forwarded to Johnson on June 10 had a striking heading to its first proposition: "NATO's Principal Political Function—Preparation for Settlement in Central Europe." This judgment was the product of hard-won experience.

Political consultation, as well as the common defense, had been viewed, since the aftermath of the Suez crisis of 1956, as a NATO function. It proved a difficult task. A few members of NATO had limited major interests beyond the area itself, but on these there was no consensus about policy. None was anxious to share America's global interests and responsibilities. In the post–Cuba missile crisis period, however, one area did emerge where consultation was of universal interest and a degree of concert was possible; that is, policy toward the Soviet Union and Eastern Europe. There was by 1966 an authentic agreement in the American government—and, more important, within NATO—that the central political task of NATO was to orchestrate the policy of its members in ways which would ease East-West relations and gradually prepare the way for a settlement whose ultimate shape and timing lay in a misty future.

All those strands were crystallized in an address by Johnson on October 7, 1966. It was the most complete statement of the new Atlantic agenda that had evolved during his administration. It applied to Europe the four principles which emerged as Johnson's way of articulating his foreign policy: deterrence of aggression ("Our first concern is to keep NATO strong and to keep it modern and to keep it abreast of the time in which we live"); economic and social progress (the Kennedy Round, international monetary reform, the development of science and technology as a common Atlantic resource, and accelerating the growth of the developing nations); regionalism (the continued vigorous pursuit of a united Western Europe); reconciliation (". . . one great goal of a united West is to heal the wound which now cuts East from West and brother from brother").

The art of the effort was to weave together abiding strands of Atlantic policy reaching back to 1947–1949, to impart to them some new forward thrust, and, on that basis, to reach beyond by ameliorative action toward the East. Johnson listed what had been accomplished in East-West relations in the two previous years and then announced seven additional measures of bridge-building around the theme, "Our aim is a true European reconciliation." The goals of a nonproliferation agreement and mutual U.S.-Soviet force reductions in Europe were reaffirmed.

It was not easy to strike precisely the right balance between strengthening the institutions of the West and reaching out to the East; and it was not easy to keep all the members of NATO in harness, as each European foreign office and foreign-trade ministry pressed its own Eastern interests and the United States conducted its complex dialogue with Moscow on nuclear matters.

Nevertheless, the Western leaders (aside from de Gaulle) managed to keep roughly together in these efforts to explore the possibilities and limits of détente. The operating consensus included Bonn, whose shift toward Ostpolitik carried some real disruptive possibilities as well as the haunting memory of interwar German-Soviet bilateral relations.

A symbol of this mature effort of the alliance to remain in at least loose harness in a phase of uncertain and ambiguous détente was the "Harmel exercise." The Belgian foreign minister, Pierre Harmel, suggested at the NATO meeting of December 1966 a study by the North Atlantic Treaty Council of changes in the international situation since 1949 and ways to strengthen the alliance "as a factor for durable peace." He was promptly made chairman of a group which filed its report on Future Tasks of the Alliance a year later. Despite the sobering setback of Soviet occupation of Czechoslovakia in August 1968, the NATO Council and the governments behind it did generate sustained political consultation on East-West matters in the period 1966–1968 and a rough concert of view on how patiently to work over the long pull for peaceful change.

Sixteen years after Johnson left Washington, the state of regional and subregional cohesion can nowhere be described as brilliant. It is still alive, even in Africa and Central America where it is hardest pressed. But, clearly, an assessment of whether in his time, Johnson backed what was to be a winning or losing cause requires a much longer perspective than any of us now commands.

What Johnson accomplished and failed to accomplish with respect to regional cohesion recalls a comment of Harold Macmillan. Referring to Macmillan's efforts with respect to arms-control arrangements with the U.S.S.R. and the entrance of Britain into Europe, an interviewer on *Firing Line* asked:

> Even when your disappointments were the most acute on
> specific things that were failing, did you feel that you were
> part of a historical process that was going to come to culmi-
> nation in the future? Or now do you have regrets to see
> other people reaping the benefits, perhaps, of what were
> things you contributed to very significantly?
>
> HAROLD MACMILLAN: Oh no. I think all of that is rather lead-
> ing into psychology, which isn't true of life. Life goes on. . . .
> I don't think you want to pull yourself up by the roots and
> see how you are working, just to go on with whatever is
> happening is great fun.[32]

Macmillan, with a fine sense of proportion, was acutely
conscious that the problems and forces confronted by statesmen of his day—and their time scale—dwarfed even those
who held the posts of greatest power. In one's time of responsibility, one could, at best, hope to nudge things in what one
hoped was a useful direction.

Whatever he believed was the right course for regional organization and policy, Johnson could not know whether he
was working with a historical process that would, one day,
come to a successful culmination. To return to Eugene Black's
phrase, there was certainly as much absurdity as inevitability
in the cause of regionalism he supported. Palpably, in an era of
intense nationalism, the forces making for violence and chaos
in all the developing regions were strong—in the Middle
East, for example, so strong as to make any immediate proposal for regional cohesion in the 1960s an evident absurdity.
But, without illusion, to use the narrow margin of influence
on history a president of the United States commanded to
promote regional stability and peaceful cooperation was, in
Macmillan's phrase, "fun." And Johnson's margin of influence
was narrow, indeed.

The U.S. power to shape the course of events in the world
has been in progressive decline since, say, 1948, when the
passage of Marshall Plan legislation assured the economic revival of Western Europe. The same can be said of the Soviet

Union, where a useful benchmark is Tito's successful defection from Soviet domination, also in 1948. Since that time, not only has Japan as well as Western Europe revived remarkably, but, fueled by powerful nationalisms, the countries of the developing regions have moved forward to assert themselves and, in different degree, have acquired increasing technical and economic capacity to make their interests felt in world affairs.

The superpowers have, of course, retained the two major concentrations of nuclear weapons and delivery capabilities as well as powerful conventional military establishments. But nuclear weapons have only two national roles: to deter the use of such weapons by others, directly or for the exertion of diplomatic pressure; and, under certain circumstances, to deter the use of conventional force for aggressive purposes. The conventional establishments of the United States and the U.S.S.R. have wider potential uses, but they must be deployed, for whatever purposes, in a world of increasingly assertive nationalism which must be taken into account; and they must be deployed with extreme sensitivity to the mortal danger of escalation across the nuclear threshold.

The diffusion of power away from both Washington and Moscow in the decades after the Second World War has altered the character and balance of the bilateral diplomatic relations with other nations of the two superpowers. And, in the present context, it reduced the U.S. capacity to determine the pace at which cooperative regional arrangements might move forward on the world scene. After all, the problems to be overcome in building such cohesion are specific to the several regions; and one objective of the exercise is to create arrangements which permit the nations of the regions to do more, the United States less. In such circumstances, the effective influence of the United States was bound to be dilute; and, indeed, it was.

The only appropriate time perspective to apply to the process of regional cooperation is very long indeed. One is dealing, for good or ill, with a world of sovereign nation-states. Each is primarily absorbed in its domestic political, social, and economic processes in unique cultural settings. There is not a great deal of political energy left over for foreign affairs; and cooperation must often overcome substantial domestic resistances and, occasionally, inherited, strongly felt neighborly quarrels. The underlying logic of regional cooperation is strong, that is, the inadequacy of nation-states as instruments for solving critical security and economic problems. But the triumph of that logic was by no means assured as Johnson made his dispositions in 1965–1968. He felt, simply, that it was the right course for an American president to pursue at that time.

Before plunging into the details of how the story of regionalism has unfolded since 1969 in Southeast Asia, the Pacific, and South Asia, I would offer a tentative, pragmatic generalization about the experience with regionalism since the end of the Second World War. This generalization does not rank as natural law, but the reader may find that it helps provide a certain logic and order to a tangled tale.

The generalization is this: The forces making for regional groupings have been strongest when three impulses converged. The first was to generate increased strength through greater unity in the face of a heightened security threat. The second was to create, through cohesion, a position of greater bargaining strength and dignity vis-à-vis a large, supportive ally (e.g., the United States) or a disproportionately large or strong member of the regional group itself (e.g., Germany, Japan, Brazil, Indonesia, India). The third was to exploit the narrow economic advantages of regional cooperation when these were perceived to be real and substantial. The role of these three impulses in the waxing and waning of regionalism in Europe and the western hemisphere can be traced now over considerable periods of time; and, as we shall see, similar forces have played and are playing a similar role in Asia and the Pacific.

4. Asian Regionalism, 1969-1975

Asian regionalism evolved in the period 1969–1985 in response to three processes:

—The alterations in policy toward Asia of the first Nixon administration, notably the Nixon Doctrine and the opening of U.S. relations with the PRC.

—Hanoi's 1975 take-over of Indochina, with Soviet backing, amidst the post-Watergate disarray of American political life, and the forces that take-over set in motion in Southeast Asia, including Soviet air and naval bases in Vietnam, the Vietnamese invasion of Kampuchea, and the engagement on the Sino-Vietnamese frontier in 1979.

—The remarkable maintenance of economic growth in East Asia during the 1970s in the face of the vicissitudes of the world economy experienced since the quadrupling of the oil price in 1973.

Taken together, these processes tended to impose on Asians increased danger and increased responsibility for shaping their own destiny while providing, to a degree, the increased resources and confidence to do so.

Against this background, the present chapter explores the evolution of Asian regionalism between 1969 and 1975. Chapter 5 takes the story down to early 1985.

The declared foreign-policy objective of the Nixon administration on coming to responsibility was to reduce direct U.S. burdens on the world scene in an orderly way, while fully maintaining the security of the United States and its vital interests as they had come to be defined in the years since 1945. This objective was to be accomplished by shifting some responsibilities to others while exploiting the possibility presented by the schism between the U.S.S.R. and PRC to develop stable and increasingly normal relations with both powers. If successful, the policy would provide not only "a generation of peace" but also an easing of tensions in American life—where there was a widespread sense that the United States was, somehow, overcommitted—and a reduction in the military budget, as well.

The critical initial expression of this policy was, of course, in Southeast Asia. Nixon inherited a situation of increased South Vietnamese military, economic, and political strength in the wake of the Communist failure in the Tet offensive of early 1968. He also inherited a weary and divided public opinion at home which, nevertheless, on balance sought an honorable end to the war.

As early as November 1967, General William Westmoreland had predicted that U.S. troops in Vietnam might safely be reduced within two years; and Johnson had refused Thieu's offer, in July 1968 at Honolulu, to announce the beginning of U.S. troop withdrawals in 1969. Johnson chose to leave his successor freedom of choice in this matter.

Nixon adopted a policy of Vietnamization in which all U.S. ground forces would be withdrawn as the South Vietnamese military establishment was built up and modernized, leaving, however, substantial U.S. air and naval forces in the region. This permitted an immediate reduction in the military budget, quite substantial in real terms when corrected for inflation. The proportion of national-defense expenditures to GNP dropped from 8.8 percent in 1968 to 6.5 percent in 1971.

There is a broad similarity between Eisenhower's military dispositions after the Korean War and Nixon's in 1969. Both were accompanied by a significant reduction in U.S. ground forces on the view that the U.S. allies, strengthened by additional military aid, would carry more of the burden of local defense. The major difference in the military budget revisions of the early Eisenhower and Nixon years was doctrinal. In cutting back conventional forces, Eisenhower announced a policy of increased reliance on nuclear deterrence, with its threat of "massive retaliation." Nixon justified his cutback wholly on the premise that America's allies were in a position to do more in deterring or dealing with conventional or guerrilla attack. It may be, however, that the Nixon administration also assumed that a conventional Chinese Communist attack was less likely than in the past, given the tension on the Sino-Soviet border and the Chinese forces committed to its defense. In crude terms, the American military establishment in conventional forces was geared to deal with one-and-a-half wars (Europe or Asia plus a small additional contingency), as opposed to the two-and-a-half-wars posture generated during the Kennedy administration.

In Asia, these developments in thought and policy were crystallized in the Nixon (or Guam) Doctrine whose emergence Henry Kissinger has described in considerable detail.[33] The new doctrine aimed to reduce the U.S. commitment in Asia without signaling to U.S. allies, friends, and adversaries that a total withdrawal of the United States was contemplated. In the course of an informal background talk with the press on July 25, 1969, Nixon broached the theme and, in response to questioning, said:

> I believe that the time has come when the United States, in our relations with all of our Asian friends, [should] be quite emphatic on two points: One, that we will keep our treaty commitments, for example, with Thailand under SEATO; but, two, that as far as the problems of internal security are concerned, as far as the problems of military defense, except for the threat of a major power involving nuclear weapons, that the United States is going to encourage and

has a right to expect that this problem will be increasingly handled by, and the responsibility for it taken by, the Asian nations themselves.[34]

In his memoir Kissinger notes:

> This still left open the question of what to do about aggression that came neither from a nuclear power nor from internal subversion. Nixon suggested that this might be dealt with by an Asian collective security system in five to ten years' time: "Insofar as it deals with a threat other than that posed by a nuclear power . . . this is an objective which free Asian nations, independent Asian nations, can seek and which the United States should support." He avoided a follow-up question as to what we would do in the intervening period before such a security system came into being.[35]

The doctrine was tersely crystallized in Nixon's *Foreign Policy Report* of February 18, 1970:

> —The United States will keep all its treaty commitments.
> —We shall provide a shield if a nuclear power threatens the freedom of a nation allied with us, or of a nation whose survival we consider vital to our security and the security of the region as a whole.
> —In cases involving other types of aggression we shall furnish military and economic assistance when requested and as appropriate. But we shall look to the nation directly threatened to assume the primary responsibility of providing the manpower for its defense.[36]

The Nixon Doctrine was, in effect, a generalization of uncertain application beyond his concrete decision to proceed with Vietnamization and the withdrawal of U.S. ground forces in Southeast Asia.

Meanwhile, starting on January 20, 1970, the channels gradually opened up which led to the process of normalization between the PRC and the U.S. government formally begun with Nixon's trip to China in February 1972.[37] The trend of events, however, was evident from, say, the Chinese invitation to an American ping-pong team to visit Peking in April 1971.

These developments stirred, of course, much reflection, discussion, and considerable anxiety in Asia. Asian leaders and citizens asked questions like these: How, precisely, did the Nixon Doctrine alter existing U.S. commitments in the region? Would the normalization of American relations with the PRC open the way for a more expansionist Chinese policy in Southeast Asia? Would it dilute U.S. ties to Japan, whose government had, quite unnecessarily, not been informed in advance of Nixon's visit to China? Would the new American-Chinese relationship lead to a takeover of Taiwan by the PRC, with all its consequences for the security structure in the Pacific?

Excepting the expulsion of Taiwan from the United Nations in October 1971, there were no substantial redispositions in Asia as the reorientation of American policy proceeded. In effect, the capacity of the United States to see through its commitments to the independence of South Vietnam was taken as the touchstone of the Nixon Doctrine.

On March 30, 1972, the North Vietnamese, their forces modernized with Soviet tanks and artillery, launched a massive invasion of South Vietnam. They had patiently waited since 1969 until no U.S. units were on the ground. The resulting battle was a test of Vietnamization and Nixon's decision of 1969 to withdraw U.S. ground forces. It was, essentially, an engagement of North Vietnamese and South Vietnamese conventional forces without a fixed front. By 1972 the Viet Cong, decimated in the 1968 Tet offensive, and the subsequent expansion of Saigon's control over the countryside, had ceased to be a significant factor in the military equation. Supported by U.S. air and naval units, the South Vietnamese held at critical points and Hanoi's offensive failed. On October 8, 1972, Hanoi's negotiator in Paris, in effect, met the terms for a settlement which had been systematically rejected since 1968: an end to the fighting and the infiltration of military forces from the North into South Vietnam, leaving the existing government in Saigon in place, and a free election to settle its future. The explicit or implicit understanding in Hanoi and Saigon was that residual U.S. forces would be withdrawn; U.S. aid to the South Vietnamese maintained at high levels; and U.S. air and naval power would be invoked if the agreement was grossly violated by Hanoi. There were difficulties in Saigon with the agreement, which left some North Vietnamese forces in border areas; and Hanoi, repeating a tactic used four years earlier, pulled away from its October agreement to test the sturdiness of the U.S. position. It was brought back to its October agreement by the B-52 bombing of Hanoi and Haiphong in December. At the time of Nixon's second inaugural, it was clear the agreement, announced on January 23, would be made.

Two different but quite consistent appraisals of the January 1973 agreement are worth quotation. First, Lee Kuan Yew, speaking at the National Press Club in Washington on April 6, 1973, on the subject "Super Power Politics and Southeast Asia in the Later '70s":

> . . . few predicted the way in which American involvement in Vietnam would end, in an orderly manner, with the South Vietnamese government of President Thieu still in charge of the principal cities and towns, and most of the populated areas of South Vietnam.
>
> There was no Vietcong victory. Hanoi will be quiet for a while, unless massive military and economic aid is again pumped in by the Soviet Union and China.
>
> However history may judge the American intervention in Vietnam, one side benefit of the conflict, and the way it has ended, is that it has broken the hypnotic spell on the other Southeast Asians, that communism is irresistible, that it is the wave of history. Communist victory was demonstrated not to

be inevitable, though at a cost no one ever contemplated. . . .

At the risk of being proved wrong, there are three scenarios I envisage as a result of the Paris agreement.

First, . . . the provisions are in the main honoured. . . . In this case, the contest will become primarily political. The South Vietnamese government stands a very fair chance in such a contest.

Second, an all-out offensive by both the North Vietnamese and the Vietcong as soon as they believe they are strong enough to overwhelm the armed forces of the South Vietnamese government. However, the North Vietnamese must weigh the possibility of an American reaction to a flagrant breach of the Paris agreement.

Third, the North Vietnamese, to avoid unnecessary risks, ostensibly honour the Paris agreement. However, they will leave it to the Vietcong, with North Vietnamese infiltrators and fresh military supplies to augment their strength, to make a bid for power in the South. . . .

But, if the worst does happen, and the Vietcong, with the help of the North Vietnamese, do gain control over the South in the middle 1970's, it does not necessarily follow that the rest of Southeast Asia will go communist. The morale of the other peoples of Southeast Asia is now very different from what it was after Dien Bien Phu in 1954. The Thais are now more prepared psychologically to face up to such a situation. . . . A crucial factor is whether they believe they can depend on American military and economic aid, as spelt out under the Guam doctrine."

For reasons no one could predict in the spring of 1973, before Watergate had progressively undermined Nixon's authority and legitimacy, it was Lee's second scenario that came to pass in the mid-1970s.

Henry Kissinger, in his memoir, comments after the event:

I believed then, and I believe now, that the agreement could have worked. It reflected a true equilibrium of forces on the ground. If the equilibrium were maintained, the agreement could have been maintained. We believed that

Saigon was strong enough to deal with guerrilla war and low-level violations. The implicit threat of our retaliation would be likely to deter massive violations. We hoped that with the program of assistance for all of Indochina, including North Vietnam, promised by two Presidents of both parties, we might possibly even turn Hanoi's attention (and manpower) to tasks of construction if the new realities took hold for a sufficient period of time. Hanoi was indeed instructing its cadres in the South to prepare for a long period of *political* competition. We would use our new relationships with Moscow and Peking to foster restraint.

We had no illusions about Hanoi's long-term goals. Nor did we go through the agony of four years of war and searing negotiations simply to achieve a "decent interval" for our withdrawal. We were determined to do our utmost to enable Saigon to grow in security and prosperity so that it could prevail in any political struggle. We sought not an interval before collapse, but lasting peace with honor. But for the collapse of executive authority as a result of Watergate, I believe we would have succeeded.[38]

As both Lee Kuan Yew and Kissinger make clear, those who were hopeful in January 1973 were quite conscious that the viability of the peace agreement with Hanoi hinged not only on the continuity of a high level of military assistance to the South Vietnamese but also on the credibility of the U.S. willingness to evoke air and naval power should the agreement, in Lee's phrase, be "flagrantly" violated.

"The collapse of executive authority as a result of Watergate," consolidated by the complexion and mood of the Congress elected in November 1974, destroyed the essential conditions for the viability of the agreement, compounded, to a degree, by the disarray of the American economy in the wake of the quadrupling of the oil price in November 1973.[39]

All this was fully understood in Hanoi and reported with admirable candor in the official account of the North Vietnamese victory in 1975 written by Chief of Staff General Van Tien Dung, summarized in the *New York Times* of April 26, 1976:

From July through October 1974 the General Staff agencies were busily and urgently working. The battlefield situation was changing to our advantage.

The morale and combat strength of the puppet troops were clearly declining. Since early that year, 170,000 men had deserted. Their total manpower had decreased by 15,000 men since 1973, with a heavy loss in combat strength.

In fiscal 1972−73 the United States had given the puppet troops $2.168 billion in military aid. This aid was reduced to $964 million in fiscal 1973−74 and to $700 million in 1974−75. Nguyen Van Thieu was then forced to fight a poor man's war.

Enemy fire power had decreased by nearly 60 percent. Its mobility was also reduced by half. The enemy had to shift from large-scale operations and helicopter-borne and tank-mounted attacks to small-scale blocking, nibbling and searching operations.

The cool fall weather of October 1974 reminded our military cadres of the coming campaign. The Political Bureau and Central Military Party Committee held a conference to hear the General Staff present its strategic combat plan.

At this conference a problem was raised and heatedly discussed: Would the United States be able to send its troops back to the South if we launched large-scale battles that would lead to the collapse of the puppet troops?

After signing the Paris agreement on Vietnam and withdrawing U.S. troops from Vietnam, the United States had faced even greater difficulties and embarrassment. The internal contradictions within the U.S. Administration and among U.S. political parties had intensified. The Watergate scandal had seriously affected the entire United States and precipitated the resignation of an extremely reactionary President—Nixon. The United States faced economic recession, mounting inflation, serious unemployment and an oil crisis.

Comrade Le Duan drew an important conclusion that became a resolution: Having already withdrawn from the South, the United States could hardly jump back in, and no matter how it might intervene, it would be unable to save the Saigon administration from collapse.

The Communist victory was complete, including Laos and Cambodia, although internecine struggle, linked to the Sino-Soviet schism, soon emerged in the latter. The impact on the world was mitigated, to a degree, by the fact that withdrawal of aid for Indochina was clearly the work of the Congress, opposed by the executive branch. This distinction in posture toward Asia was underlined by Ford's vigorous response to the capture by Cambodian Communists of the U.S. merchant ship *Mayaguez* sixty miles off the Cambodian coast in May 1975. But, for the moment, the *Frankfurter Allgemeine Zeitung* accurately captured the image projected by the United States with the headline over an editorial on its front page: "America—A Helpless Giant"; so did the *Economist*, in less Wagnerian terms, with the cover of its issue of April 5, 1975: "The Fading of America."

Why the American Congress behaved as it did with respect to Southeast Asia in 1973–1975 is a complex story which I shall leave for other historians to sort out.[40]

I would merely observe that a powerful political action of the kind taken by the Congress in destroying the foundations of the January 1973 settlement, at a time when U.S. military forces were no longer engaged in Vietnam, almost always results from a convergence of quite different forces. Among them were, clearly, these: an institutional congressional instinct to exploit an interval of gross weakening in the powers of the presidency brought on by Watergate; a desire of the congressional doves to deny the hawks an outcome that the former had believed impossible; annoyance with Thieu and his government or lack of faith in the long-run viability of a non-Communist Vietnam; a desire among some former hawks to be, quite simply, rid of the problem; and, at the margin, a quite purposeful campaign, with some elements of Communist activism in the media and with respect to Congress, focused sharply on the objective of reducing aid to South Vietnam. But all those elements in the equation were framed by three others which, I suspect, were quite influential.

First, at no stage did Nixon ever define and assert a clear and positive, direct and abiding U.S. strategic interest in Southeast Asia itself and in the outcome of the war. He argued, simply, that he had inherited a commitment it would be dangerous not to see through to an honorable conclusion because of its effects on the strategic balance elsewhere.

Second, Nixon failed to consult with and associate Congress with the commitments he made to Thieu to achieve the settlement of January 1973. Congressional commitment in January 1973 might or might not have avoided the debacle of 1973–1975; but, clearly, the effort to achieve that commitment should have been made. Moreover, the timing was propitious. Nixon, in the wake of the 1972 election, was at the peak of his prestige and influence in January 1973.

Third, the movement of the U.S. toward a normalization of relations with China appeared to remove the major strategic danger which had shadowed the conflict in Indochina over the previous quarter century. Subliminally, many Americans felt they could leave Indochina—which for twenty years had cost the U.S. so much blood, treasure, and political agony—to its fate without paying a significant price in terms of the Asian balance of power or other vital U.S. interests. Neither the executive branch nor the Congress conceived of the possibility—to use the phrase of a Soviet diplomat in 1969—that the U.S.S.R. would move into the empty chairs left by American diplomacy and, quite particularly, into the bases in Cam Ranh Bay and Danang.

However historians may weight these and other elements, the fact is that, in the spring of 1975, "the worst had happened," to use Lee Kuan Yew's phrase spoken two years earlier; but, again referring to his assessment of 1973, it did not necessarily follow that the rest of Southeast Asia would go Communist. The morale of the peoples of the region did, indeed, prove to be "very different from what it was after Dien Bien Phu in 1954," or what it would have been if Johnson had failed to meet the challenge in July 1965.

To understand this outcome, one must examine what happened in Southeast Asia between 1969 and 1975; notably, the evolution of ASEAN and the economic performance of the region.

After the initial ministerial meeting at Bangkok of August 5–8, 1967, which created ASEAN, sessions of the foreign ministers took place every year except 1970. They were held successively in each member country.[41]

A central secretariat was created only in 1975. Until that time the staff work for ASEAN was conducted by coordination among designated officials in each foreign office. Aside from the ministerial meetings, substantive work was carried forward by functional committees in which those bearing domestic responsibility in each field participated. At this early stage of ASEAN's history, the direct engagement of members of the governments, at both high-policy and technical levels, had an important virtue. It diffused a widespread sense of responsibility for the organization and the habit of thinking cooperatively, even when practical results were meager.

In addition to certain ad hoc committees, eleven permanent committees were created as follows: Food and Agriculture, Shipping, Civil Air Transportation, Communication/Air Traffic Services/Meteorology, Finance, Commerce and Industry, Transportation and Telecommunication, Tourism, Science and Technology, Socio-Cultural Activities, and Mass Media. Between 1967 and 1975 projects were designed and completed in the fields of commerce and industry, food and agriculture, communications and transport, and finance and banking.

The economies of ASEAN represent a wide and diversified spectrum with distinctive linkages to the world economy. It required patient, pragmatic efforts to identify precisely what the members of ASEAN could productively do together. The results were modest but serious—for example, workshops on a considerable range of shared agricultural problems, the creation of package tours and collective travel documents, cooperation in bulk shipping, and, perhaps most important of all, improved telecommunications linkages among the members via new microwave installations. In addition, there was a wide range of meetings and informal contacts among representatives of private sectors.

Speaking in Boston on November 11, 1981, the Malaysian foreign minister Tan Sri M. Ghazali Shafie reflected thoughtfully on the significance of this phase of ASEAN's evolution in relation to the 1975 debacle in Indochina.

In its early years, specifically between 1968 and 1975, ASEAN activity was conducted through eleven Permanent Committees which encompassed the social and economic goals of the Association. Basically this was a learning stage of getting to know each other's systems, their strength and weaknesses and their procedures. The going was slow, because each party was treading gingerly along so as to avoid sensitivities which were generally created by different colonial pasts, or to avoid disrupting a basic process so critical to the strength and resilience of the other.

They were very useful years to further bind the member countries together. Besides, in the less sensitive areas of culture exchanges, tourism, research and development, and training on existing institutions, major advances were made. Travel controls within ASEAN were relaxed, special ASEAN package tours were developed—harmonisation of port procedures were initiated; radio and television programmes were exchanged; several festivals of the mass-media were launched. Indeed, a popular movement on ASEAN was launched to emphasise the strength of the Association and to relate its activities with the daily life of the people—so as to break down the ramparts of history and of prejudice. It was important that our peoples understood the need for togetherness so as to garner support for our efforts to strengthen the system of free enterprise which was serving them well. Indeed one of the earliest results and heartening features of ASEAN are the growing number of conferences and projects undertaken by private organisations and the business community.

In 1975 North Vietnamese tanks rolled past Danang, Cam Ranh Bay, and Ton Son Nut into Saigon. The United States withdrew their last soldiers from Vietnam, and the worst of ASEAN's fears which underscored the Bangkok Declaration of 1967 came to pass. But ASEAN by then had seven solid years of living in neighbourly cooperation. Call it foresight, or what you will, the fact remains that with ASEAN solidarity there were no falling dominoes in Southeast Asia following the fall of Saigon to the Communists, and the United States withdrawal from Southeast Asia.[42]

Something else was happening in the first decade of ASEAN's existence: extraordinarily high rates of economic growth were sustained throughout the region (see Table 1). There was some retardation under the impact of the global recession of 1974–1975, but a sharp rebound in 1976.

The expansion of real GNP and GNP per capita was accompanied by a shift to manufactures and manufactured exports which expanded unevenly but, generally, at even higher rates (see Table 2 and Chart 1). In all cases, for example, there was a rise in per capita calorie and protein supply between 1967 and 1974.[43] Education levels and indicators of health and health services also generally responded positively (see Tables 3 and 4).

This kind of sustained, palpable progress, experienced in a region which also contained parallel examples of high growth and modernization in South Korea, Taiwan, and Hong Kong—let alone the continuing astonishing momentum of Japan—strengthened the sense of confidence among the members of ASEAN that history had not automatically destined them to fall under one kind or another of Communist dominance. The economic and social vitality of the individual countries also contributed to the will to assert certain shared diplomatic positions through ASEAN.

TABLE 1. Patterns of Growth Performance in ASEAN (Per Capita GDP and Real GDP Growth)

	GNP at Market Prices		Per Capita Growth Rates		Real per Capita GDP in 1970 Constant U.S. $			GDP Growth Rates at Constant Prices % *					
	Per Capita 1975 (U.S. $)	Index	(1960– 1974)	(1965– 1974)	1970	1974	Compound Growth Rates 1970– 1974 %	1969– 1973	1972	1973	1974	1975	1976
Indonesia	260†	32	2.4	4.1	77	140	12.3	8.7	8.2	12.8	6.6	5.2	(7.9)
Malaysia	750	91	3.9	3.8	320	380	4.4	7.8	6.7	11.3	8.0	3.5	8.5
Philippines	350	43	2.4	2.7	175	200	3.4	6.5	4.2	10.1	4.8	6.6	6.4
Singapore	2,500	292	7.6	10.0	930	1,320	9.1	12.8	11.3	11.1	6.8	4.1	6.8
Thailand	350	43	4.6	4.3	180	210	3.9	7.2	4.3	10.3	4.6	5.5	6.3
ASEAN Average	842	100	—	—	—	—	—	—	—	—	—	—	—

*The starting levels for constant market prices differ for individual ASEAN countries: Indonesia, 1973; Malaysia, 1970; Philippines, 1972; Singapore, 1968; Thailand, 1962. The growth series for each country is indicative of the historical growth performance of that country, though it is not quite so useful for inter-country comparison.

†It has recently become known that previous national income estimates have been understated by over 20 percent. This new figure is based on the new "input-output table 1977." See Olch Nugroho, "Table Input-Output Indonesia 1971," *Ekonomi dan Kellangan Indonesia*, June 1977.

Sources: *World Bank Atlas 1976*, supplemented by national sources: for Indonesia, Biro Pusat Statistik, *Statistik Indonesia, 1974–75* (Jakarta, 1976), and *Bulletin of Indonesian Economic Studies*, March 1977; for the Philippines, National Census Statistics Office, *Philippine Yearbook 1975* (Manila, 1976), and NEDA, *Philippine Economic Indicators*, September 1976; for Malaysia, The Treasury of Malaysia, *Economic Report* (Kuala Lumpur, various years), and Bank Negara Malaysia, *Annual Report and Statement of Accounts, 1976* (Kuala Lumpur, 1977); for Singapore, Ministry of Finance, Singapore, *Economic Survey of Singapore, 1976* (1977); and for Thailand, Bank of Thailand, *Monthly Bulletin*, March 1977.

Secondary source: John Wong, *ASEAN Economies in Perspective* (Philadelphia: Institute for the Study of Human Issues, 1979), p. 135.

TABLE 2. Growth of Manufacturing Production in ASEAN (at Constant Prices) (%)

	Value added 1960–1969 (Average)	Production 1960–1969 (Average)	1969	1970	1971	1972	1973	1974	1975	1976 (First Half)
Indonesia	5.9	2.8†	—	15.0‡	10.1	—	15.2	16.1	—	—
Malaysia (West)	10.4*	—	15.6	12.3	6.2	22.8	21.0	15.3	0.0	18.5
Philippines	4.6	5.9	3.0	1.5	10.6	9.3	10.7	−2.2	−0.8	3.1
Singapore	19.5	12.7	52.7	7.8	14.3	15.8	17.0	4.2	−2.3	7.7
Thailand	10.9	—	—	12.1	10.8	9.7	13.8	4.2	6.9	7.5
ASEAN	10.3	—	—	—	—	—	—	—	—	—
For comparison:										
All developing countries	—	—	—	—	6.6	9.2	10.0	6.4	3.9	—
World	—	—	—	—	4.0	7.5	9.6	3.7	−2.2	—

* 1960/1961–1969/1970.
† 1960–1968.
‡ Value-added.

Sources: UN ESCAP, *Mid-term Review and Appraisal of the International Development Strategy in the Second United Nations Development Decade in the ESCAP Region, 1974*, p. 83; *Economic and Social Survey of Asia and the Pacific, 1976* (March 1977); UN, *World Economic Survey, 1975.*

Secondary source: Wong, *ASEAN Economies in Perspective*, p. 166.

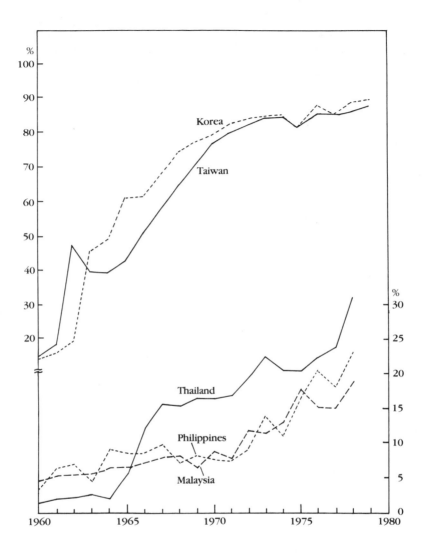

CHART 1. Percentage Shares of Manufactures in Total Exports of ASEAN and Asian New Industrial Countries (NICs), 1960–1979 (after Miyokei Shinohara, *Industrial Growth, Trade, and Dynamic Patterns in the Japanese Economy* [Tokyo: University of Tokyo Press, 1982], p. 100)

TABLE 3. Indicators of Education Levels: ASEAN, 1960, Mid-1970s, and 1981

| | Number Enrolled as % of Age Group | | | | | | Number Enrolled in Higher Education as % of Population Aged 20–24 | | | Adult Literacy Rate (%) | |
| | Primary School | | | Secondary School | | | | | | | |
	1960	1977	1981	1960	1977	1981	1960	1977	1981	1960	1975
Indonesia	71	86	100	6	21	30	1	2	3	39	62
Malaysia	96	93	92	19	43	53	1	3	5	53	60
Philippines	95	105	110	26	56	63	13	24	26	72	87
Singapore	111	110	104	32	55	65	6	9	8	—	75
Thailand	83	83	96	13	27	29	2	5	20	68	84

Sources: World Bank, *World Development Report, 1980* (Washington, D.C., 1980), Table 23, pp. 154–155; *World Development Report, 1984* (Washington, D.C., 1984), Table 25, pp. 266–267.

TABLE 4. Health-Related Indicators: ASEAN, 1960 and 1977

| | Population per: | | | |
| | Physician | | Nursing Person | |
	1960	1977	1960	1977
Indonesia	46,780	11,530	4,520	2,300
Malaysia	7,060	7,910	1,800	940
Philippines	6,940	7,970	1,440	6,000
Singapore	2,380	1,150	650	320
Thailand	7,900	7,100	4,830	2,400

Source: World Bank, *World Development Report, 1984*, Table 24, pp. 264–265.

TABLE 5. Asian Development Bank Loan Approvals by Sector: Three-Year Moving Averages, 1968–1970 through 1978–1980

	Total Lending	Agriculture and Agro-Industry	Energy	Industry and Non-Fuel Minerals	Development Banks	Transport and Communications	Water Supply	Urban Development Education and Health
Average (U.S. $ millions)								
1968–1970	128.4	25.0	15.4	19.3	30.0	30.9	6.8	1.0
1969–1971	199.3	40.8	50.6	17.3	39.0	43.2	7.4	1.0
1970–1972	271.9	42.7	89.9	13.7	38.0	58.4	27.0	2.2
1971–1973	330.5	52.1	106.4	1.4	51.2	78.9	37.1	3.4
1972–1974	428.4	80.4	114.4	17.2	64.5	91.4	57.1	3.4
1973–1975	543.2	151.3	125.1	23.1	90.9	96.0	49.8	7.0
1974–1976	661.3	193.6	141.2	36.2	115.3	109.9	59.9	5.2
1975–1977	774.2	236.2	170.5	32.4	119.7	131.4	65.2	18.8
1976–1978	940.4	257.9	202.5	68.2	135.2	150.2	84.3	42.1
1977–1979	1,098.9	328.1	264.0	61.7	129.8	133.4	95.7	86.2
1978–1980	1,282.0	396.7	319.0	50.3	140.5	159.5	103.2	112.8
Cumulative (1968–1980)[a]	8,093.3	2,264.4	1,963.3	362.2	1,106.1	1,283.6[b]	705.8	407.9

[a] Inclusive of refinanced Technical Assistance loans.
[b] Inclusive of Multiproject loans.
Source: *Asian Development Bank Annual Report, 1980* (Manila, 1981), p. 33.

In addition, it was during these years that the seriousness and depth of the economic problems confronted by the PRC became increasingly clear and were, indeed, acknowledged with admirable candor by the authorities in Beijing. In fact, looking about on the world scene, the members of ASEAN had no reason to believe that models for economic and social development existed better than those they were evolving on their own.

One other regional institution moved forward with élan in these years: the ADB (see Table 5). Corrected for the approximately 45 percent price increase between 1969 and 1975, average annual lending, in real terms, increased by three and a half times in this first phase of the ADB's history. Like the region it served, the ADB was a going concern by 1975, an instrument of multilateral cooperation respected widely within Asia and beyond.

Thus, the six-year interval between the enunciation of the Nixon Doctrine and the fall of Saigon was well used by the peoples and governments of the western Pacific.

5. Asian Regionalism, 1975–1985

Reacting promptly to the debacle in Indochina, the governments of ASEAN began to prepare for a summit meeting in the second half of 1975 to chart a common course under the circumstances in which they found themselves. The heads of the five governments met in Bali February 23–25, 1976, launching a new, more purposeful phase in the history of the organization. Before dealing with the evolution of ASEAN at and since the Bali sessions, it is necessary to outline the changes in the structure of power in Asia within which ASEAN has operated and sought to protect its common interests.

The Communist take-over of Indochina in 1975 was a major event for all the nations of Asia, to which, in one way or another, they have all reacted; but it was part of a process which can be arbitrarily dated from 1969. We have already sketched the evolution of the Guam Doctrine and the opening of U.S. contacts with the PRC. But there was also a Soviet dimension to the process. It was against the background of Sino-Soviet border clashes in 1969 that a series of contacts between U.S. and Chinese officials took place. All this suggested that a new phase in the Asian balance of power was about to open. At its center was a determined thrust of the Soviet Union to enlarge its power and influence in the whole arc from East Africa to the Sea of Japan.

The Soviet government had been giving its future policy in Asia and the region bordering on the Indian Ocean a good deal of systematic thought since the mid-1960s at least. The palpable schism in American political life over policy toward Southeast Asia, gathering intensity since 1966, evidently had wider implications for the future shape of U.S. policy in Asia and elsewhere; and this process was accompanied by British withdrawal east of Suez. On May 28, 1969, an article was published in *Izvestia* by Vikenty Matveyev to which Soviet officials referred questioners when, ten days later, Brezhnev proposed a system of collective security pacts between the U.S.S.R. and the non-Communist states of Asia.[44] Noting that a vacuum would be created by the British withdrawal east of Suez and the possible U.S. withdrawal of forces from Vietnam, Matveyev, as reported in the *New York Times*, went on to say, "Judging by what the Peking press says, Mao and his henchmen entertain quite definite designs on a number of countries in this part of the world. . . ."

> . . . Matveyev [then argued that] the withdrawal of foreign forces "should pave the way for the laying of the foundation of collective security, in which case the countries that have gained their freedom would, by pooling efforts, consolidate peace and repulse all machinations of imperialist expansionist forces."
>
> He pledged that the Soviet Union and other socialist countries "will contribute, as they have always done, to every effort helping to insure firmer dependable peace and security in Asia despite the anti-popular designs of bellicose reaction."
>
> The Matveyev article listed India, Pakistan, Afghanistan, Burma, Cambodia, and Singapore among the Asian countries "striving to consolidate their sovereignty and economic independence."

The *New York Times* correspondent then noted:

> Some diplomats believe the suggestion of a collective security system is primarily an effort to strengthen Soviet influence in Asia, using fears about Chairman Mao as a basis of improving relations with countries bordering on China.

"Earlier this month, Aeroflot, the Soviet airline, began flights to Singapore and a study group from the Soviet Union is visiting the Philippines, with which Moscow up to now has had no diplomatic relations. Moreover the Soviet Union is doing nothing to dampen speculation about the possibility of improving relations with the Nationalist Chinese regime in Taiwan.[45]

On June 7, Brezhnev, addressing a group of Communist leaders at an international conference, formally proposed his new Collective Security System for Asia. It is an odd fact that neither Nixon's nor Kissinger's memoirs refer to Brezhnev's plan, although its purpose and rationale were clearly explained by Soviet sources, and it was subsequently pursued with high seriousness as opportunity offered. There appears to have been no substantial consciousness of its meaning in Congress or in American public opinion, although, of course, various tactical moves within Brezhnev's broad strategy were noted.

In effect, the Soviet Union set out to establish a chain of alliances, naval bases, and areas of enlarged political influence which would permit the projection of its military power and influence in the arc from Vladivostok to the Persian Gulf and the East African ports via the strategic straits of Southeast Asia (see Map 1). The strategy also provided a way of enveloping and isolating China, of forestalling an extension of Chinese power and influence in Asia, and an alternative, of sorts, for the possible direct military assault on China which the Soviet government contemplated seriously in 1969 but abandoned when Nixon communicated his unwillingness to acquiesce.

The new policy was related not only to signs of U.S. retraction in the Pacific and the Sino-Soviet cold war but also to the progressive buildup of the Soviet fleet. Table 6 captures one useful reflection of Brezhnev's policy: the expansion in visits of Soviet operational naval vessels to the Indian Ocean in the period 1968–1976.[46]

The first major result of the new strategy was the twenty-

MAP 1. Sea Routes through the Strategic Straits of Southeast Asia

TABLE 6. Soviet Operational Ship Visits in the Indian Ocean, 1968–1976[a]

Country	1968	1969	1970	1971	1972	1973	1974	1975	1976
Somalia	—	2	7	22	20	42	61	54	75
S. Yemen	—	4	5	15	7	14	37	34	18
Iraq	—	4	1	2	8	15	17	8	12
Sri Lanka	1	2	1	—	6	2	5	6	6
Mauritius	—	1	7	1	9	1	2	2	1
India	—	1	6	2	—	3	2	4	2
Kenya	—	1	4	—	—	2	4	1	—
N. Yemen	—	1	2	—	—	—	1	2	3
Pakistan	—	5	2	—	—	—	—	1	—
Maldives	—	—	—	3	—	—	—	1	1
Iran	—	2	—	—	—	—	—	—	1
Tanzania	—	—	2	—	—	—	—	—	—
Ethiopia	—	1	—	—	—	—	—	—	—
Kuwait	—	1	—	—	—	—	—	—	—
Madagascar	—	1	—	—	—	—	—	—	—
Sudan	—	—	1	—	—	—	—	—	—
Totals	1	26	38	45	50	79	129	113	119

[a]Excluding visits by oceanographic research/space support ships.

Source: Richard B. Remnek, "Soviet Policy in the Horn of Africa: The Decision to Intervene," in *The Soviet Union in the Third World: Successes and Failures*, ed. Robert H. Donaldson (Boulder, Colorado: Westview Press, Inc., 1981), p. 130.

year Soviet-Indian Treaty of Peace, Friendship, and Cooperation on August 9, 1971, which, Kissinger reports, struck Washington like a bombshell.[47] Moscow evidently exploited the Indian sense of isolation, as Nixon moved to a new relationship with China, and Kissinger held forth on equilibrium among the five serious centers of power: the United States, the U.S.S.R., Western Europe, Japan, and China. The Indians were bound to ask where they stood in a world thus conceived. The Indian decision to move closer to the Soviet Union was, no doubt, also influenced by the distinctly warmer relations of the Nixon administration with Pakistan than India and, quite particularly, by the crisis between the west and east wings of Pakistan which began on March 25, 1971, with the decision of the Pakistani government to suppress by force the movement in East Pakistan for a higher degree of independence. The upshot was a tense, protracted crisis involving China and the Soviet Union, a brief war between India and Pakistan in December 1971, and the emergence of an independent Bangladesh in its aftermath.

While the closer connection with India appeared to offer Moscow significant advantages, it did not provide reliable military bases. The victory of the North Vietnamese in 1975 was another matter. Soviet naval forces soon moved into the enormous installations built by the United States in Cam Ranh Bay, Soviet air units into the airfield complex near Danang. The U.S. air and naval bases in the Philippines, at Clark Field and Subic Bay, were thus directly confronted and potentially neutralized; the sense of Soviet encirclement was heightened in China; and the countries of Southeast Asia came within the range of direct Soviet attack. The leaders of the region had not forgotten that it was from Indochina that the Japanese assault of Malaya and the British base at Singapore had been launched. (In the course of a tour of duty in Cambodia in the summer of 1961, Mr. Richard Howland, an American Foreign Service officer, came upon an overgrown, abandoned airfield in Pong Puk from which Japanese aircraft had taken off in December 1941 to attack successfully the battleship *Prince of Wales* and the cruiser *Repulse*, opening the way to the capture of Singapore.)

The Soviet position in Indochina was further consolidated with the entrance of Vietnam into the Council for Mutual Economic Assistance (COMECON) and the signing of a defense treaty with the Vietnamese on November 3, 1978. All this was part of the prelude to Hanoi's invasion of Kampuchea on December 25, 1978, to overthrow the Chinese-oriented Communist government installed in 1975.

Meanwhile, further to the west a coup mounted by a consortium of Communist groups overthrew President Mohammed Daud of Afghanistan in April 1978; a Soviet-Afghan Treaty of Friendship and Cooperation was signed on December 4; and, after various vicissitudes with Daud's contentious Communist successors, Moscow took on the unenviable task of consolidating Soviet power by invading Afghanistan on December 17, 1979.

Soviet positions in South Yemen and Ethiopia were, for a time at least, consolidated by coups followed, in the case of South Yemen, by a Soviet–South Yemen Treaty of Friendship and Cooperation signed on December 4, 1978, and, in the case of Ethiopia, by increasingly strong military support in the wake of the coup of February 1977.

In short, a decade after the enunciation of Brezhnev's concept of a Soviet-led collective security system for Asia designed to fill the vacuum left by the retraction of British and American power east of Suez and to counter the new Sino-U.S. ties, the strategy had acquired a good deal of substance. It has been a serious enterprise, backed by a rapidly expanding naval strength and a determination to make the Soviet Union a true global—not merely a Eurasian—power. On the other hand, it has not proceeded smoothly.

In general, the last half of the twentieth century has been a rather poor time to set up, expand, and maintain an empire. There is something authentically old-fashioned about the Soviet effort. But this is the phase in the life of Russia when its relative strength has tempted its leaders to make the effort. The Soviet problem is that it must not only challenge the interests of the United States and of the other technologically advanced powers, it must not only strain and weaken its domestic economic base to make the effort, but it also confronts in the developing regions not traditional or quasi-traditional societies, but increasingly competent and ambitious young nations driven by a passionate nationalism. Thus, from East Africa to Cam Ranh Bay none of the Soviet naval bases or other imperial connections are truly secure in the long run or to be regarded as reliable, even now, in a time of combat. And in some dimensions the Soviet effort has already generated strong nationalist resistance, including not only the resistance of the Afghans but also the brief Chinese attack on Vietnam in response to the latter's invasion of Kampuchea. The Japanese, frustrated by protracted Soviet unwillingness to negotiate the return of four Japanese islands taken after the Second World War, and threatened by an enlargement of Soviet forces on two of those islands, signed a treaty of friendship with China on August 12, 1978; accelerated somewhat the expansion of their naval and air forces; and threw their political and economic support behind ASEAN. These Japanese decisions have heightened, to a degree, tensions between Tokyo and Moscow. Perhaps most significant (and most uncertain) of all, Soviet policy may have set in motion forces which could, in time, lead to a new set of relations between India and its neighbors, including China.

This is the interacting process among the larger powers which has framed ASEAN's efforts to protect its common interests since the fall of Saigon. All of it could not, of course, be perceived when the chiefs of governments of ASEAN met in Bali in late February 1976. What they could perceive were strong forces at work in their region, all of which bore directly on the fate of each member nation:

—A retraction of American power, the limits of which they could not foresee—a power on which they had explicitly or implicitly relied for their independence and security.

—A consequent vacuum which the Soviet Union, having generously backed Hanoi in its victorious campaign of 1975, was in a strong position to fill in further association with the Vietnamese.

—A PRC, locked in a cold war with the U.S.S.R., deeply concerned in the short run about Soviet encirclement, in the long run about its own power and influence in Asia.

—An American policy which, having apparently turned its

back on Southeast Asia, was pursuing détente with the Soviet Union and seeking a normalization of relations with China, both powers regarded (in differing proportion) with well-earned suspicion by the several leaders and peoples of Southeast Asia.

It was, thus, not difficult to envisage a situation, with the United States reduced to impotence by self-inflicted wounds, in which the PRC and U.S.S.R. would contest for dominance in Southeast Asia. This was an old theme in the region, for, except at rare moments such as the Korean War, the two major Communist powers did not act in concert. They had systematically struggled for a dominant role in relation to the Asian Communist parties, notably the Vietnamese. And as the Malaysian foreign minister recalled in 1981, ASEAN's birth was, in part, associated with a desire of Indonesian and Malaysian leaders to escape from the Sino-Soviet rivalry which had contributed to the confrontation between the two countries and nearly resulted in the Communist take-over of Indonesia in 1965.[48]

Conscious of the limited military capacities they commanded individually and collectively, but conscious also that they represented dynamic societies containing some 240 million human beings, they decided to face the crisis together and to assert even more strongly than in the previous nine years their determination to create a Zone of Peace, Freedom, and Neutrality (ZOPFAN). As Lee Kuan Yew said in his opening statement at Bali, "As never before, the future of non-communist Southeast Asia rests in the hands of the leaders and peoples of non-communist Southeast Asia."

Two carefully prepared documents were signed by the heads of government at Bali: the Declaration of ASEAN Concord (reaffirming the Bangkok Declaration), and the Treaty of Amity and Cooperation in Southeast Asia. These are reproduced in Appendix A. They also signed an agreement establishing a permanent ASEAN Secretariat. Aside from the creation of a permanent secretariat, four substantive decisions were taken in February 1976: to play an active role in trying to settle the problems of Indochina in ways which avoided a threat to Thailand and ASEAN as a whole; to consolidate their commitment to harmonizing peacefully all problems among the member states; to accelerate economic cooperation within ASEAN, notably with respect to problems of energy and food supply; and to strengthen ties between ASEAN and other states and widen acceptance of the ZOPFAN doctrine.

With respect to the latter, discussions were held in 1977 at the Kuala Lumpur summit conference with the heads of government of Australia, Japan, and New Zealand; and similar strengthening collective bilateral contacts were envisaged with Canada, the EEC, the United States, and the countries of West Asia.

Clearly, the most urgent of ASEAN's political and security problems was its relations with Vietnam and the other Indochinese states. At the Bali meeting there was extended confidential discussion of a common policy toward Indochina and, especially, of the danger implicit in the situation in Kampuchea where, under Chinese tutelage, the egregious Pol Pot was in authority, generating, as seen in Hanoi and Moscow, a threat to the consolidation of Vietnam. As the Malaysian foreign minister said in 1981, ASEAN, after the Bali sessions, gave Vietnam "a heavy dose of peaceful intentions."[49] What ASEAN wanted was an Indochina, independent of both the Soviet Union and the PRC, which might widen the Zone of Peace, Freedom, and Neutrality, lifting, in particular, the real and present danger to Thailand represented by an Indochina either dominated by a major power or riven by Sino-Soviet rivalry via their surrogates. The Vietnamese invasion of Kampuchea in December 1978 foreclosed the possibility of Indochina's adherence to ZOPFAN for some time.

In its most serious venture on the world scene, ASEAN responded strongly: by taking sustained collective leadership at the United Nations, starting in November 1979, in support of a withdrawal of Vietnamese forces and the creation of an authentically representative government in Kampuchea; and by organizing a third-force, nationalist grouping which might one day bring Kampuchea to a position of authentic independence. Although its objectives have not been attained, ASEAN's sustained dual initiative was widely supported by non-Communist countries, North and South; and it may constitute a possible resolution of the problem of Kampuchea in which the PRC would acquiesce. If and when it will prove acceptable in Moscow and Hanoi remains to be seen.

The evolution of ASEAN, clearly the most vital multilateral grouping in Asia, has never been easy. All the factors which led Eugene Black to ask if Asian regional cooperation was "absurd" have been present and active. Like other governments in Asia and elsewhere, the first and most powerful criterion governing policy is national interest narrowly and conventionally defined. Every major agreement has been, therefore, a patient and imaginative exercise in overcoming those abiding parochial forces. Only vivid memories of painful past experience and an awareness of potential danger have yielded this rather surprising organization, although the habit of cooperation has evidently grown with the passage of time and a sequence of positive, if modest, achievements.

There have, of course, been disappointments. For example, the ASEAN collective industrial program, which Japan offered to support at Kuala Lumpur in 1977, has not gone well. Indeed, cooperation by the private sectors of the ASEAN countries has yielded thus far better results than industrial cooperation among the ministries (see below, p. 93).

But the underlying major problems of ASEAN lie in the continued military vulnerability of the region and in the potential political and social instability of certain of its member states.

In July 1981 the Senate Subcommittee on East Asian and Pacific Affairs held three days of hearings on U.S. policy in Southeast Asia, a great deal of which was devoted to ASEAN.

On July 21, the chairman of the subcommittee (Senator Hayakawa) posed the following question to Richard L. Armitage of the Office of International Security Affairs at the Department of Defense:

> THE CHAIRMAN: Singapore's Lee Kuan Yew said in 1979, "The first unhappy admission we must make is that for at least ten years there is no combination of military forces in ASEAN that can stop or check the Vietnamese army in any open conflict."
>
> Is this still true? Does this correspond to the U.S. assessment of the military balance between the Vietnamese and the armed forces of the ASEAN nations?
>
> MR. ARMITAGE: . . . I think President Lee Kuan Yew's statement basically is correct. Although the ASEAN countries are modernizing their forces, I find it very unlikely that they will be able to do other than find themselves in a less disadvantageous position rather than actually become equal to or superior to the Vietnamese.[50]

The fact is that with arms supplies from abroad and improved training, the countries of ASEAN command an increasing technical capacity to control subversion and guerrilla operations within their territories; and there are limited potentials for mutual support in such circumstances. Even more important, perhaps, the unity of ASEAN and its prestige in the world community contribute an important deterrent as compared, for example, to a situation of fragmentation in the region which might permit piecemeal intrusion. But an invasion of Thailand by massive regular North Vietnamese units from Cambodia may well be beyond their individual and collective capacity to contain on their own. Unless the United States or China (or both) brought its forces directly into play, such an invasion is likely to result in Vietnamese occupation. Similarly, only U.S. naval and air strength in the region is capable of deterring or coping with the Soviet forces mounted in or easily accessible to Southeast Asia.

As of early 1985, however, the preoccupations of both the

Vietnamese and the Soviet Union with other matters suggest that the more immediate danger lies in Communist efforts of subversion. At one time or another, every member of ASEAN has experienced a serious phase of externally supported Communist insurrection seeking to exploit domestic dissidence. Retarded growth induced by the relative stagnation of the world economy in the period 1979–1983 has heightened the possibility of such exploitable dissidence. There is thus a sense of priority for the maintenance of economic, social, and political conditions within the ASEAN societies, such as will prevent a subversive potential from emerging which might induce substantial external support from one or more of the Communist states. The Indonesians have formalized this notion in the phrase *ketahanan nasional* (national resilience).[51] In different terms, this doctrine is accepted by each of the members of ASEAN.[52]

As we shall see, the stance of the United States in Asia and the Pacific altered substantially after the Communist takeover of Indochina in 1975. If current U.S. guarantees in Southeast Asia remain credible in Hanoi, Moscow, and Beijing, domestic instability capable of external exploitation remains the greatest threat to the individual and collective security of the ASEAN countries.

U.S. policy toward Asia and the Pacific since 1975 can be defined as a gradual, partial recovery from the shock of the fall of Indochina to the Communists. It was one thing to cut aid to South Vietnam, criticize Thieu's regime, and argue that the United States should rid itself of obligations in an obscure and distant part of the world where we should never have become committed. It was a quite different matter to see on television the disarray of the evacuation of Americans from Saigon and the plight of the South Vietnamese. The anatomy of raw defeat, even if self-inflicted, was not pleasant; nor was it easy to observe Americans leaving an ally of some thirty years to its fate. There was shock, confusion, and a widespread sense of humiliation even among those who had advocated U.S. withdrawal. As one who was drawn into a public discussion at the time, I can attest that a good many in the Congress who had supported, in effect, the destruction of non-Communist South Vietnam turned promptly to the question of how to limit the damage done to U.S. strategic interests there and elsewhere in the world. It was not an easy task.

Psychologically, Ford's vigorous response to the seizure of the *Mayaguez* in May 1975 began the reaction in U.S. public life; and, despite considerable U.S. casualties, it had wide public support in the United States. But, for Southeast Asians, it was a small gesture of uncertain meaning in the face of the gross change in the balance of power taking place in the region.

Speaking in Hawaii on December 7, 1975, thirty-four years after the Japanese attack on Pearl Harbor, Ford sought to reassure non-Communist Asia in a more substantial way with "a new Pacific Doctrine." He asserted that "American strength is basic to any stable balance of power in the Pacific"; that "the partnership with Japan is a pillar of U.S. strategy"; and that the United States had "a continuing stake in the stability and security of Southeast Asia."[53] He also addressed himself explicitly to ASEAN:

> I can assure you that Americans will be hearing much more about the ASEAN organization. All of its members are friends of the United States. Their total population equals our own. While they are developing countries, they possess many, many assets—vital peoples, abundant natural resources, and well-managed agricultures. They have skilled leaders and the determination to develop themselves and to solve their own problems. Each of these countries protects its independence by relying on its own national resilience and diplomacy. We must continue to assist them. I learned during my visit that our friends want us to remain actively engaged in the affairs of the region. We intend to do so. . . .
>
> . . . Our relations with the five ASEAN countries are marked by growing maturity and by more modest and more realistic

expectations on both sides. We no longer approach them as donor to dependent. These proud people look to us less for outright aid than for new trading opportunities and more equitable arrangements for the transfer of science and technology.

There is one common theme which was expressed to me by the leaders of every Asian country that I visited. They all advocate the continuity of steady and responsible American leadership. They seek self-reliance in their own future and in their own relations with us.[54]

Satisfying as the rhetoric may have been, Ford's doctrine left unanswered a fundamental question for ASEAN: what would the United States do if the North Vietnamese launched a direct major military attack on Thailand? It was, of course, a question Ford could not answer with confidence given the War Powers Act; and, with the Chinese-oriented Communists in control of Kampuchea, the issue did not immediately arise so far as the Thai-Kampuchean border was concerned. The Vietnamese invasion of Kampuchea in December 1978, however, posed the issue unmistakably.

Although SEATO had been dismantled as an organization in June 1977, the Carter administration responded to the new situation by asserting on several occasions the continued validity of the Southeast Asia Treaty of 1955 for the defense of Thailand, as well as bilateral U.S. commitments made in 1962 which declared that the United States would act in the defense of Thailand in accordance with its constitutional processes, whether or not other signatories of the Southeast Asia Treaty responded.

In May 1978, Vice President Mondale, during his visit to Bangkok, stated the U.S. position as follows: "Circumstances have changed, but our commitments of both a regional and bilateral nature under the Manila Pact are still valid."

In February 1979, during the visit of Thai Prime Minister Kriangsak to Washington, President Carter stated:

Our nation is intensely interested and deeply committed to the integrity and the freedom and the security of Thailand. And as you well know, the bilateral commitment and the multilateral commitments made in the Manila Pact are the basis for our security agreements with you and your people.

And in July 1979, at the meeting with ASEAN foreign ministers in Bali, Secretary Vance reaffirmed the president's statement, and Secretary Muskie did the same during Thai Foreign Minister Sitthi's visit to the United States in June 1980.

U.S. military aid to Thailand was increased during the Carter years.

On October 6, 1981, Reagan, on the occasion of the visit to Washington of the Thai prime minister, said: "The Manila Pact, and its clarification in our bilateral communique of 1962, is a living document. We will honor the obligations it conveys." The fine print of U.S. policy includes two reservations to which Reagan referred: implementation of the Manila Pact would "depend upon circumstances," and it would follow "full consultation with the Congress."

Perhaps more persuasive than such formal diplomatic pronouncements was the emergence of a strong bipartisan consensus, in the wake of the Soviet invasion of Afghanistan, that the proportion of U.S. resources devoted to military expenditures had to be increased. Changes in public sentiment of this kind translated into military hardware do not, in themselves, determine the outcome of political debates at moments of crisis; but there is a significant degree of legitimacy in the attention devoted by both the friends and adversaries of the United States to the course of the American military budget. It is an imperfect but not irrelevant index of the nation's mood and will.

Thus, so far as ASEAN (and the rest of non-Communist Asia) is concerned, the posture of the United States toward the region in 1985 was more reassuring than had appeared likely when Saigon fell to the Communists in the spring of 1975. The memory of what had transpired in U.S. policy in 1974–1975 was, of course, not forgotten; and the Asian view of the U.S. role in their region would never again be quite the same. Nevertheless, no other power was capable of deterring a Soviet drive for Asian hegemony; and the time for such an effort was, in any case, not propitious. The Soviet Union faced intractable problems in Poland, Afghanistan, and in its domestic economy, as well as with an India taking its distance from Moscow and, at last, articulating its concern for Afghanistan. The Vietnamese were unlikely to move in force across the Mekong without active Soviet support; and, in any case, they were bogged down equally in Kampuchea and in their efforts to generate economic viability in their nominally unified nation. With the correlation of forces not likely to be judged propitious in Moscow and Hanoi, the ASEAN members, all of whom had lived for many years with varying degrees of insecurity, counted their blessings and went about their business.

And business, in its economic sense, went tolerably well despite some disappointments. One of the most difficult tasks of all regional economic organizations of developing countries is to allocate industrial projects among themselves—to permit one country to produce on a large scale for all, so that the benefits of efficiency can be shared. As nations move through the drive to technological maturity, generating increasingly diversified and sophisticated industrial structures, intensified two-way trade of mutual advantage, based on comparative advantage, naturally emerges. This process is well documented, for example, in the classic League of Nations study *Industrialization and Foreign Trade* (1945). But it is difficult to negotiate or impose patterns of industrial location believed to be based on comparative advantage at earlier stages of development. Thus, the unsatisfactory fate of Japan's major ASEAN initiative of the 1970s.

On the occasion of the bilateral discussion of the ASEAN leaders with Prime Minister Takeo Fukuda on August 7, 1977, the Japanese government announced it "would consider favorably the request for a total of one billion U.S. dollars" in assistance to industrial projects, provided that each project was established as an ASEAN (rather than purely national) project and that its feasibility was confirmed. On August 18 in Manila, Fukuda, in the course of a wide-ranging review of Japan's policy in Asia, asserted his country would be "an especially close friend of ASEAN." But despite Japanese support and some subtlety in the design of projects and their financing, the ASEAN industrial program has had limited results; and much the same is true of the two other formal dimensions of ASEAN economic cooperation: intraregional trade preferences and "complementation schemes," in which private firms within the region cooperate to permit particular firms to specialize and benefit from economies of scale for the benefit of all.[55] As in Latin America, private-sector collaboration among manufacturing, banking, and service firms has thus far proved more promising than formal intergovernmental efforts.

Nevertheless, growth in Southeast Asia and its trade with the advanced industrial countries accelerated from 1975 to 1979, as the world economy recovered from the first oil price shock and real oil prices declined. Like other developing regions, ASEAN came under severe pressure with the second oil-price shock and the marked deceleration in the advanced industrial countries. Rates of increase in real GNP and in foreign trade sharply declined in response to reduced sales in advanced countries and, in some cases (e.g., Malaysia and Indonesia), reduced raw-materials prices. Nevertheless, the ASEAN countries maintained higher rates of growth than the advanced industrial countries, and intra-ASEAN trade as a proportion of total trade increased.

Unless the advanced industrial countries continue to conduct the kind of essentially suicidal economic policies implemented in the period 1979–1982, the non-Communist countries of the Pacific Basin are likely to remain the most dynamic and resilient group in the world economy.

6. The Future Organization of the Pacific Basin and of South Asia

Before turning to some concluding reflections on the evolution of regional organization in Asia, it may be useful to consider one organization that does not exist (an intergovernmental institution to embrace the Pacific Basin) and one that was born on August 2, 1983 (the Standing Committee to Monitor and Coordinate South Asian Regional Cooperation).

The issue of whether or not the Pacific Basin should be organized has been on the international agenda since 1965, when Professor Kiyoshi Kojima proposed a Pacific free-trade area comprising the United States, Canada, Japan, Australia, and New Zealand to balance the EEC and European free-trade area. Subsequent discussions, intergovernmental and private, have led to proposals for a wide range of institutions differing in function and membership. The Japanese government formally supported some kind of organization of the Pacific Basin as early as 1967; and the Japanese and Australian governments set in motion in 1980 a series of meetings, the third of which took place in Java in November 1983. This joint initiative, which we shall examine later in this chapter, may, perhaps, prove productive in time; but thus far it can be said that rarely has a concept been so intensively and systematically studied with so little result.[56] In the words of the old Chinese proverb, there has been a great deal of noise on the staircase, but no one has come into the room.

Much less thought and effort has thus far been devoted to

the question of organized economic cooperation among the countries of South Asia. Nevertheless, the sequence of meetings of South Asian foreign secretaries between April 1981 and July 1983, climaxed by the foreign ministers' meeting of August 1983, reflects the existence of strong forces which could increase the cohesion of the region; although the obstacles to be overcome are evidently formidable.

Turning first to the Pacific Basin, it should be noted that—as with the OECD, the EEC, ASEAN, and a potential South Asian grouping—important noneconomic interests are in play. Indeed, a good many statements about the economic organization of the Pacific Basin have had political and security overtones. The current consensus, however—which I share—is clearly that, should an institution be set up, it should deal exclusively with economic matters. Nevertheless, this chapter, while primarily concerned with the possibilities and problems of an economic organization, also includes tentative and preliminary observations on the possible future organization of the Pacific Basin for security purposes.

From the beginning, it was the remarkable rate of growth of the economies of the Asian rimland and the equally remarkable expansion in their foreign trade that set in motion the idea that the region would benefit from a framework of organization. Tables 7–11 suggest the scale that foreign trade within the Pacific Basin had achieved by the second half of the 1970s. Among the key features of those tables are the historic fact of U.S. trade with East Asia exceeding that with Western Europe by 1976; the extraordinary mutual trade dependence of Japan and the other countries of the Pacific Basin; and the substantial trading role of Taiwan in the region. As of 1977, 66 percent of Australia's total exports flowed to countries within the Pacific Basin; 59 percent of Japan's; 73 percent of South Korea's; 70 percent of the Philippines'; 67 percent of Thailand's; 45 percent of the United States'.[57] The import percentages were, with exception of Australia,

TABLE 7. U.S. Two-Way Trade with Western Europe and East Asia, 1976–1979 (U.S. $ millions)

	1976	1977	1978	1979
Western Europe				
Austria	449	543	690	723
Belgium	4,180	4,685	5,528	7,036
Denmark	1,035	1,147	1,319	1,481
France	6,118	6,750	8,514	10,699
West Germany	11,659	13,680	17,519	20,093
United Kingdom	9,344	11,416	14,040	19,141
Greece	747	727	881	1,014
Iceland	160	203	222	268
Ireland	499	628	866	1,035
Italy	5,789	6,070	7,828	9,737
Netherlands	5,806	6,402	7,394	8,921
Norway	1,185	1,349	1,813	2,027
Portugal	548	723	730	965
Spain	3,095	3,061	3,362	4,054
Sweden	2,007	2,160	2,503	3,268
Switzerland	2,234	2,969	3,611	5,802
Total	54,855	62,513	76,820	96,264
East Asia				
Australia	3,554	3,695	4,764	7,152
China (PRC)	348.8	391.5	1,129.8	2,486
China (ROC)	4,933	5,834	8,034	9,699
Hong Kong	3,751	4,424	5,389	6,388
Indonesia	4,313	4,501	4,635	4,906
Japan	27,066	30,724	39,347	45,742
Republic of Korea	4,661	5,533	7,247	8,539
Malaysia	1,530	1,951	2,324	3,183
New Zealand	794	816	1,010	1,324
Philippines	1,813	2,112	2,385	3,218
Singapore	1,693	2,094	2,616	3,876
Thailand	654	889	1,106	1,608
Total	55,110.8	62,964.5	79,986.8	98,112

Source: Direction of Trade Yearbook, published by the International Monetary Fund.

Secondary source: Tables 7–12 are from *Forum on the Pacific Basin: Growth, Security & Community*, a conference sponsored by the Asia and World Forum, the Center for the Study of Security Issues, the Foreign Policy Research Institute, and the Institute of International Studies, Taipei, Taiwan, May 28–30, 1980, pp. 13–17.

TABLE 8. Japan's Two-Way Trade with Western Europe, East Asia, and the United States, 1976–1979 (U.S. $ millions)

	1976	1977	1978	1979
Western Europe				
Austria	185	220	260	385
Belgium	881	1,015	1,293	1,465
Denmark	382	490	1,348	610
France	1,507	1,588	1,876	2,455
West Germany	3,475	4,309	5,695	6,800
United Kingdom	2,246	2,930	3,752	4,744
Greece	772	1,143	935	828
Iceland	24	21	27	51
Ireland	139	172	269	307
Italy	903	917	1,154	1,662
Netherlands	1,340	1,617	1,934	2,077
Norway	828	970	624	589
Portugal	158	200	176	201
Spain	682	619	637	858
Sweden	799	839	1,020	1,064
Switzerland	1,077	1,201	1,662	1,769
Total	15,398	18,251	22,662	25,865
East Asia and the United States				
Australia	7,682	7,673	8,058	8,830
China (PRC)	3,081	3,568	5,240	6,712
China (ROC)	3,475	3,871	5,379	6,796
Hong Kong	2,186	2,691	3,613	4,312
Indonesia	5,737	6,845	7,398	10,836
Republic of Korea	4,747	6,273	8,686	9,562
Malaysia	2,069	2,449	3,079	4,728
New Zealand	872	960	1,066	1,382
Philippines	1,909	2,012	2,625	3,182
Singapore	2,181	2,425	3,223	4,118
Thailand	1,921	2,124	2,390	2,862
United States*	27,788	32,481	40,286	46,732
Total	63,648	73,372	91,052	110,052

*The discrepancy between the U.S.-Japan trade figures here and those in the U.S. trade table is because of the differing statistics reported to the IMF by individual countries. This is also the case in Japan-Australia trade figures.

Source: *Direction of Trade Yearbook*, published by the International Monetary Fund.

TABLE 9. Australia's Two-Way Trade with Western Europe, East Asia, and the United States, 1976–1978 (U.S. $ millions)

	1976	1977	1978
Western Europe			
Austria	38	45	52
Belgium	292	261	269
Denmark	47	50	64
France	482	503	541
West Germany	1,136	1,296	1,471
United Kingdom	1,915	1,918	2,166
Greece	35	32	35
Iceland	13	12	11
Ireland	26	28	37
Italy	598	671	666
Netherlands	400	362	408
Norway	93	71	70
Portugal	17	23	25
Spain	152	117	118
Sweden	283	283	275
Switzerland	145	148	212
Total	5,672	5,820	6,420
East Asia and the United States			
China (PRC)	64	585	624
China (ROC)	354	438	594
Hong Kong	505	520	643
Indonesia	272	258	357
Japan	6,810	6,810	7,079
Republic of Korea	289	351	552
Malaysia	362	364	491
New Zealand	995	1,059	1,083
Philippines	160	213	224
Singapore	444	508	546
Thailand	96	107	141
United States	3,516	3,773	4,659
Total	14,167	14,986	16,993

Source: *Direction of Trade Yearbook*, published by the International Monetary Fund.

TABLE 10. Canada's Two-Way Trade with Western Europe, East Asia, and the United States, 1976–1979 (U.S. $ millions)

	1976	1977	1978	1979
Western Europe				
Austria	78	78	95	128
Belgium	614	635	602	784
Denmark	109	122	141	164
France	850	839	1,016	1,205
West Germany	1,546	1,639	1,777	2,460
United Kingdom	3,036	3,035	3,159	3,890
Greece	66	62	82	93
Iceland	2	3	5	9
Ireland	59	68	76	109
Italy	926	846	885	1,161
Netherlands	639	667	700	1,024
Norway	290	277	177	282
Portugal	42	58	58	100
Spain	237	233	238	340
Sweden	368	348	390	471
Switzerland	251	305	355	444
Total	9,113	9,215	9,756	12,664
East Asia and the United States				
Australia	677	719	690	880
China (PRC)	290	424	525	701
China (ROC)	338	371	438	537
Hong Kong	352	329	378	487
Indonesia	97	87	95	90
Japan	3,975	4,058	4,667	5,339
Republic of Korea	435	440	508	707
Malaysia	80	89	97	142
New Zealand	133	136	149	194
Philippines	83	109	108	142
Singapore	111	125	143	229
Thailand	48	63	71	103
Subtotal	6,619	6,950	7,849	9,551
United States	52,179	56,914	63,158	76,259
Total	58,798	63,864	71,007	84,810

Source: Direction of Trade Yearbook, published by the International Monetary Fund.

TABLE 11. Republic of China's Two-Way Trade with Western Europe, East Asia, and the United States, 1976–1979 (U.S. $ millions)

	1976	1977	1978	1979
Western Europe				
Austria	23	13	16	37
Belgium	93	123	157	203
Denmark	20	19	38	56
France	123	177	222	311
West Germany	775	695	985	1,377
United Kingdom	329	450	567	702
Greece	12	20	29	40
Iceland	1	2	1	3
Ireland	4	12	15	22
Italy	117	143	211	343
Netherlands	218	235	331	453
Norway	11	11	36	29
Portugal	10	2	4	7
Spain	30	34	42	74
Sweden	66	73	117	146
Switzerland	88	71	124	175
Total	1,920	2,080	2,895	3,978
East Asia and the United States				
Australia	407	460	657	875
China (PRC)	0	0	0	0
Hong Kong	712	903	1,010	1,344
Indonesia	421	503	625	850
Japan	3,557	3,776	5,269	6,825
Republic of Korea	160	193	287	349
Malaysia	159	219	314	458
New Zealand	41	48	57	76
Philippines	110	132	213	274
Singapore	251	324	379	545
Thailand	172	198	229	259
United States	4,861	5,843	7,418	9,059
Total	10,851	12,599	16,458	20,914

Source: *Direction of Trade Yearbook*, published by the International Monetary Fund

TABLE 12. Measures of International Involvement of Six Pacific Basin Countries, 1950–1977

Country	Goods and Services Exports as a % of GNP						
	1950	1955	1960	1965	1970	1975	1977
Australia	15	13	14	15	18	16	17
Japan	n.a.	8	9	11	13	15	18
Korea	2	1	2	5	15	28	36
Philippines	17	17	13	17	14	19	19
Thailand	24	20	17	19	17	19	22
United States	4	4	5	5	6	8	7

n.a. Not available.

Sources: World Bank, *World Tables 1976*; Hugh Patrick and Henry Rosovsky, eds., *Asia's New Giant: How the Japanese Economy Works* (Brookings Institution, 1976), p. 399; OECD, *Main Economic Indicators*, March 1979; IMF, *International Financial Statistics*, vol. 32 (July 1979).

Secondary source: Lawrence B. Krause and Sueo Sekiguchi, eds., *Economic Interaction in the Pacific Basin* (Washington, D.C.: Brookings Institution, 1980), p. 17.

systematically higher. Table 12 exhibits the generally high proportion of goods and services exports to GNP for countries of the region, excepting the United States.[58]

In the Western Pacific, then, we are dealing with countries geared to high growth rates and rapidly increasing mutual trading interdependence, with heavy reliance on foreign trade for their continued growth and prosperity.

The pace of real growth and trade expansion in the region has been accompanied by increased capital flows within it and the emergence of increasingly sophisticated banking and capital market institutions.

There was also important structural change captured in Chart 1 (see above, p. 72). In the course of the 1970s the proportion of manufactured goods to total exports moved up strongly in Thailand, the Philippines, and Malaysia, suggesting that they might, over the decade ahead, follow something like the remarkable path pioneered earlier by South Korea and

Taiwan. As Miyokei Shinohara has pointed out, a "horizontal" or "intra-industry" division of labor is emerging in the western part of the Pacific Basin to supersede the classical "vertical" division of labor in which manufactured goods are traded against foodstuffs and raw materials.[59]

In this transition opportunities are emerging for intensified trade in various kinds of manufactures, a process which occurred as between the pre-1914 United Kingdom and Germany, and, in the post-1945 world, within the Common Market, between Western Europe and the United States, and between Japan and the United States.

On the face of it, then, the current importance of the region, the complexities of its interdependence, and its prospects as the most dynamic region of the world economy over the next generation all suggest that an organization performing for the Pacific Basin roughly the function of the OECD in the Atlantic world would be useful.

Why has it not happened? What are the obstacles that must be overcome if some such institution is to come to life? I shall deal with these questions in a somewhat unorthodox way. I shall first list the six major obstacles to the economic organization of the Pacific Basin exactly as I perceived them in Austin when I completed a draft of this book in April 1983. I shall then restate my view as it was altered by my talks in the region down to November 1983.

First, international institutions are not easy to create; but, in this respect, the OECD was uniquely fortunate. Its predecessor institution, the Organization for European Economic Cooperation (OEEC), set up to manage the Marshall Plan, already existed and had, for more than a decade, generated the habit of economic consultation and cooperation within Europe and across the Atlantic. It was not difficult, therefore, to convert the OEEC to a different agenda as the need for U.S. aid ended but new problems of common concern emerged; for example, in trade, monetary affairs, and assistance to developing countries. This was done in 1960. An organization for the Pacific Basin must be created *de novo*; although, as we shall see, the ADB might play a useful central role.

Second, the initial members of the OECD, while amply variegated, were relatively homogeneous with respect to levels of development, culture, and political institutions. Asia is much more diversified. In particular, an organization for the Pacific Basin would have to accommodate the interests of countries over a much wider spectrum of development and technological sophistication than the OECD.

Third, there are a variety of questions posed by the concept, especially in its present somewhat amorphous state, that relate, in one way or another, to security concerns of countries of the region. Would membership draw them into unwanted, more explicit security relations within the United States? If Communist governments were permitted to join—and took up the option—would the organization permit unwanted contacts with and influence by such governments?

Fourth, some countries of the region fear that an economic organization of the Pacific Basin would inevitably be dominated by Japan, the United States, or, worst of all, by both in concert. Without extensive experience of multilateral economic institutions, the fact that they normally provide more evenhanded treatment than conventional bilateral relations to less powerful nations is not universally appreciated.

Fifth, a major stumbling block: Would a Pacific Basin organization dilute the slowly developing but important elements of economic cohesion within ASEAN?[60] Or could an institution for the Pacific Basin be so designed as to strengthen the cohesion of ASEAN and accelerate its rate of progress in cooperative economic ventures? ASEAN is regarded with such respect and hope as a stabilizing institution in Asia that few would advocate proceeding with the organization of the Pacific Basin at the cost of reducing or damaging its prospects.

Sixth, there is the question of Taiwan's place in an organization of the Pacific Basin. On the one hand, it would be quite irrational on economic grounds to exclude this significant component (about 8 percent) of the region's trading system. On the other hand, Taiwan's inclusion might pose problems for relations of a Pacific Basin organization and some of its members with the PRC.

In talking to government officials throughout Asia and the Pacific in July–November 1983, I found that all six of these problems proved to have a certain reality. Indeed, that should have been the case because I defined them after reading a good many statements by government officials and analyses by responsible academic figures, quite often based on interviews with public servants. But I would now put the problem in a somewhat different way.[61]

Throughout the Pacific Basin there is an awareness that the concept of an embracing economic organization for the region will not go away. There is even a widespread sense of inevitability that, some day, it will come about. There are a few governments which, for somewhat differing reasons, are actively searching for a positive outcome soon; notably, South Korea, Japan, and Australia. A good many governments, however, resist moving ahead at the present time as they engage in an effort to assess the likely costs and benefits of such an enterprise in rather narrow national terms.

Even though the Pacific Basin is now primarily discussed in economic terms, the governments take political costs and benefits into account. In pursuing this kind of cost-benefit analysis the governments are gravely hampered because no proposition was formally on the table until, as we shall see, July 12, 1984. The difficulty is particularly acute for officials in the developing countries of the Pacific Basin. They are simply not in a position to define what the Pacific Basin has to offer their countries. They greatly fear, for example, that if the Pacific Basin were organized along European Common Market lines, or even as a looser free-trade area, they would lose out to Japan and the United States in industrial sectors which have moved forward in developing Asia in a quite promising way in recent years behind protecting barriers.

The heart of the resistance to an economic organization of the Pacific Basin clearly lies, then, in fear among the less-developed countries of the region that it would lead, in one way or another, to dominance by the United States, Japan, or by both in concert; and this fear transcends a simple anxiety that the more advanced industrial countries of the region will dominate trade in manufactures. The fear extends to looser formulations of the Pacific Basin in which it is envisaged that the group would not commit itself to a common market or free-trade area, but feel its way pragmatically toward an agreed agenda. As Prime Minister Mahathir of Malaysia put it in October 1981:

> In the case of the Pacific Community, our main stand is that it is difficult enough to work within the framework of ASEAN, which is only a five-member community. We feel that it would really not work out; the end result would most probably be dominance by the more forceful members of the group. So I think in that sort of situation the credibility would be gone. It would not be a regional grouping, it would be a region under the influence of some of them.[62]

Conscious that progress toward agreement on a Pacific Basin concept was being impeded equally by inappropriate formulations derived from European experience and by proposals so vague and amorphous that they invited suspicion of hidden motives, the Japanese and Australian prime ministers set in motion in January 1980 an effort to achieve an informal consensus on what a Pacific Basin institution might do and how it might be organized so that a proposition could be laid before the governments for decision.[63] This joint effort has yielded a series of Pacific Economic Cooperation Conferences (PEEC).

Each country appointed three participants: a public official (to operate in his personal capacity), a representative of the private sector, and an academic analyst of the Pacific Basin problem. It is pretty well agreed that, at the first two conferences at Canberra (1981) and Bangkok (1982), the tripartite group made little progress in resolving the central problem, which was defined with admirable clarity at the initial seminar in Australia by Thanat Khoman. As an elder statesman of Asia and the Pacific, he perhaps felt more free to be blunt than a working prime minister like Mahathir:

> . . . the most important factor which stands in the way of implementing the Pacific basin co-operation concept is the unequal and disparate stages of economic development among Pacific rim states. It is a fact that the region comprises highly developed countries as well as much weaker states. Such differences in economic and industrial advancement lead to fears on the part of less developed nations of being dominated by more powerful ones, who may exercise their hegemony over the former or exert unjustified pressures, to the former's detriment.[64]

One official participant described the proceedings in Bangkok as follows:

> The academics put forward different and conflicting concepts of the Pacific Basin; the representatives of the private sector said: "Give us the parameters, give us a structure the governments want, and we can work constructively within it"; the foreign office officials said: "What's the proposition? How can we decide if there is no proposition?"

Evidently, the public servants present, lacking instructions, did not feel free to assume the responsibility for laying clearcut proposals on the table and seeing if they could be brought by discussion and negotiation to a working consensus.

Nevertheless, an important decision was made at Bangkok; that is, to build a third PEEC around four functional subjects, each defined to underline the strong trade orientation of the region's development: agriculture and renewable-resource goods trade; minerals and energy trade; manufactured goods trade; and investment and technology transfer. Papers were prepared on these subjects at major institutions in Thailand, Australia, Korea, and Japan, respectively. They were reviewed at a meeting in Bali November 21–23, 1983.

The group decided that progress along these functional lines was sufficient to justify a further session in 1985 in Seoul.

The fate of this tripartite exploratory exercise will, evidently, be determined, in the end, by the governments of the region; and the outcome is not clear as this book is completed in 1985. What is reasonably clear is the sequence of concepts which have been applied to the Pacific Basin. First, there was the analogy to Europe; that is, a common market or free-trade area for the advanced industrial countries of the Pacific region, framed by the wider concept of a Pacific Community. It was soon perceived that trading unions would create more problems than they might solve in relations between the more- and less-developed countries; and they might, indeed, obstruct the process of heightened interdependence clearly underway between them. Second, there were various versions of an organization for the Pacific Basin analogous to the OECD in Paris. As this idea was pursued indecisively, a third concept gradually emerged based on two insights. It became clear, as one formulation put it, "that issues ought to be handled by specific functional task forces."[65] It also became clear that, if it were to succeed, a Pacific Basin organization would have to conceive of itself primarily as a regional organization constructively linking more- and less-developed countries. And, I would add, if it has not become clear it will become clear that the developing countries of the region will, in the end, only be seriously interested in functional task forces if they result in increased investment, increased trade, or accelerated acquisition of technologies.

That it should take almost twenty years to arrive at this still-incomplete degree of consensus on a functional North-South approach to the Pacific Basin is not surprising. By and large, things have gone pretty well for the economies of the Pacific Basin; and when they have not gone well remedy could be sought in bilateral relations or one or another existing multilateral organization. As an Australian parliamentarian put it to me: "When things have gone well, the governments asked, 'Why do we need a Pacific Basin organization?' When there were crises they were too distracted with immediate problems to think about it." The Pacific Basin has been regarded by most governments as an interesting and potentially important concept; but it has not been accorded steady, high priority. In addition, it was natural but misleading to begin by applying to the Pacific Basin concepts derived from earlier experience in Europe. Finally, once it was accepted that the Pacific Basin organization would have to be, essentially, a regional North-South institution, there was no agreed model on which to build. Indeed, since the early 1970s North-South relations have been frustrated in the Pacific Basin and sometimes enflamed by the efforts of the South to install on a global basis the concepts of a New International Economic Order. There was, quite sensibly, no impulse to echo in a regional organization the sterile North-South dialogue conducted within the United Nations; but no viable alternative concept for North-South cooperation has been agreed upon.

Nevertheless, it is worth noting that the formulation that has gradually emerged from the protracted pragmatic dialogue about the Pacific Basin, more or less crystallized at the tripartite meeting at Bali, has both significant precedents and a reasonably coherent historical and theoretical rationale.

For example, the report of the Brandt Commission, *North-South*, devoted several chapters to certain functional problems (agriculture, energy, raw materials, and the environment) as appropriate areas for concerted effort between more-advanced and developing countries, although these functional and sectoral strands in the report were overwhelmed in their public impact by a plea for a massive transfer of resources from North to South on the dubious grounds that the North lacked adequate investment opportunities to achieve full employment. The report of the Herrera Commission, appointed by the secretary general of the OAS to define areas for economic cooperation in the western hemisphere for the 1980s and beyond, isolated agriculture, energy, raw materials, and certain environmental problems among its seven priority tasks.[66] ASEAN has defined energy and agriculture as the two top-priority areas for joint action. Indeed, at Cancun, in a little-noted intervention, President Reagan showed an awareness of the need to move in this direction. Among the five principles he set out to guide North-South economic relations, he included as his third point "guiding our assistance towards the development of self-sustaining productive activities, particularly in food and energy." Unfortunately, neither Mr. Reagan's colleagues at Cancun nor his own administration has pursued this insight seriously and systematically.

These resource problems are, in fact, endemic and not confined to the non-Communist world. Any analysis of the problems and prospects for the Soviet Union and the People's Republic of China over the next generation would have to include energy and agriculture high on the list of priority tasks.

An approach in terms of these resource-related functional areas has one simple, powerful virtue: it can answer lucidly the key question in the minds of the governments of the developing countries of the Pacific Basin. The question is: "What's in it for us?" The answer is: enlarged external investment.

Studies by the World Bank and the regional development banks have, for some time, indicated that greatly enlarged domestic and foreign investment in these sectors will be required if the world economy and the developing regions resume reasonably high and steady rates of growth.

With respect to energy, for example, a World Bank estimate suggested that energy production investment requirements in the developing regions for the 1980s would approximate

$683 billion (in 1980 U.S. dollars), with an annual investment growth rate of 12.3 percent, lifting the proportion of investment allocated to this purpose from 2.3 percent of GNP in 1980 to 3.2 percent in 1990. A good deal of this capital would have to come from abroad.

For Latin America alone, the Inter-American Development Bank estimated that in the course of the 1980s something of the order of $300 billion (in 1980 U.S. dollars) would be required for investment in energy production, about 45 percent of which would have to come from abroad. The proportion of GNP allocated to energy investment would, on these calculations, rise from something like 3 percent to 4.4 percent.

A study sponsored by the ADB, to which we shall later refer at greater length (see below, pp. 119–120), estimated that energy production investment would have to double in its developing member countries (excepting India) in the period 1980–1985 relative to the level of 1975–1980, if high growth rates are to be sustained. With respect to agriculture, the inescapable increase of population in the developing regions due to age structures, despite current declines in birth rates, may add something like 2 billion human beings to the planet in the next generation; and, overall, the rate of increase in agricultural production in those regions is not yet matching the rate of increase in the demand for food, inducing an annual rate of growth in grain imports of more than 3 percent per annum. Although investment requirements for the 1980s have not been estimated, few would disagree that in this historic generation of maximum tension between population increase and food supply enlarged domestic and foreign investment in agriculture will be required in the developing regions.

As for raw materials, there is evidence of underinvestment in recent years and distorted patterns of investment. In Latin America, for example, the tension between an understandable nationalist desire to control fully natural resources and an understandable desire of foreign investors for stable and reasonable terms for their outlays has resulted in a number of countries in reduced rates of raw-material development. If the world economy revives, we may encounter raw-material bottlenecks. Taking precisely this view of raw-material prospects, the World Bank has estimated that 1977–2000 capital requirements for additional capacity in seven key minerals would come to $278 billion (in U.S. 1977 dollars), of which $96 billion constitutes investments in the developing countries. (In 1982 dollars the figures would be about $342 billion and $118 billion, respectively.)

There is another major form of resource-related investment that should be included in this array; that is, investment in rolling back degradation of the environment and maintaining for the long pull supplies of clean air and water, arable land, the forests, and irreplaceable areas for recreation and wild life. These are tasks for both advanced industrial and developing countries. Over the past generation, the flow of investment for these purposes has greatly increased and there have been some notable areas of progress, including, for example, the Chinese reforestation program. Indeed, concerted regional programs for reforestation should be considered high on the potential agenda for regional cooperation in South Asia as well as the Pacific Basin.

Historically, there is good reason to believe that increased priority for and investment in these basic resource sectors conforms to the underlying forces at work in the world economy since the end of 1972.[67] The rise in grain prices at that time and in oil prices in the autumn of 1973 signalled the close of a generation in which the relative prices of basic commodities had fallen 25 percent. That process lifted urban real incomes and provided one major pillar for the uniquely powerful boom in the world economy of the 1950s and 1960s. The turning point of 1972–1973 had been clearly foreshadowed by stock and reserve ratio movements in grain and energy markets during the second half of the 1960s and the first three years of the 1970s.

Since that turning point, the world economy experienced a period of oil-price remission (1975–1978); a second oil-price shock; and a second period of remission (1980–1983). There have been important shifts to other energy sources and economies in energy use as well as a radical deceleration in average rates of growth which affected the demand for industrial raw materials as well as energy. There have also been wholesome changes in agricultural policy in India, China, and some other developing nations. As of 1985, prices of these commodities are relatively soft as compared to their peak levels of the 1970s. But in my view at least and, more important, in the view of those who have carefully examined supply-demand prospects in particular sectors under the assumption that the world economy breaks out of its recent phase of stagnation, the period of relatively expensive basic resources has not ended. And, pulling back from the details, this assessment makes reasonable sense. We are at a stage of history when the rate of population increase is pressing hard against agricultural and other resources, but also a period when many developing countries have come to levels of modernization when they can absorb quite rapidly the existing unapplied backlog of technologies. As we could see in the 1950s, 1960s and even the troubled 1970s, the natural growth rates of substantial portions of Latin America, North Africa, the Middle East, and Asia are high. It would, indeed, be surprising if this was not an era of some strain on global resources.

Put another way, it will take very large resource-related investments in the world economy over the next generation if growth is not to be bottlenecked, especially in the developing regions, by a resumption of relatively high resource prices, the progressive degradation of arable land, and other degenerative processes.

This brings us to a question put to me several times in ASEAN countries. It is a question leaders in the advanced industrial countries will have to answer not only to them but also to their own citizens if the Pacific Basin or any other

North-South partnership venture begins to become a potentially serious proposition. The question put to me was: "What's in it for you? Why should you in the North care?" There are religious, moral, or simple human reasons why individuals in advanced industrial countries may care about the fate of men, women, and children in developing countries. And these currents of thought and feeling should not be callously ignored or set aside, because they are a part of political reality, as the popular response to famine in Africa in 1984–1985 demonstrated. But they are only a part. Leaders and citizens in developing regions are, therefore, justified in asking what the operating motives are in the North, not only because they feel their histories have given them the right to be suspicious of the North but also because no partnership is going to be viable unless it provides solid, recognizable benefits to both parties in conventional national-interest terms.

The interests of the North in high and regular economic growth in the South are, essentially, two.

—First, the South is becoming an increasingly important trading partner of the North. Between 1972 and 1982 U.S. exports to developing countries rose from 30 percent to 40 percent of total exports, imports from 27 percent to 42 percent. Because at this stage of history the average growth rates in the South should be higher than in the North (due to larger backlogs of unapplied technologies), one might expect this trend to continue.

—Second, the rate of growth in the South is one factor determining the capacity of the developing countries to undergo change with minimum internal and external violence as well as a factor determining their vulnerability to external intrusion. This second point requires some elaboration. Putting aside the Berlin crises of 1948–1949 and 1961–1962 and the chronic European-theater missile crisis of 1979–1984, all the most difficult, dangerous, and bloody Cold War crises of the past thirty-five years have been interwoven with the inherently volatile process of modernization in the developing regions; for example, the crises in Korea, Indochina, Indonesia, Afghanistan, the Middle East, Africa, the Caribbean, and Central America. High and steady economic growth would certainly not have prevented all these crises. The enormous drama of modernization in the developing regions is evidently many sided. But economic weakness, frustration, and distortion have surely contributed to the crises experienced in the developing regions and their vulnerability to external intrusion.

It would be naive and unrealistic for governments in the North to believe that high and steady growth in the developing countries would insulate them from crises with strategic implications or, indeed, that it lies wholly in the power of the North to guarantee high and steady growth in the developing regions. But it would be equally naive and unrealistic for the North not to recognize its strategic interest in high, steady growth in the South and to exploit its real but limited margin of influence to contribute realistically to that objective.

These broad observations may appear only dimly related to the question of an economic organization for the Pacific Basin. And indeed, issues of this type do not figure significantly in the massive literature on the subject. But that is one reason almost twenty years of discussion have failed to yield a positive result. Once one accepts Thanat Khoman's North-South definition of the central problem of the Pacific Basin, these issues must be faced. Put another way, the problem of bringing to life a Pacific Basin organization is not primarily a matter of ASEAN resistance or fear of dilution. It is mainly a question of whether the advanced industrial nations of the Pacific Basin, most notably the United States and Japan, are prepared to enlarge the flows of public as well as private capital to the region for purposes that commend themselves to all the parties concerned. I may, of course, be wrong; but it is my clear impression that all the other obstacles to the creation of a Pacific Basin economic organization are manageable if the United States and Japan are prepared to enlarge the investment resources they make available in the kind of resource-related fields isolated in the Bali report. And I agree with Hahn-Been Lee that the time has come for a U.S. initiative.

> In the final analysis, it is political will which creates a new international structure. The Japanese Government did take the first official initiative on the Pacific Basin. It was a precious initiative, coming from a country which has not, at least in recent years, been noted for taking the initiative on any international matter. Unfortunately, this valuable initiative has lost momentum because of reservations expressed by ASEAN, and the singular lack of an official response from the United States. The United States has not met the challenge. . . . A revival of the past momentum is now needed. In my view, it is the turn of the United States to make a more positive response to the earlier Japanese initiative. Fortunately, ASEAN is reacting in a cautiously positive manner. The reaction, however, is too cautious to generate new momentum. There seems to be a kind of gentle stalemate in the triangular relationship between Japan, ASEAN and the United States.[68]

So much by way of background. How should one proceed? In the face of the Bali report the governments may act in terms of Jean Monnet's dictum: ". . . people only accept change when they are faced with necessity, and only recognize necessity whan a crisis is upon them."[69] There is no palpable crisis forcing governments toward a Pacific Basin organization; and Hahn-Been Lee's "gentle stalemate" may persist. It is also possible that the Bali report and the sustained effort of which it is a part will in time break the stalemate and the Pacific Community will proceed from concept to action on a wide front based on a lucid and firmly agreed consensus having, at last, been found.

But there is a third possibility. Even after further PEEC sessions, the governments of the region may not be ready for the long-term commitment implied by the setting up of a Pacific Basin organization. They may be closer to the judgment of

Hadi Soesastro of Indonesia: ". . . the paradigm for Pacific economic cooperation must be one involving 'the art of having an affair' which may or may not lead to 'marriage.'"[70] They may judge it wiser that a Pacific Basin organization start modestly and pragmatically and proceed step by step as it is demonstrated that useful results can be produced and the anxieties outlined above allayed.

And, indeed, the "affair"—or at least a bit of "dating"—may have been initiated on July 12, 1984, in Djakarta. As noted earlier, it has become something of a tradition that foreign ministers of ASEAN meet collectively with each of their "dialogue partners" in the wake of their annual meeting. The partners are: the EEC, dealt with collectively; Australia; Canada; Japan; New Zealand; and the United States. At the 1984 meeting ASEAN, through its current chairman, the foreign minister of Indonesia (Mochtar Kusumaatmadja), suggested a joint meeting with its five Pacific dialogue partners. The meeting thus became the first intergovernmental gathering based explicitly on the principle of economic cooperation in the Pacific Basin.

At this multilateral session, ASEAN proposed that cooperation should begin in the field of human-resource development with an inventory of existing programs, and that a meeting of senior officials of the eleven governments involved (six ASEAN plus five Pacific dialogue partners) take place in about six months; that is, early in 1985. The purpose of this session would be to discuss concrete proposals in the light of the inventory. The problems of human-resource development in the Pacific islands were underlined as an important area of universal concern.

A good deal hinges on the seriousness and effectiveness with which the Djakarta initiative is pursued, notably by Japan and the United States. ASEAN has placed on the Pacific agenda an item which was, evidently, carefully chosen. It is both serious and of universal interest. It is neither particularly sensitive nor threatening to the developing countries of the region, which are already familiar and generally comfortable with external assistance in education and technical training. Moreover, a Pacific Basin human-resource development program is unlikely to require large-scale additional governmental outlays by Japan, the United States, and the other advanced industrial countries of the Pacific Basin. Finally, by beginning the Pacific enterprise between ASEAN and its dialogue partners, complex issues of membership were, for the time, avoided; for example, the possible participation of the PRC, Taiwan, the U.S.S.R., South Korea, and so on. Political life will, thus, not be placed under great strain in the countries of the region if a conventional program evolves supplementing existing national and international efforts in education and technical training.

On the other hand, the field of human-resource development, taken seriously, poses fundamental questions of great importance because it requires a reasonably clear vision of each nation's path of development over the coming generation. For example, human-resource development in the Pacific islands requires some kind of answer to the question of how a viable economic life can be built on the islands. Human-resource development also poses a question discussed with passionate interest throughout the Pacific Basin: How should each country, taking into account its stage of growth and economic prospects, prepare to make the most of the new technologies; for example, microelectronics, genetic engineering, robots, lasers, new industrial materials, and new methods of communication?

If the Pacific human-resource development program should come effectively to grips with these two problems, it would be immediately recognized as a serious venture; pressure for expansion of the initial exploratory group would intensify; a demand for similar programs in other regions would soon emerge; and the Pacific Basin countries would be led on to consider a wider agenda, perhaps even making the transition from dating to an affair, or, perhaps, even to marriage.

TABLE 13. Primary Energy Consumption, 1971–1981, Asia and Pacific Basin

| | Million Tons Oil Equivalent | | | Annual Average Rate of Increase (%) | |
	1971	1976	1981	1971– 1981	1976– 1981
United States	1,701	1,804	1,806	0.6	—
Canada	168	207	221	2.8	1.4
South Asia	95	114	155	5.0	6.2
Southeast Asia	106	145	200	6.6	6.6
Japan	301	345	354	1.6	0.5
Australia	62	76	89	3.7	3.2
China	321	432	500	4.5	3.0
Subtotal	2,754	3,123	3,325	1.9	1.7
of which:					
Developing Asia	522	691	855	5.1	4.3
Developed Pacific Basin	2,232	2,432	2,470	1.0	0.3
World total	5,387	6,286	6,849	2.4	1.7

Source: Derived from British Petroleum Company, *PB Statistical Review of World Energy, 1981*, p. 32.

The problem of energy supply is a prime candidate for a major next step beyond human-resource development. Table 13 suggests why this is the case.[71]

Table 13 dramatizes a simple but exceedingly important point: at this stage of their evolution developing nations experience, under normal circumstances, much higher rates of growth in energy consumption than advanced industrial countries and higher marginal energy-to-GNP ratios. Among the reasons for this phenomenon are the following: higher real growth rates; higher rates of population expansion in energy-intensive cities; the rapid absorption of energy-intensive technologies such as steel, metal-working, and chemicals; higher rates of expansion in motor vehicle use.

Between 1971 and 1981 the proportion of energy consumption by the countries of developing Asia to the total for the Pacific rose from 19 percent to 26 percent.

History is seldom linear; but, if the 1971—1981 differential rates were to persist, by the year 2000 developing Asia would require 2,200 million tons of oil equivalent in energy consumption, developed Asia, 2,984 million tons. The proportion of energy used in developing Asia would rise from 26 percent to 42 percent of the total for the region. The absolute increment that would have to be generated in or for developing Asia would be 1,345 million tons of oil equivalent and only 514 million tons for developed Asia.

It is calculations like these which have led the World Bank and the regional development banks to the estimates for large increases in energy investment on behalf of the developing regions cited earlier (see above, pp. 110—111).

With the help of an international expert group and an international review panel, the ADB published in 1982 a detailed equivalent study for Asia, *Asian Energy Problems.* The study, reaching as far to the west as Afghanistan (but excluding India), covers all the ADB's developing member countries (DMCs). It projects energy demand and supply by energy sources, down to 1990, assuming an average annual rate of increase in energy consumption of 7.6 percent, as compared to 8.5 percent for 1973—1978. It concludes that the average annual investment needs of the energy sector of the DMCs will be more than double in the 1980—1985 period as compared to the average level (in real terms) of 1975—1980; that in most DMCs almost all the needed equipment has to be imported; and that the task of mobilizing the necessary external financial resources will require heavy support from international financial agencies.

The study also notes that many DMCs do not have energy

supply and consumption data organized in such a way that they are amenable to economic and statistic evaluation.

These pioneering calculations are cited not only to indicate that the ADB has made a preliminary canvass of the energy problem but also to suggest the order of magnitude of the task confronted in the Pacific Basin if the rapidly growing countries of the region are to provide themselves, through their own resources and external assistance, with the energy base they will require if high real-growth rates are to be maintained.

The operational question is: What could a Pacific Basin energy organization do that could not be done just as well on a national and bilateral basis?

An energy program for the Pacific Basin might begin with agreement that, in a standard format, each country project its energy requirements, domestic production, export capabilities, and import needs down to, say, 1990 and to the year 2000. Alternative explicit assumptions about real growth rates and marginal energy-to-GNP ratios might be used. Members of ASEAN might prepare their estimates in common and present them on a consolidated basis, for reasons discussed below. The secretariat of the energy program (organized by the ADB) would pull together these projections, assure their comparability, and present a broad statistical picture of the region's energy problems and potentialities.

On the basis of such data, responsible energy officials of the government (as well as officials of the World Bank, ADB, and possibly the International Energy Agency [IEA]) would meet and isolate certain key areas for action. The experience with energy projections since 1974 does not justify firm reliance on particular numbers generated by analyses of even the highest professionalism and sophistication. The initial projections would have to be regularly revised in the light of unfolding experience. On the other hand, certain major problems and areas for action are likely to emerge so substantial that they transcend any likely range of uncertainty; for example, the need for enlarged coal exports from Australia and the United States, the need for increased use of nuclear energy, the likelihood of reduced Indonesian oil (but possibly expanded liquified natural gas) exports, the need for continued energy conservation, the importance of exploiting, when cost effective, the generation of energy from biomass, photovoltaic cells, and so on.

Out of a pragmatic examination of the major elements in the region's energy balance sheet a lucid and specific energy working agenda might emerge which might well require further detailed analysis by functional subcommittees; for example, on coal, oil, gas, atomic energy. In part, action on that agenda, when refined, could be undertaken by individual nations acting on their own or bilaterally. ASEAN, which has already identified energy as a key problem on its common agenda, might proceed to examine in a heightened way the possibilities for intra-ASEAN cooperation in this field. Above all, the outcome should be a certain number of energy investment projects which require and justify external financing, private and/or public. In the case of ASEAN, a special fund might be provided (perhaps by the ADB and the World Bank) to support intensified energy cooperation among the members.

Thus, the exercise as a whole would, if successful, have the following characteristics: it would require the governments to examine their energy prospects on a long-term basis; lead governments to act domestically with a longer time horizon than that induced by the oscillations of the international oil market; stimulate ASEAN to heighten its collective efforts in the field of energy and provide special resources for that purpose; and enlarge the flow of external capital, private and public, to expand the region's energy base.

In addition, the exercise would provide an occasion for heightening attention to the possible relevance of new or unorthodox energy sources and technologies and accelerating their diffusion when cost effectiveness was established.

The enterprise would not initially, or perhaps ever, involve new structures or institutions: the ADB could sponsor the gathering of the relevant data on an ad hoc basis; its secretariat could service the meetings; the World Bank and other relevant global institutions could attend and contribute; participation within the Pacific Basin, flexibly defined, would be on the basis of the interest of governments in participating.

Underpinning the project would be a simple, shared perception: energy investment lead times are long; there is a need for the region to gear its energy policies systematically to a horizon that looks beyond the current situation in international energy markets; and, in so doing, it is wise to exploit such practical opportunities for international cooperation as may emerge from sustained multilateral consultation.

As suggested earlier, energy is, of course, not the only candidate for such pragmatic multilateral Pacific Basin programs. Agriculture, already identified by ASEAN as a key priority area, is another, as is raw-material supply, including the maintenance and systematic cultivation of the forests. There may well be substantial opportunities to exploit current and emerging technologies to improve, by multilateral cooperation, communications throughout the Pacific Basin. Krause and Sekiguchi (and others) argued that regular multilateral consultation on trade could mitigate or avoid some of the difficulties and tensions generated in recent years by unilateral actions in that field.[72]

In addition, the countries of the Pacific Basin may wish, at some stage, to consider setting up an equivalent for their region of the European Atomic Community (EURATOM).

The fundamental point made here is that, unless a major crisis or some other event produces a solid consensus, a Pacific Basin organization is most likely to emerge successfully by demonstrating, case by case, that it is a useful supplement to national, bilateral, and existing multilateral economic relations, and the way to begin is to go to work on a major problem—or perhaps a few problems—of palpable common interest. Once that demonstration is made, there will be no shortage of other problems to be tackled; and the appropriate shape for the organization will evolve naturally, in an unforced way.

It may well be asked: Why should problems as universal as enlarged energy or agricultural investment or reforestation be dealt with on a regional basis? Why not proceed in a global forum? The answer is that the isolation and implementation of investment projects is most unlikely to proceed successfully with some 150 governments sitting around the table. Such large gatherings can listen to speeches or professional papers and, perhaps, with some strain, emerge with more-or-less agreed resolutions of greater or lesser ambiguity. They are simply too large for serious pragmatic business. It was precisely such considerations which shaped the OAS Herrera Report cited earlier (see above, pp. 111–112).

There is an additional North-South function that a Pacific Basin organization would be well equipped to undertake at an early stage. It relates to a particular aspect of the transfer of the new technologies which I group together under the rubric of the Fourth Industrial Revolution, and to which I referred in relation to the ASEAN proposal for human-resource development.[73]

The Fourth Industrial Revolution has three distinctive characteristics. First, the new innovations are linked to areas of basic science which themselves are evolving rapidly. This was true of only a few major innovations in the past. We are, therefore, likely to see new linkages develop between the operating economic sectors of our economies on the one hand and the research universities and institutions on the other. Indeed, this is already happening in many countries. Moreover, success in generating and absorbing the new technologies is likely to be closely related to each nation's ability to bring its scientists, engineers, and producers into close working association. Second, the new technologies are likely to be ubiquitous, affecting virtually all sectors of the economy: the old basic industries; agriculture, forestry, and animal husbandry; and the service sectors, from medical care to education. This is a technological revolution on a wider front than its three predecessors. Finally, in different degree, the new technologies are immediately relevant to the economies of the developing countries as well as to those of the advanced industrial economies.

The least-advanced developing countries may initially find relevant only new technologies related to agriculture, forestry, animal husbandry, medicine, and communications. The technologically most-advanced developing countries (e.g., South Korea) may have to move into the new technologies rapidly and over a wide front if they are to maintain their momentum of recent decades. A good many of the developing countries (e.g., China, India, most of the Latin American countries) will find themselves in between, with some regions and sectors still absorbing older technologies that are still relevant but have not yet been introduced, while others are caught up at or close to the frontiers of the Fourth Industrial Revolution.

The North-South job I have in mind is not that embraced in the broad but rather empty discussions of "the transfer of technology" which are a regular feature of United Nations debates. Nor do they relate to the serious dimensions of the transfer of technology which go on every day through education, multilateral research institutions, international scientific and technical meetings, and normal international commercial transactions. What I believe I have learned is that there is an information gap which is troubling not only the dozen or so developing countries I visited in 1983 but also New Zealand, Australia, and the smaller countries of Europe. The gap can be summarized in the following question: "What is going on in these new areas of innovation that is likely to be relevant to our country in five, ten, or fifteen years?" Without being able to answer that question, governments, research institutes, and major private and public producing units cannot begin to make intelligent decisions with respect to the training of personnel or, even, decide in which directions to look with respect to commercial possibilities. What is required are sustained series of sessions, engaging on both sides first-rate scientists, engineers, and entrepreneurs to discuss both the likely areas where R&D activities will yield cost-effective innovations and the range of possible applications of the new technologies to developing countries at different stages of modernization.

In dealing with this matter the question may well be asked (and often was): "Why should the developing countries concern themselves now with these arcane new innovations? They have quite enough to do absorbing the familiar backlog of the Third Industrial Revolution; that is, metal-working, chemicals, the internal-combustion engine, radio, television, and so on." The answer is not only, as suggested earlier, that many of the new technologies are immediately relevant, but also that leapfrogging is possible. Developing countries do not have to repeat in a rigid sequence the technological history of the more-advanced countries. For example, many developing countries bypassed much of the railway age and moved directly to the more flexible truck and bus for freight and passenger haulage. Moreover, the likely regenerative effects of the new technologies on the older basic industries (motor vehicles, machine-tools, electrical machinery, etc.) may require the developing countries to move into the new technologies faster than they might now envisage if they are to retain the comparative advantage of lower wages in international trade.

The capacity of the developing countries to absorb the new technologies is greater than many now think. The pace at which scientists, engineers, and modern entrepreneurs have been trained over the past generation in most of the Asian countries is impressive. In India, for example, the number of scientists and engineers increased more than tenfold between 1960 and 1984 (from approximately 190,000 to 2.4 million), while the increased flow of talent to private enterpreneurship has been a dramatic feature of the country's social life. The effective linkage of a scientist, engineer, and producer has occurred, however, in only a relatively few sectors. It is my impression that in India and elsewhere in developing Asia the key to the successful absorption of the relevant technologies of the Fourth Industrial Revolution lies in the better linking of these three domains. It is also the key to the reversal of the brain drain.

Be that as it may, the potential meaning and relevance of the new technologies for the Pacific Basin are, I am confident, important potential items for the agenda of any organization that may be set in motion; and the Asian Development Bank might undertake the responsibility for helping organize and structure the work.

Now a few observations on the possible organization of the Pacific Basin for security purposes. At the present time the security structure of the Pacific Basin consists, on the Soviet side, of its own forces plus those of the Vietnamese, linked since December 1978 by a formal mutual-security pact. North Korea signed mutual-security treaties with both the U.S.S.R. and the PRC in July 1961. The PRC stands, in fact, alone but, for many years, in a confrontation with the Soviet Union which may or may not be eased by the somewhat erratic bilateral discussions begun in 1982. The United States is deeply involved in a network of commitments to Australia and New Zealand via ANZUS; to Thailand via the reaffirmation of the Manila Pact, explicitly interpreted since 1962 as a bilateral commitment; to Japan, the Philippines, and South Korea via bilateral arrangements; and to Taiwan, less explicitly, via U.S. unilateral assertion of a vital interest that Beijing-Taipei relations be settled peacefully and via some continued arms supply. The United States has extensive security links to Canada via NATO and certain bilateral arrangements; but these do not extend significantly into the Pacific. Although the capabilities of the non-Communist nations of the region have greatly increased since 1975, the United States alone commands the nuclear, naval, and air forces to deter Soviet strength in the Pacific or to act effectively against those forces should deterrence fail.

There are serious reasons why these arrangements have assumed, essentially, bilateral forms. Japan has been inhibited by its constitution and, thus far, by the memory of the Second World War from playing a truly regional security role. The other countries of the area are limited by their military capabilities, their location, their politics—or by all in combination—from entering into commitments far beyond their own territory and the immediate sea approaches to them. Nevertheless, there have been joint Malaysian-Thai military operations against elements of the Malaysian Communist party near their borders and other forms of security cooperation. Australia has quietly expanded military advisory programs to five ASEAN members. In Vietnam, between 1965 and 1973, there was, of course, a significant degree of concerted multilateral effort under the rubric of the SEATO Treaty, with an additional substantial contribution by South Korea. But the outcome in 1975 is not likely to encourage further commitments of that kind. In particular, the governments of the region understand the likely resistance in the American political process to engaging large ground forces on the Asian mainland.

Indeed, as a matter of practical realism, the instinct of governments in the Pacific Basin is likely to be to leave things as they are. And that may well be the wise course. No government is now pressing for a general multilateral security organization of the region, although in September 1982 Lee Kuan Yew proposed that members of ASEAN join in multilateral military exercises.

Nevertheless, four factors may, in time, place the issue of a security organization for the Pacific Basin on the common agenda.

First, there is the shared, fundamental interest of the nations of the region that the sea lanes remain open in the face of the increasing capacity of the Soviet Union to threaten that interest. The Soviet exercise of that capacity, in fact or as an instrument of diplomatic pressure, would be a grave matter, indeed, setting in motion possibilities of escalation difficult to control. It is not inevitable that the Soviet Union do so. On the other hand, the existence of those expanding capabilities constitutes a potential threat governments of the region are likely to take increasingly into account in their own dispositions.

Second, the rising military capabilities of Japan may make possible a larger Japanese contribution to the maintenance of freedom of the seas in the region. It will, however, simultaneously generate anxieties among some of the Asian nations recalling World War II. As in the case of the German contribution to NATO, an integrated regional command may increasingly commend itself as a solution to this problem.

Third, the smaller and less-developed countries of the region are not only expanding rapidly their real income and capacity to absorb and use efficiently sophisticated technologies, they are also determined, as the existence of ASEAN suggests, to take a larger hand in shaping their destinies. But the brute scale of the problem of keeping the sea lanes of the Pacific Basin open transcends the capacity of any one power of the region. Therefore, the concept of a concerted effort by nations with a shared interest may well emerge.

Finally, such an enterprise may come to be seen as a solution to a dilemma increasingly confronted by the United States since, say, the late 1950s. On the one hand, economic power and political influence have been in a process of progressive diffusion away from both Washington and Moscow. On the other hand, only the United States (or a coalition including the United States) is capable of deterring the concentration of nuclear and conventional forces, including expanded naval force, commanded by the Soviet Union. Thus, the United States military role, already multilateralized in Europe, may well, in time, assume collective forms in Asia.

It should be noted that a gathering and organization of the forces in Asia which share an abiding interest in the freedom of the sea lanes by no means solves all the presently foreseeable threats to peace in the region; for example, the potential threat to Thailand along the borders of Kampuchea. We shall consider that matter in Chapter 7.

We turn now, briefly, to South Asia. Since its countries achieved independence it has been the scene of chronic tension and war. There is no long bibliography, no array of symposia to cite on the virtues and possible instruments for economic cooperation in South Asia. Nevertheless, the Joint Communique of the Foreign Ministers of the South Asian Governments and the Final Declaration of their meeting of August 1−2, 1983 (reproduced in Appendix F), may prove in time to be of historic significance. The meetings were devoted to South Asian Regional Cooperation, which they helpfully designate as SARC. If the governments persist in the objectives enunciated and the agreed SARC program of action, they might, indeed, to use Tarlok Singh's phrase, "reverse past trends":

> Earlier generations of Indians had looked upon India's freedom as a means to the liberation of a large portion of humanity, including specially countries in Asia and Africa which had come under the sway of imperial power. It is an accident of history that, owing to the combination of events that marked the advent of freedom and later developments arising from the cold war, this original purpose came to be overlaid with short-term policy objectives based on considerations of immediate security.
>
> The decades lost and the greater dangers that now loom large make it imperative that, reversing past trends, India and her neighbors, individually and together, make serious

efforts to go back once again to earlier aspirations and values. If they could do so, there is no obstacle to rapid economic and social development that cannot be overcome; failing this, their poverty will persist and every constructive aim will continue to recede." [74]

Institutionally, SARC can trace its history back to early 1976 with the informal coming together of scholars working on development problems in several countries in South Asia. They thought it made sense to compare experiences based on continuing confrontations with similar economic problems and to explore possibilities of regional cooperation for development. The process was initiated with evident government approval, but no formal commitment. In September 1978 their effort was formalized when academic institutions in six South Asian countries agreed to set in motion a concerted and systematic program of studies under a Committee on Studies for Co-operation in Development in South Asia (CSCD).[75] CSCD, now including seven member institutions, held eight meetings between 1978 and January 1983.

Against the background of this ferment, professional and technical in form but suffused with the large considerations evoked in the quotation above from Tarlok Singh, governments in the region were prepared to go further. At the initiative of the late Ziaur Rahman, then president of Bangladesh, diplomatic movement toward South Asian regional cooperation was launched in 1981. The form was a series of what proved to be five SARC meetings at the level of foreign secretary; that is, the highest diplomatic level short of meetings of foreign ministers. Seven governments have participated: Bangladesh, Bhutan, India, Maldives, Nepal, Pakistan, and Sri Lanka. Three countries usually regarded as part of South Asia have not participated: Iran, Afghanistan, and Burma. The final foreign secretaries meeting toward the end of July set the framework for the potentially historic gathering of the foreign ministers on August 1–2, 1983.

What accounts for the emergence in the late 1970s and early 1980s of an apparently serious South Asian impulse to work together? I am certainly not competent to pronounce with authority on that question; and I have found no South Asian analysis addressed systematically to it. I would guess that the following factors, at least, were in play:

—The continued seriousness of the development problems of the region, exacerbated by the deterioration of the world economy in the late 1970s and early 1980s.

—The failure equally of the advanced industrial countries, themselves hard pressed, to offer remedy and of the global negotiations designed to create a New International Economic Order. "Collective Self-Reliance" at the regional level emerged not merely as a phrase to be used at international development gatherings of a political character but, in fact, as a last refuge. And in a move of potential significance, the 1983 Seventh Non-Aligned Summit meeting at New Delhi explicitly sanctioned the kind of South-South regional and sub-regional cooperation envisaged by SARC.

—A rising awareness of increased capacity in South Asia to deal with economic and technical problems.

—A gathering sense in South Asia that continued fraternal quarreling and confrontation were not only costly in narrow economic terms but also contributed to both domestic political instability and national insecurity.

—Finally, in Tarlok Singh's phrase, "the greater dangers that now loom large"; the unsettling events in Iran, the Soviet invasion of Afghanistan, and the rise of Soviet assertiveness in East Africa and the Indian Ocean.

The depth of the concern about these larger developments—most notably the invasion of Afghanistan—is greater in South Asia than most pronouncements by governments of the region would suggest. The seven SARC countries are non-aligned and committed to the stance and vocabulary that goes with that option. Moreover, the largest country in the region, India, long ago made the Faustian choice that it would rely on its own military strength and the Soviet veto in the U.N. Security Council rather than negotiate with Pakistan to settle the Kashmir question. But the events of recent years have suggested to many South Asian leaders that forces might be gathering which nonalignment could not fend off; that formal alignment with the West was neither a desirable nor realistic option, unless the security situation in South Asia gravely deteriorated; and, therefore, a reversal of past trends toward confrontation and fragmentation within the region was desirable.

I cannot weigh the importance of these security concerns as against other factors; but I am convinced that they have been a force pushing the South Asian countries toward mutual accommodation and economic cooperation.

A careful reading of the documents in Appendix F suggests that the SARC foreign ministers sedulously avoided evoking strategic concerns or interests in presenting their agreed conclusions; but they included in their statement of agreed principles some phrases that transcend the business narrowly in hand: "sovereign equality, territorial integrity, political independence, non-interference in internal affairs of other states. . . ." These phrases are not merely diplomatic boilerplate in a region which includes Afghanistan.

Tables 14–17 suggest some of the key characteristics of the South Asian economies, including in Table 14 some comparisons with other economies in Asia. With Sri Lanka a quite systematic exception, their real per capita growth rates are low, the decline in rates of population increase small, the reduction in the role of agriculture in GDP modest, and adult literacy rates low. There has been clearly some positive net real growth per capita in most of the region as well as an expansion in the role of industry and manufacturing. Even more important has been the increase in the technical sophistication of industry. Aside from Bhutan, educational enrollment rates are quite high and extraordinarily high for India in higher education. These figures promise quite rapid future

TABLE 14. Growth Performance of the Asian Economies in Real GDP: 1960–1970, 1970–1981 (%)

	GNP per Capita, 1981 (U.S.)	1960– 1970	1970– 1981	1960– 1978
A. NICs in East Asia				
Taiwan	2,577	9.3	9.5*	
Korea, Rep. of	1,700	8.6	9.1	
Hong Kong	5,100	10.0	9.9	
Singapore	5,240	8.8	8.5	
Average	3,634	9.2	9.3	
B. ASEAN				
Indonesia	530	3.9	7.8	
Malaysia	1,840	6.5	7.8	
Philippines	790	5.1	6.2	
Thailand	770	8.4	7.2	
Singapore	5,240	8.8	8.5	
Average	1,834	6.5	7.5	
C. South Asia				
Bangladesh	140	3.7	4.2	−0.4
India	260	3.4	3.6	1.4
Nepal	150	2.5	2.1	0.8
Pakistan	350	6.7	4.8	2.8
Sri Lanka	300	4.6	4.3	2.0
Average	240	4.2	3.8	1.3

*Refers to 1960–1980.

Sources: ADB Key Indicators, April 1982 (1972–1981); ADB Key Indicators, April 1981 (1971); World Bank, *World Development Report 1983*; For Taiwan, Executive Yuan, *Statistical Yearbook of the Republic of China* (Taipei, 1982).

Secondary source: John Wong, "ASEAN Economies: Growth and Adjustment," a Report prepared for the "Study Prospectus: Southeast Asia" (mimeo, Table 1), organized by Oxford Analytica, Oxford, England, August 1983. The per capita GNP calculations are from *World Development Report 1980*, pp. 83, 110, as reported in M. L. Qureshi; for which full reference is given in notes to Table 15, below.

TABLE 15. Distribution and Growth of Population of South Asian Region by Country

Country	Population (Mid-year) 1979	Proportion of Population in South Asia 1979	Population Growth Rate (% per Annum)		Projected Population in Year 2000 (Millions)
			1960–1970	1970–1977	
Bangladesh	87.83	10.36	2.9	2.5	153.5
Bhutan	1.50	0.18	2.3	2.3	2.1
India	650.98	76.76	2.3	2.1	1,017.7
Maldives	0.15	0.02	—	—	0.2
Nepal	13.71	1.62	1.8	2.3	23.0
Pakistan	79.48	9.37	2.8	3.0	145.1
Sri Lanka	14.42	1.70	2.4	1.6	20.4
Total	848.07	100.00	2.4	2.2	1,362.0

Sources: Mid-year population for 1960, 1970, and 1977 from ESCAP Survey 1978, Table 45, p. 187; mid-year population for 1979 from Asian Development Bank, Key Indicators, Table 1, p. 1; population growth rates for Bangladesh from World Bank, World Development Report 1979, Table 17, p. 159; for other countries from ESCAP Survey 1978, Table 45, p. 187; population estimates for Maldives, UN World Population Trends and Prospects by Country 1950–2000 Summary Report for the 1978 assessment; projected population from Population Reference Bureau Inc., 1978, Population Data Sheet.

Secondary source: M. L. Qureshi, *Survey of Economic Resources and Prospects of South Asia* (Colombo: Marqa Institute in association with Third World Foundation for Economic and Social Studies, London, 1981), p. 15.

TABLE 16. Structure of Production in South Asian Countries

| | Distribution of Gross Domestic Product (%) | | | | | | | |
| | Agriculture | | Industry | | Manufacturing | | Services | |
Country	1960	1978	1960	1978	1960	1978	1960	1978
Bangladesh	61	57	8	13	6	8	31	30
India	50	40	20	26	14	17	30	34
Nepal	—	62	—	12	—	10	—	26
Pakistan	46	32	16	24	12	16	38	44
Sri Lanka	34	35	22	31	17	23	44	34

Source: *World Development Report 1980*, World Bank, Table 3, p. 114.
Secondary source: Qureshi, *Survey*, p. 41.

progress in reducing illiteracy and elevating the capacity of the region to absorb and manage sophisticated, diversified technologies.

Nevertheless, in terms of conventional canons of growthmanship, South Asia belongs near the bottom of the league. In World Bank parlance, we are dealing with Low Income Developing Countries. Moreover, taken as a whole they are all suffering from a complex set of pathological circumstances whose symptoms are: excessively intrusive state bureaucracies; excessive subsidies, price controls, and protectionism; and excessive idle industrial capacity. This is not the occasion to analyze the causes of these problems or their remedy. Their existence is increasingly acknowledged and discussed in South Asia; and it is recognized that they contribute to relatively slow growth rates.

On the other hand, India, containing three-quarters of the region's population, is, at the margin, one of the most technologically advanced of the developing countries. This capacity is not only reflected in Indian nuclear and space activities and certain aspects of military production but also in the manner in which scientists, technicians, and producers have been organized in agriculture. The diffusion throughout the

TABLE 17. Distribution of Education-Related Statistics of South Asian Region by Country

Country	Adult Literacy Rates 1975	Numbers Enrolled in Primary School as % of Age Group 1977	Numbers Enrolled in Secondary Schools as % of Age Group 1977	Numbers Enrolled in Higher Education as % of Age Group 1976	1979
Bangladesh	26	81	23	2	3
Bhutan	—	11	1	—	—
Nepal	19	71	14	2	3
India	36	80	28	6	9
Pakistan	21	51	17	2	2
Sri Lanka	78	86	47	1	3

Source: World Bank, *World Development Report, 1980*, Table 23, p. 154; literacy rate for Sri Lanka from Key Indicators, Asian Development Bank, October 1979, Table 2, p. 3.

Secondary source: Qureshi, *Survey*, p. 171; 1979 figures for higher education proportion added from *World Development Report, 1983*, Table 25, p. 196.

country of the best possible agricultural practice under Indian circumstances still has a long way to go; but the success of India in rendering itself self-sustaining in food has more substantial underpinnings than is generally understood. Moreover, if the Indian private sector was both challenged to compete internationally and simultaneously had lifted from it a good part of the heavy bureaucratic weight it now carries, there is reason to believe it might give a good account of itself, generating throughout industry the kind of technological partnerships now to be observed in only a few Indian sectors.

In differing degree both Pakistan and Bangladesh are also more technologically sophisticated countries than their real per capita income figures would suggest; and, by almost all modernization measures, Sri Lanka is a developing nation of promise.

In short, the sense in South Asia that the region is not without resource in confronting its still formidable problems is quite correct.

As the Joint Communique of the Foreign Ministers notes, they accepted the consensus which emerged from the protracted efforts of the foreign secretaries and launched an "Integrated Program of Action" in the following areas: agriculture, rural development, meteorology, telecommunications, scientific and technological cooperation, health and population activities, transport, postal services, and sports, arts, and culture. This is an ambitious effort.

Aside from wishing the program well, one can only state some of the problems that will have to be overcome. They are both technical and political.

Technically, one critical question is whether meetings in these fields which exchange information and experiences along the lines of many similar meetings under ESCAP auspices will be judged sufficiently fruitful to sustain SARC. Perhaps the greatest hope for progress may lie in the isolation of multilateral investment projects in fields like reforestation, river development, and telecommunications, which would justify application for financial support from outside the region. The SARC program provides explicitly for that possibility. An early success in formulating and financing such a multilateral project would go far to generate confidence within the region in SARC as a whole; and a world community, grateful to observe South Asian cooperation, is likely to be rather generous in its support.

The most serious obstacles to the success of SARC are, of course, political, just as the major payoffs for success are likely to be political; and this is well understood in the region. The first political problem is the relative size of India, which contains about three-quarters of all South Asia in both population and GNP. India generates the same kind of anxiety in South Asia that Japan and the United States together generate in the Pacific Basin; and India is not in a position to provide the possibility for greatly enlarged flows of capital. Indian officials are quite well aware that their role in SARC, if it is to be viable, will require extraordinary sustained restraint and concern for the anxieties and suspicions of their partners. In addition, the SARC effort will have to go forward against a counterpoint of chronic intervals of bilateral tension as between South Asian countries and of domestic political difficulties in particular countries; and quite often the two will be related even if, in fact, the governments of this intimately fraternal region practice strict noninterference in each other's domestic affairs.

Clearly SARC will not succeed unless the political leaders of the region firmly decide and explain to their peoples that SARC is an absolutely essential long-run commitment that must go forward step-by-step, whatever may be happening in the conventional short-run world of bilateral diplomacy. Events in 1984—notably, heightened India-Pakistan tension over Kashmir and other matters—cannot be judged encouraging.

7. Some Reflections

The account of the emergence of regional institutions in Asia in Chapters 1–5 and the speculations about the future in Chapter 6 suggest a number of themes for final reflection. I have, quite arbitrarily, selected three: certain particular features of the American role in the rise of Asian regionalism and its future; the character of certain ingrained U.S. ambiguities concerning its interests in the area; and, looking further down the road, the potential significance of China-India relations for South and Southeast Asia and stable peace in Asia as a whole.

As a case study around the theme of Ideas and Action, Lyndon Johnson's elevation of Asian regionalism as a major strand in American policy has some distinctive aspects. Unlike Eisenhower in Books 1, 3, and 4 of this series (bombing policy, policy after Stalin's death, and Open Skies), unlike Byrnes in Book 2 (focused on a 1946 plan to avoid the division of Europe), but like John Kennedy in Book 5 (development aid policy), Johnson was directly in touch with those who generated the concepts underlying a new U.S. emphasis on Asian regionalism. He did not rely on a creative honest broker like C. D. Jackson or Nelson Rockefeller. He was personally engaged in clarifying the concept as well as in trying to bring it to life. In 1965, as he formulated the Johns Hopkins speech, he actively reached out beyond the conventional executive branch chains of command to those who might contribute. But as early as May 1961, in his report on Asia to Kennedy, Johnson had already outlined the sort of concerted trans-Pacific partnership he was later to press forward as president (see above, pp. 32–33).

In his vigorous effort to generate and bring to life a new concept in Asia in the last three years of his responsibility, Johnson reflected a general aspect of his working style. In the course of his administration he set up some 100 task forces instructed to come up with new ideas in specific fields: 60 within the government, 40 made up of outside experts. A good many presidents understood better than their hard-pressed bureaucracies the importance of new ideas in government. This includes even so instinctively conservative a president as Dwight Eisenhower. Only a very few, however, made the search for new ideas a central aspect of their administration; and none went about the linking of policy invention to political innovation with more passion or energy than Johnson.

In the case of regionalism in Asia (and elsewhere), an American president in the 1960s and beyond faced, however, a built-in limitation. After all, what Johnson sought to set in motion was a process in which the governments of Asia and the Pacific, on an organized basis, would assume increased responsibility for their own destiny, while the United States drew back in degree from its abnormal and inherently transient dominating role of the immediate post-1945 years. The United States evidently retained—and will retain for the foreseeable future—certain irreducible responsibilities in Asia, in its own interest and in that of the many Asian countries whose destiny matters to the United States. But the diffusion of economic capacity and political stature proceeding in the world decrees that while an American president can propose in the matter of Asian regionalism, the Asian governments will dispose.

With respect to the ADB and the Mekong Committee, the problem of generating cooperation among Asian governments in the 1960s was not difficult. Indeed, at the time of

the Johns Hopkins speech the concept of a regional development bank was being pressed forward by Asian and Pacific
leaders and the United Nations had already initiated work on
the potentialities of the Mekong. Economic development was
an almost universally shared interest of the region, Burma
being a kind of exception; and, in any case, international cooperation in the orderly distribution of resources provided
by others is the easiest kind of enterprise to organize, as
the United Nations Relief and Rehabilitation Administration
(UNRRA) and the Marshall Plan have long since demonstrated.

ASEAN was another matter. Here the influence of the United
States was substantial, although certainly not unique; but it
was not Lyndon Johnson's rhetoric that moved the governments of Southeast Asia to come together in 1967, but a
heightened sense of danger as they observed the rising tensions in American political life reflecting the painful attri-
tional war proceeding in Vietnam. In fact, the 1961 coming
together of Malaya, the Philippines, and Thailand in ASA had
already reflected anxiety about external support from Great
Britain, France, and a United States actively negotiating in Geneva an uncertain neutralism for Laos. By 1967 it seemed
likely to the political leaders of the vulnerable potential
dominoes of Southeast Asia that the extraordinary degree of
responsibility for the region assumed by the United States in
1965 was bound to be transient. Thus, Lee Kuan Yew's dictum of June 1966: ". . . if we [in Asia] just sit down and believe people are going to buy time for ever after for us, then
we deserve to perish."

There were other good reasons for ASEAN to emerge; for
example, the need to settle differences between Malaysia and
post-Sukarno Indonesia and the limited but real potentialities
for economic cooperation, and a sense of acute asymmetry in
bilateral economic negotiations with resurgent Japan. But
fundamentally, it was an awareness that if they did not hang
together they might well be destined to hang separately.
Thus, the central figures in the creation of ASEAN had to be—

and were—Asians: Thanat Khoman in Bangkok, Tunku Abdul Rahman in Kuala Lumpur, Adam Malik in Djakarta, and the other pioneers of the 1960s. Collectively they played a role in Southeast Asia equivalent to the collective post-1945 role in Europe of Monnet, Schumann, Adenauer, and De Gasperi. In Asia, as in Europe, the U.S. part in the process was complex and even paradoxical; the Asians wanted U.S. support for their efforts to achieve unity, which were inspired, in part, by fears of excessive U.S. withdrawal; but they also sought unity to avoid excessive dependence on the United States and to stand with greater strength and dignity vis-à-vis Japan, China, and other powers.

From the narrow perspective of the governments of ASEAN, U.S. policy in the period 1965–1975 has a meaning rarely discussed in the United States or elsewhere beyond the region: it bought valuable time not only for ASEAN to find its feet but also for an additional decade of extraordinary economic and social progress to occur. ASEAN's total real output was probably more than twice its 1965 level in 1975. More important, this interval of sustained rapid progress, combined with the increasingly serious character of ASEAN, suffused the region with a degree of inner confidence which made the trauma of the take-over of South Vietnam much easier to surmount in 1975 than a decade earlier.

In each of the five preceding studies around the theme of Ideas and Action, the timing of events proved significant. This is also the case with respect to the struggle in Vietnam and the emergence of ASEAN.

The security of the states joined together in ASEAN is by no means automatically assured as of the mid-1980s. One can envisage circumstances in which they could fall even if they hang together. But should they survive as independent non-Communist states, the decade of time painfully bought by the South Vietnamese, American, and allied forces is likely to be reckoned, among many other variables, in the calculus of historians, as they move forward in what seems destined to be an endless debate over the pre-1975 role of the United States in Southeast Asia.

As for the future, U.S. policy remains a critical component in the fate of the region in two dimensions: economic and military. As noted earlier (see above, pp. 87–88), ASEAN recognizes quite formally that a failure to maintain reasonable domestic political and social harmony within each nation could result in crises with profound security implications. The problem of sustained political and social stability within developing nations is by no means a simple function of their real rate of growth. On the other hand, reasonably high and steady growth rates appear to be a necessary but not sufficient condition for stability. The high population growth rates of most developing countries, combined with age structures heavily concentrated in the younger age brackets, decree that large cohorts enter the working force annually. High growth rates are required to avoid unmanageably high levels of unemployment and underemployment, with all their attendant corrosive frustrations. Thus, the virtual stagnation of the world economy in 1979–1982 was, in all the developing regions, a powerful destabilizing force. It had its impact in four distinct ways. It reduced export volumes; reduced export prices; generated protectionist barriers to exports; and reduced the flows of long-term official lending, as elected officials had to weigh the urgent claims of their constituents against the interests incorporated in foreign aid. In addition, anxieties about the servicing of private loans contracted in the 1970s—anxieties substantially generated, in turn, by the impact of the global recession on developing countries—reduced the flow of new private lending. In varying degree, all the developing countries of the Pacific Basin experienced retardation in their growth or absolute contraction since 1979. There was a stronger rebound in East Asia and the Pacific than in the other developing regions in 1983–1985; but its staying power was uncertain.

This essay is not an appropriate occasion to explore fully

this dangerous degenerative process or to prescribe long-run remedy. (I have tried to contribute to that objective in *The Barbaric Counter-Revolution: Cause and Cure* [1983]). It is highly germane, however, to note that a resumption of steady growth in the advanced industrial countries is a necessary condition for the viability of the developing countries of the Pacific Basin; and, as a nation which still produces something like 20 percent of the world's real GNP (about 38 percent of the GNP of the advanced industrial countries of OECD), the United States bears a special responsibility in this regard. Aside from all the other palpable reasons for seeking a resumption of steady growth in the United States, with inflation controlled by means other than an exclusive reliance on monetary stringency and high real interest rates, the strategic interests of the United States in the developing regions require that outcome. It is not an exaggeration to say that U.S. domestic economic policy did more to destabilize the developing regions of the non-Communist world in the period 1979–1983 than all the fervent efforts of the Soviet Union and its agents in Havana, Hanoi, and elsewhere.

The military task facing the United States in the Pacific Basin over the years ahead, as it confronts Soviet dispositions, is also real and challenging; and it will not be removed from the American agenda by even a wholly successful achievement of steady non-inflationary growth in the United States and a resumption of rapid growth in the rest of the Pacific Basin. The successful execution of that task, however, lies not in the assembly of the requisite mass of military hardware, although hardware is clearly relevant. It lies rather in a more lucid resolution in American public opinion and policy of two related conceptual problems which have bedeviled the nation for a long time: the relation of naval and air power to the balance of power on the Asian land mass; and the abiding nature of the U.S. interest in the continued independence of the countries of Southeast Asia.

A minor incident in the 1960s dramatizes, after a fashion,

the first and most fundamental of these conceptual problems. In the wake of Johnson's speech to the Alumni Council on July 12, 1966 (see above, pp. 10–11), Senator Mike Mansfield included the following passage in a letter to the president dated July 27.[76]

> In my judgment, there is a world of difference between thinking of the United States as a Pacific power and as an Asian power. The two concepts are distinct even though they may overlap somewhat along the littoral of the Asian mainland. As a Pacific power, we would have a primary concern in whatever happens in the Pacific ocean and should be prepared to assume in that area all necessary security responsibilities, unilateral, bilateral or whatever. But being a Pacific power does not call for a heavy and permanent military involvement on the Asian mainland. Historically, in fact, we have rejected such involvement. As a Pacific power, of course, we would still join with other nations in all sorts of constructive, social and economic endeavors in Asia, but we would not necessarily accept and, much less, seek heavy and permanent military responsibilities on the Asian mainland.
>
> If we see ourselves as an Asian power, on the other hand, we would have a primary concern and involvement in all that transpires on the continent from Pakistan to the Soviet Maritime provinces. As necessary, we would accept unilateral and permanent military responsibility on the Asian continent.
>
> We are clearly a Pacific power even as we are an Atlantic power, but we are not and, in my judgment, ought not to aspire to be an Asian power any more than we ought to think of ourselves, basically, as a European power. The difference between the two, in my judgment, is not merely a matter of semantics; it is quite fundamental.

Mansfield accurately reflected a deeply rooted distinction in the mind of many Americans, rarely articulated. Clearly, most Americans are prepared to accept the fact that the United States is a Pacific power; but the notion that the United States has abiding interests on the Asian mainland is a quite different matter, summoning up as it does visions of ground force engagement with Asian hordes.

The reconciliation of the two images requires a mature facing up to the reciprocal nature of sea (and air) power to what transpires on land. Specifically, it requires clarification of issues reflected in certain phrases in Mansfield's letter where, conscious of the complexity of the problem, he somewhat blurs the distinction he seeks to make; for example, "the two concepts . . . may overlap somewhat along the littoral of the Asian mainland" and "As a Pacific power . . . we would not necessarily accept . . . permanent military responsibilities on the Asian mainland." In effect, Mansfield implies that, as a Pacific power, there might be serious U.S. strategic interests on the Asian littoral and, selectively, permanent U.S. military commitments on the Asian mainland. The key question is: If one agrees that the primary interest of the United States is in the freedom of the Pacific sea lanes, how deeply must it concern itself with the balance of power on the Asian mainland?

In American history issues of the kind Mansfield raised go back to the pre-1914 generation and the debates initiated by the writings of Alfred Thayer Mahan. Mahan served the nation well when he published in 1890, as the frontier came to an end, *The Influence of Sea Power upon History, 1660–1783.*[77] From his opening observations on the role of the Roman navy in the ultimate defeat of Hannibal to his closing reflections on the role of the French and British navies in the American War of Independence, Mahan never lost sight of the relation between naval operations and the course of battles on land: from Scipio and the decisive battle of the Metaurus to Washington at Yorktown and, later, Wellington at Waterloo.

Mahan's writings had a powerful direct effect on the thought of certain key American leaders, notably Theodore Roosevelt and Henry Cabot Lodge; and part of his doctrine was much more widely diffused among those who never read his texts. But, in its net impact on pre-1914 U.S. thought, Mahan's views were curiously distorted. They played an important part in achieving acceptance of the need for the United States to generate significant independent sea power; but Mahan failed in his central effort, which was to illuminate the complex relation between sea power and the balance of power on land in Europe and Asia.

The principal elements in Mahan's thought can be rearranged and summarized in the following sequence:

1. The balance of the world's power lies in the land mass of Eurasia; and it is subject to unending competitive struggle among nation-states.

2. Although the balance of world power hinges on the control of Eurasian land, the control over the sea approaches to Eurasia has been and can be a decisive factor in the balance of power on land, as the history of many nations, most notably Britain, demonstrates.

3. In the end, naval power consists in the ability to win and to hold total dominance at sea, which, in turn, requires a naval force in being capable of meeting and defeating any likely concentration of counterforce. A naval power must, therefore, maintain as a concentrated tactical unit at readiness an adequate fleet of capital ships with requisite underlying support.

4. Support for such a force includes forward bases, coaling stations, a merchant fleet adequate for overseas supply, and, perhaps, certain territories whose friendship is assured at a time of crisis. It follows, therefore, that a naval power should be prepared actively to develop an empire as well as a substantial foreign trade and pool of commercial shipping.

5. The United States stood at a moment in its history and in its relation to the distribution of world power when the full-scale development of its navy was urgent.

6. The pursuit in times of peace of the prerequisites for naval power would have the following ancillary advantages: the challenge of commercial and imperial competition would maintain the vigor of the nation; acceptance of responsibility for Christianizing and modernizing the societies of native

peoples within the empire would constitute a worthy and elevating moral exercise; and the whole enterprise would be commercially profitable.

As the Japanese moved vigorously into sustained industrialization after 1885 and the German curve of steel production crossed that of Britain in the 1890s, there were signs of underlying shifts in the locus of power in Europe and Asia. But these shifts and their meaning were difficult to dramatize for the American people despite the Japanese victory over the Chinese in 1895, and increased German activism in China and Latin America. Even after 1900, when the German threat to the European balance of power was more palpable and the Japanese defeated the Russian fleet, it would have been impossible to make Americans accept consciously the notion that the buildup of naval strength was ultimately required in order that American influence be exerted not merely defensively in the Atlantic and the Pacific, but also to assure that no single power achieved hegemony on the mainland of either Europe or Asia. In Mahan's own writing, the full significance of propositions 1 and 2 were thus obscured and slighted; for if they were taken seriously, what was called for was not an exuberant American effort to assert itself unilaterally on the high seas, ceasing to rely on a protective British navy, but an expansion in total military power—an army as well as navy— in alignment with those other nations which shared its interest in avoiding a dominant concentration of power on the Eurasian land mass, with all this might imply for control over the seas.

Mahan was not himself a simple lobbyist for a large American navy. He steadily advocated Anglo-American understanding, and, later, as the First World War approached, he helped articulate the nature of the American power interests in its outcome; but, generally speaking, propositions 3–6 became detached from 1 and 2, leaving Mahan, in his net influence, mainly a propagandist for the expansion of the American navy and its forward bases, for the creation of the Isthmian

Canal, and for the concentration of the battle fleet, rather than a consistent philosopher of the American interest in the balance of power in Europe and Asia and an expositor of its strategic position on the world scene.

Projected out into national policy, the comfortable ambiguities left in the exposition of Mahan and his followers had an important consequence. Whereas the technical requirements of the American strategic position called for the rapid development of the concepts and attitudes of alliance, the new doctrine was shaped to fit the mood of national assertiveness which welled up toward the end of the ninteenth century. Not only such figures as Senator Lodge but also many key American naval officers permitted themselves, for example, the luxury of being both advocates of Mahan and twisters of the lion's tail. And traces of this attitude persisted in the navy down to the early stages of the Second World War.

The ambiguity between what might be called Mahanism and a correct interpretation of Mahan's principles was crystallized by the somewhat ironic role of the American navy in the First and Second World Wars. Thought in the U.S. Navy for long had been focused around a decisive, direct engagement of the battleships which would determine who commanded the seas. In fact, over the past seventy years it has had to devote itself overwhelmingly to convoying, antisubmarine patrol, submarine operations, and amphibious landings.

History in the twentieth century required, in short, that the United States, in its own interest, along with allies with parallel interests, exert power directly on the Eurasian mainland with massive ground force units to sustain a balance of power. The American navy played an indispensable and effective role in support of this process; and this outcome was in no way inconsistent with Mahan's fundamental propositions. But, as Mahanism gained ground, toward the end of the nineteenth century, there were no premonitions of the trenches of

1917–1918; of the battles of North Africa, Italy, France, and the Pacific Islands of 1941 to 1945; or of Korea and Vietnam.

In these harsh experiences, the United States, at moments of acute crisis, but not before, recognized its interest in the balance of power on the European and Asian continents. And, in substantial part—by no means exclusively—that recognition was based on the perceived consequences for control of the sea lanes of the achievement of hegemony by a single potentially hostile power in Europe or Asia. Unrestricted German submarine warfare in 1917 and the arrival of German submarines in bases on the French coast in 1940 evidently played an important role in altering U.S. popular as well as official attitudes. Indeed, in both wars the struggle against German submarines was a close thing. The hardening of Franklin Roosevelt's stance toward the Japanese, as they moved from northern to southern Indochina in 1941, was explicitly related to its implications for the Pacific sea lanes (see Appendix B).

With respect to Europe, the United States came reluctantly to accept and to institutionalize its abiding multiple interests in the continental balance of power through NATO and, particularly, the commitment of U.S. ground forces to Supreme Headquarters, Allied Powers in Europe (SHAPE) in 1951.

Although SHAPE was, in a sense, created by the assault on South Korea in 1950, there has been no equivalent commitment in Asia, excepting in Korea itself. In part, this is because, over the past half-century, the American perception of the potential hegemonic power has shifted three times: from Japan to China to Russia. The character of the actual or potential military threat differed markedly in each case (see Appendix B). This fact flows from the greater complexity of the balance of power in Asia than in Europe. There is no simple equivalent in Asia of, say, the contemporary central front in Europe. There is a group of critical and strategically sensitive areas to which U.S. post-1945 policy has responded separately: there is the northwest Pacific, where there are the bilateral security links to Japan and the Republic of Korea, including the decision to continue to maintain ground forces in the latter (a littoral exception Mansfield's doctrine might, in theory, admit); there is the forward naval and air base structure, notably in the Philippines, to protect the sea lanes on the South China Sea and the straits linking the Pacific Basin to the Indian Ocean, as well as generally to secure supply lanes from the United States; and there is ANZUS, with its mantle of protection for two important island allies. For one of the sensitive strategic areas—the Sino-Soviet border—the United States has no explicit military policy. It has, at certain moments, sought through diplomacy to discourage a Soviet attack on China; and the existence of relatively normal relations between the PRC and the U.S. government leaves open the possibility of some kind of U.S. military assistance if a Sino-Soviet war should occur. But one can doubt that anyone in either Beijing or Washington is clear about what, in fact, the United States would do in the face of that eventuality.

There is, finally, the now old and still enflamed problem of Southeast Asia and, in particular, the potential confrontation between the Soviet-backed Vietnamese and Thailand (see Map 2). As noted earlier (see above, pp. 90–91), the United States has recommitted itself to the defense of Thailand, in both the Carter and Reagan administrations, in the post-1975 years. Here the ambiguities of the United States as a Pacific, rather than Asian, power converge with a striking paradox. On the one hand, over a span of forty-three years, nine successive U.S. presidents, from Franklin Roosevelt to Reagan, have, with great reluctance, made serious U.S. commitments in Southeast Asia. On the other hand, there is still no clear national consensus—equivalent, for example, to those on Europe, the Middle East, or South Korea—as to why Southeast Asia is an area of critical strategic interest to the United States.

As Appendix B seeks to make clear, a major aspect of that

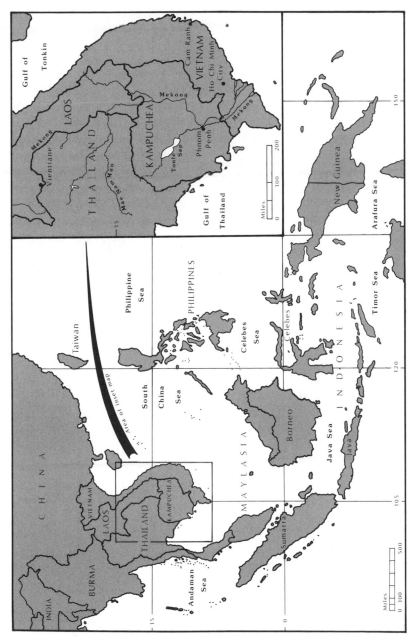

MAP 2. Thailand and Its Vulnerable Borders

153

interest concerns the sea lanes, and it illustrates, in effect, the reciprocal of Mahan's doctrine: not only can sea power influence the course of affairs on land, but control over the land can affect the degree of security of the sea lanes. The Soviet sea and air bases in Vietnam and Kampuchea have already altered, but not yet shifted decisively, the degree of security of the sea lanes of the South China Sea and the Indian Ocean. On the other hand, to use Mansfield's phrase, the defense of Thailand is much more than a matter of protecting a littoral. The critical line of battle could lie a considerable distance from the sea.

It would be wholly inappropriate in a book of this kind to attempt to outline a war plan to defend Thailand in case of a Soviet-backed Vietnamese assault across the Mekong, from Laos and/or Kampuchea. Evidently, the first objective of ASEAN policy and of those who support that policy is to act so as to minimize the temptation in Moscow and Hanoi to launch such an attack. Positively, the objective is to work toward a state of affairs in which Kampuchea is ruled by an authentically independent government and policy in Hanoi shifts toward a concentration of its political energies and resources on the long-delayed development of Vietnam, perhaps even in association with its non-Communist Southeast Asian neighbors; for example, in the development of the Mekong. It is by no means inevitable that Thailand will be attacked by Vietnam with Soviet support. But it is a possibility.

Should it come about, I would only observe that the possibility of effective American participation in the defense of Thailand, with congressional and popular support, is likely to be substantially determined by the response of the countries of ASEAN and the scale of the response of other countries of the Pacific Basin. The enterprise would have to be a truly multilateralized Pacific Basin effort, with no one cheering from the sidelines.

As noted earlier, unlike the massive literature on the Pacific Basin, there is little published discussion of the possible security dimensions of South Asian cooperation. (In fact, so far as Americans are concerned there appears to be little awareness that the SARC effort is under way.) And I doubt that the issue is likely to arise unless the somewhat anxious security situation in the region greatly degenerates. Nevertheless, a few observations may be useful on the security dimensions of the problem of South Asia if only to underline its inescapable linkage to the problems of East Asia and the Pacific.

American thought, in particular, tends sharply to separate East Asia from South Asia.[78] They are dealt with in different parts of the State Department, South Asia being grouped with the Middle East. The distinction is crystallized in academic life as well, where regional studies and research institutes are rather sharply divided at the western border of Burma. It was surprising as well as refreshing, therefore, when an American scholar and public servant, Edwin F. Black, evoked the name and ideas of Homer Lea to write a paper entitled "Defense of the Center: The Indian Subcontinent."[79] Commenting on the accompanying map, Black wrote:

> Long before the U.S. Navy was able to get funds to establish a base in the Indian Ocean—decades even before John Foster Dulles sought to identify some mutuality of Western self-interest in the defense of Southwest Asia through the organization of the Central Treaty Organization (CENTO)—a short, hunchbacked American military genius, who devoted his short life to helping Dr. Sun Yat-sen "topple the Manchus from their ancient Dragon Throne," was plotting geopolitical triangles across the face of this vast buffer zone, the Indian subcontinent.
>
> This was in 1912, and Homer Lea, in his book *The Day of the Saxon*, was using these triangles as a method of explaining the strategic importance of the Center to the survival of the Anglo-Saxon community [see Map 3]. As can be seen, he had, with extraordinary prescience, fixed the apex of several of these triangles on Diego Garcia, which today plays an important role in U.S. deployments through the Indian Ocean.

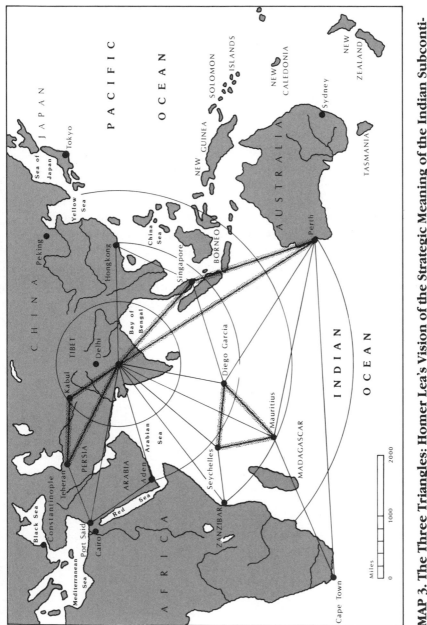

MAP 3. The Three Triangles: Homer Lea's Vision of the Strategic Meaning of the Indian Subcontinent (after Homer Lea, *The Day of the Saxon* [New York: Harper & Brothers, 1942], p. 64)

To Homer Lea, Russian expansion into the Indian subcontinent was inevitable. His fear was that, in the continuing global struggle between the Saxon (England at that time) and the Slav (Russia), the Saxon might not recognize that without India, his position of power throughout the world would crumble. As Lea saw it, the loss of the Center would mean Russian dominance of the globe. . . .

. . . India's Achilles' heel is its northwest frontier region. Lea warned that Russia must not be allowed to pass the Kabul-Tehran line. Its defense, he argued, rests on friendly control of three geopolitical triangles: in the west, the triangle Delhi-Kabul-Tehran; in the east, Delhi-Singapore-Perth; and in the south, the islands of Seychelles-Mauritius-Diego Garcia. Once the Russians consolidate their position in Afghanistan, the only obstacle between them and the plains of India is Pakistan.

The coming together of Pakistan, China, and India is a process the U.S. government can quietly cheer on from the outside; and it can help finance South Asian multilateral development projects of serious worth as it once helped finance through the World Bank the Indus Waters scheme. As presidents, John Kennedy tried hard, but without much hope, to induce Nehru and Ayub to settle Kashmir, and Lyndon Johnson was quite accurate, in terms of diplomatic effort, when he used to say, "I was at Tashkent, but you couldn't see me." But only the peoples in that part of the world can decide that they confront dangers that require new dispositions and the ending of old quarrels, as, for example, the British and French decided early in this century in the face of the rise of Germany. Strong hortatory support for those new dispositions from outside the region is likely to be counterproductive.

Similarly, at this stage, there is no basis for a change in the basic security relations between South Asia and the United States; and, as with a Sino-Soviet war, it is difficult to see now with any precision what security arrangements might make sense in a direct Soviet thrust into South Asia. But a potential convergence of strategic interests palpably exists between

South Asia, the United States, and others with a vital interest in the Eurasian balance of power and the freedom of the seas.

What is important is to understand the strategic view from Moscow of the great arc from East Africa to Vladivostok and the linkage of the problem of freedom of the seas in the Indian Ocean to freedom of movement in the Pacific and South China Sea. Thus, Soviet-dominated forces in Afghanistan, like Soviet-dominated forces on the Mekong, have brought us close to a major global strategic crisis. The coming of such a crisis is by no means inevitable. But it will not be avoided by pretending that it could not happen.

Now a final word about these matters as they may appear much further down the road in history—say, in the year 2050. Assuming that economic development is not throttled by a global Malthusian or nuclear tragedy, the relative stature in Asia of India and China will be much greater than it is at present. Rates of population increase should decelerate, as they already are, more rapidly at present in China than India. But still, these two giant nations will probably contain well over two billion human beings. If the normal S-shaped path of growth prevails, both countries should experience some acceleration, yielding real incomes per capita in the range of $1,000–1,500 (in 1980 dollars), four to six times present levels. By that time, great progress should have been made in their greatest common task; that is, the modernization and elevation of productivity in their vast rural sectors. Most important of all, with the likely further diffusion of education, these countries are likely to command a much higher proportion of then-current technologies than at present; although their current technological capacity is greater than their relatively low real income per capita levels would suggest.

All this will increase the military potential of China and India and their capacity to project it. The economies of other nations in the Pacific Basin will, of course, also expand over this period; but, as nearly as one can calculate, the relative as well as absolute power and influence of China and India will be considerably greater than it is at present.

A great deal depends, therefore, on their future policies and, especially, their policies toward each other. At two extremes, they could enter a phase of systematic rivalry, like France and Germany in Europe in the century before 1945; or they could consciously forego that option and use their combined influence to stabilize the region, as the statesmen of France and Germany have done in the past thirty-five years.

Operationally, the outcome will depend not only on whether or not they achieve a joint stance toward Soviet pressure on South Asia and the Indian Ocean but, quite particularly, on the policies they adopt toward Southeast Asia.

From an Indian point of view (see Appendix B), Burma is a kind of equivalent to the Ardennes for France; and the independence of Burma runs with the independence of Thailand, Malaysia, and Singapore. From a Chinese point of view, Southeast Asia is also a region of great sensitivity. If controlled by a potentially hostile power, Southeast Asia can threaten not only China's southeastern land frontier but also the ports and sea lanes of the South China Sea. In an active effort to protect these vital interests, one can conceive of circumstances in which China and India could clash.

The outcome which would satisfy the vital interests of both nations would be solid agreement that they will jointly support the independence of Southeast Asia from intrusion or military exploitation by any major power. Indeed, even now an unambiguous Sino-Indian agreement to support ASEAN's object of a Zone of Peace, Freedom, and Neutrality would contribute greatly to rendering it a reality.

The vision held up here of the critical future role of India-China relations may appear in 1985 to be far-fetched and unrealistic, not least in the hard-pressed governments of the two countries. Both confront difficult problems of domestic reform which require them to alter concepts and arrangements that became embedded in policy in the 1950s and sub-sequently generated strong vested interests in their perpetuation. Both confront foreign policy and security problems much more pressing from day to day than Sino-Indian bilateral relations. An improvement in the latter is seen as part of the current foreign-policy agenda in both New Delhi and Beijing; but, probably with some relief, the matter is not judged to be a pressing issue of high priority. Perhaps most important of all, the leaders of both countries are acutely conscious of their limited economic and military potential relative to the potentials of the United States and the U.S.S.R.

In suggesting the long-run importance of Sino-Indian relations to public officials in both countries, I found them a bit surprised that I assessed their prospects so hopefully by the middle of the next century. It seems far away, although most children now being born will then still be alive. But, even if prepared to contemplate abstractly such a time of potential responsibility and authority in Asia, they did not see how it related to difficulties they had to fend off or problems they had to solve today or next week—the normal working horizon of public officials.

The reason the issue deserves quiet thought and discussion now goes to the rationale for this series of books. Decisions of governments are not taken simply by choosing one concept versus another. Personalities, vested interests, inertia, accident, and Murphy's Law are always at work. Ideas nevertheless do play a part in decisions. They matter because consciously or unconsciously they help determine the way the choices open to those making decisions are defined and the option actually chosen. They help determine priorities and the arraying of priorities is the heart of government. One set of ideas that already matters—and will matter increasingly—is the explicit or implicit image of long-run Sino-Indian relations in each of the two capitals and, ultimately, among the peoples of the two countries. It would not be difficult—and, indeed, it would be historically understandable—if a latent image of long-run rivalry developed in both countries. But with sufficient reflection and, ultimately, statesmanlike leadership, both peoples might conclude that, as latecomers to modernization, their long struggles to free themselves from colonial and quasi-colonial relationships were a sufficient lesson in the limitations of imperial power and rivalry; that the century ahead was not, in any case, a propitious time for two powers with nuclear capacities to conduct such a rivalry, which would inevitably require alliances and other associations which would dilute their freedom of action; and that their increasing potential capacity to shape the course of events in Asia would, therefore, be maximized if they chose to act in concert to damp rather than exacerbate the potential sources of conflict in their region.

Appendix A.

Three Basic ASEAN Documents

[*Note*: This appendix contains the texts of the ASEAN Declaration (Bangkok, August 8, 1967); the Declaration of ASEAN Concord (Bali, February 24, 1976); and the Treaty of Amity and Cooperation in Southeast Asia (Bali, February 24, 1976). They are accessibly reproduced in *10 Years ASEAN*, published in 1978 by that organization.]

THE ASEAN DECLARATION
(BANGKOK DECLARATION)

The Presidium Minister for Political Affairs/ Minister for Foreign Affairs of Indonesia, the Deputy Prime Minister of Malaysia, the Secretary of Foreign Affairs of the Philippines, the Minister for Foreign Affairs of Singapore and the Minister of Foreign Affairs of Thailand:

MINDFUL of the existence of mutual interests and common problems among countries of South-East Asia and convinced of the need to strengthen further the existing bonds of regional solidarity and cooperation;

DESIRING to establish a firm foundation for common action to promote regional cooperation in South-East Asia in the spirit of equality and partnership and thereby contribute towards peace, progress and prosperity in the region;

CONSCIOUS that in an increasingly interdependent world, the cherished ideals of peace, freedom, social justice and economic well-being are best attained by fostering good understanding, good neighbourliness and meaningful cooperation among the countries of the region already bound together by ties of history and culture;

CONSIDERING that the countries of South-East Asia share a primary responsibility for strengthening the economic and social stability of the region and ensuring their peaceful and progressive national development, and that they are determined to ensure their stability and security from external interference in any form or manifestation in order to preserve their national identities in accordance with the ideals and aspirations of their peoples;

AFFIRMING that all foreign bases are temporary and remain only with the expressed concurrence of the countries concerned and are not intended to be used directly or indirectly to subvert the national independence and freedom of States in the area or prejudice the orderly processes of their national development;

DO HEREBY DECLARE:

FIRST, the establishment of an Association for Regional Cooperation among the countries of South-East Asia to be known as the Association of South-East Asian Nations (ASEAN).

SECOND, that the aims and purposes of the Association shall be:

1. To accelerate the economic growth, social progress and cultural development in the region through joint endeavours in the spirit of equality and partnership in order to strengthen the foundation for a prosperous and peaceful community of South-East Asian Nations;
2. To promote regional peace and stability through abiding respect for justice and the rule of the law in the relationship among countries of the region and adherence to the principles of the United Nations Charter;
3. To promote active collaboration and mutual assistance on matters of common interest in the economic, social, cultural, technical, scientific and administrative fields;
4. To provide assistance to each other in the form of training and research facilities in the educational, professional, technical and administrative spheres;
5. To collaborate more effectively for the greater utilization of their agriculture and industries, the expansion of their trade,

including the study of the problems of international commodity trade, the improvement of their transportation and communication facilities and the raising of the living standards of their peoples;

6. To promote South-East Asian studies;
7. To maintain close and beneficial cooperation with existing international and regional organizations with similar aims and purposes, and explore all avenues for even closer cooperation among themselves.

THIRD, that, to carry out these aims and purposes, the following machinery shall be established:

(a) Annual Meeting of Foreign Ministers, which shall be by rotation and referred to as ASEAN Ministerial Meeting. Special Meetings of Foreign Ministers may be convened as required;

(b) A Standing Committee, under the chairmanship of the Foreign Minister of the host country or his representative and having as its members the accredited Ambassadors of the other member countries, to carry on the work of the Association in between Meetings of Foreign Ministers;

(c) Ad-Hoc Committees and Permanent Committees of specialists and officials on specific subjects;

(d) A National Secretariat in each member country to carry out the work of the Association on behalf of that country and to service the Annual or Special Meetings of Foreign Ministers, the Standing Committee and such other Committee as may hereafter be established.

FOURTH, that the Association is open for participation to all States in the South-East Asian Region subscribing to the aforementioned aims, principles and purposes.

FIFTH, that the Association represents the collective will of the nations of South-East Asia to bind themselves together in friendship and cooperation and, through joint efforts and sacrifices, secure for their people and for posterity the blessings of peace, freedom and prosperity.

DECLARATION OF ASEAN CONCORD

A COMMON BOND EXISTING AMONG THE MEMBER STATES OF THE ASSOCIATION OF SOUTHEAST ASIAN NATIONS,

The President of the Republic of Indonesia, the Prime Minister of Malaysia, the President of the Republic of the Philippines, the Prime Minister of the Republic of Singapore and the Prime Minister of the Kingdom of Thailand.

REAFFIRM their commitment to the Declarations of Bandung, Bangkok and Kuala Lumpur, and the Charter of the United Nations;

ENDEAVOUR to promote peace, progress, prosperity and the welfare of the peoples of member states,

UNDERTAKE to consolidate the achievements of ASEAN and expand ASEAN cooperation in the economic, social, cultural and political fields;

DO HEREBY DECLARE:

ASEAN cooperation shall take into account, among others, the following objectives and principles in the pursuit of political stability:

1. The stability of each member state and of the ASEAN region is an essential contribution to international peace and security. Each member state resolves to eliminate threats posed by subversion to its stability, thus strengthening national and ASEAN resilience.

2. Member states, individually and collectively, shall take active steps for the early establishment of the Zone of Peace, Freedom and Neutrality.

3. The elimination of poverty, hunger, disease and illiteracy is a primary concern of member states. They shall therefore intensify cooperation in economic and social development, with particular emphasis on the promotion of social justice and on the improvement of the living standards of their peoples.

4. Natural disasters and other major calamities can retard the pace of development of member states. They shall extend, within their capabilities, assistance for relief of member states in distress.

5. Member states shall take cooperative action in their national and regional development programmes, utilizing as far as possible

the resources available in the ASEAN region to broaden the complementarity of their respective economies.

6. Member states, in the spirit of ASEAN solidarity, shall rely exclusively on peaceful processes in the settlement of intra-regional differences.

7. Member states shall strive, individually and collectively, to create conditions conducive to the promotion of peaceful cooperation among the nations of Southeast Asia on the basis of mutual respect and mutual benefit.

8. Member states shall vigorously develop an awareness of regional identity and exert all efforts to create a strong ASEAN community, respected by all and respecting all nations on the basis of mutually advantageous relationships, and in accordance with the principles of self-determination, sovereign equality and non-interference in the internal affairs of nations.

AND DO HEREBY ADOPT

The following programme of action as a framework for ASEAN cooperation:

A. Political

1. Meeting of the Heads of Government of the member states as and when necessary.

2. Signing of the Treaty of Amity and Cooperation in Southeast Asia.

3. Settlement of intra-regional disputes by peaceful means as soon as possible.

4. Immediate consideration of initial steps towards recognition of and respect for the Zone of Peace, Freedom and Neutrality wherever possible.

5. Improvement of ASEAN machinery to strengthen political cooperation.

6. Study on how to develop judicial cooperation including the possibility of an ASEAN Extradition Treaty.

7. Strengthening of political solidarity by promoting the harmonization of views, coordinating position and, where possible and desirable, taking common actions.

B. Economic

1. Cooperation on Basic Commodities, particularly Food and Energy

(i) Member states shall assist each other by according priority to the supply of the individual country's needs in critical circumstances, and priority to the acquisition of exports from member states, in respect of basic commodities, particularly food and energy.

(ii) Member states shall also intensify cooperation in the production of basic commodities particularly food and energy in the individual member states of the region.

2. Industrial Cooperation

(i) Member states shall cooperate to establish large-scale ASEAN industrial plants, particularly to meet regional requirements of essential commodities.

(ii) Priority shall be given to projects which utilize the available materials in the member states, contribute to the increase of food production, increase foreign exchange earnings or save foreign exchange and create employment.

3. Cooperation in Trade

(i) Member states shall cooperate in the fields of trade in order to promote development and growth of new production and trade and to improve the trade structures of individual states and among countries of ASEAN conducive to further development and to safeguard and increase their foreign exchange earnings and reserves.

(ii) Member states shall progress towards the establishment of preferential trading arrangements as a long term objective on a basis deemed to be at any particular time appropriate through rounds of negotiations subject to the unanimous agreement of member states.

(iii) The expansion of trade among member states shall be facilitated through cooperation on basic commodities, particularly food and energy and through cooperation in ASEAN industrial projects.

(iv) Member states shall accelerate joint efforts to improve access to markets outside ASEAN for their raw material and finished products by seeking the elimination of all trade barriers in those markets, developing new usage for these products and in adopting common approaches and actions in dealing with regional groupings and individual economic powers.

(v) Such efforts shall also lead to cooperation in the field of technology and production methods in order to increase the production and to improve the quality of export products, as well as to develop new export products with a view to diversifying exports.

4. Joint Approach to International Commodity Problems and Other World Economic Problems

(i) The principle of ASEAN cooperation on trade shall also be reflected on a priority basis in joint approaches to international commodity problems and other world economic problems such as the reform of international trading system, the reform of international monetary system and transfer of real resources, in the United Nations and other relevant multilateral fora, with a view to contributing to the establishment of the New International Economic Order.

(ii) Member states shall give priority to the stabilisation and increase of export earning of those commodities produced and exported by them through commodity agreements including buffer stock schemes and other means.

5. Machinery for Economic Cooperation

Ministerial meetings on economic matters shall be held regularly or as deemed necessary in order to:

(i) formulate recommendations for the consideration of Governments of member states for the strengthening of ASEAN economic cooperation;

(ii) review the coordination and implementation of agreed ASEAN programmes and projects on economic cooperation;

(iii) exchange views and consult on national development plans and policies as a step towards harmonizing regional development; and

(iv) perform such other relevant functions as agreed upon by the member Governments.

C. Social

1. Cooperation in the field of social development, with emphasis on the well being of the low-income group and of the rural pop-

ulation, through the expansion of opportunities for productive employment with fair remuneration.

2. Support for the active involvement of all sectors and levels of the ASEAN communities, particularly the women and youth, in development efforts.

3. Intensification and expansion of existing cooperation in meeting the problems of population growth in the ASEAN region, and where possible, formulation of new strategies in collaboration with appropriate international agencies.

4. Intensification of cooperation among member states as well as with the relevant international bodies in the prevention and eradication of the abuse of narcotics and the illegal trafficking of drugs.

D. Cultural and Information

1. Introduction of the study of ASEAN, its member states and their national languages as part of the curricula of schools and other institutions of learning in the member states.

2. Support of ASEAN scholars, writers, artists and mass media representatives to enable them to play an active role in fostering a sense of regional identity and fellowship.

3. Promotion of Southeast Asian studies through closer collaboration among national institutes.

E. Security

Continuation of cooperation on a non-ASEAN basis between the member states in security matters in accordance with their mutual needs and interests.

F. Improvement of ASEAN Machinery

1. Signing of the Agreement on the Establishment of the ASEAN Secretariat.

2. Regular review of the ASEAN organizational structure with a view to improving its effectiveness.

3. Study of the desirability of a new constitutional framework for ASEAN.

TREATY OF AMITY AND COOPERATION
IN SOUTHEAST ASIA

PREAMBLE

The High Contracting Parties;

CONSCIOUS of the existing ties of history, geography and culture, which have bound their peoples together;

ANXIOUS to promote regional peace and stability through abiding respect for justice and the rule of law and enhancing regional resilience in their relations;

DESIRING to enhance peace, friendship and mutual cooperation on matters affecting Southeast Asia consistent with the spirit and principles of the Charter of the United Nations, the Ten Principles adopted by the Asian-African Conference in Bandung on 25 April 1955, the Declaration of the Association of Southeast Asian Nations signed in Bangkok on 8 August 1967, and the Declaration signed in Kuala Lumpur on 27 November 1971;

CONVINCED that the settlement of differences or disputes between their countries should be regulated by rational, effective and sufficiently flexible procedures, avoiding negative attitudes which might endanger or hinder cooperation;

BELIEVING in the need for cooperation with all peace-loving nations, both within and outside Southeast Asia, in the furtherance of world-peace, stability and harmony;

SOLEMNLY AGREE to enter into a Treaty of Amity and Cooperation as follows:

CHAPTER I
PURPOSE AND PRINCIPLES

Article 1

The Purpose of this Treaty is to promote perpetual peace, everlasting amity and cooperation among their peoples which would contribute to their strength, solidarity and closer relationship.

Article 2

In their relations with one another, the High Contracting Parties shall be guided by the following principles:

a. Mutual respect for the independence, sovereignty, equality, territorial integrity and national identity of all nations;
b. The right of every State to lead its national existence free from external interference, subversion or coercion;
c. Non-interference in the internal affairs of one another;
d. Settlement of differences or disputes by peaceful means;
e. Renunciation of the threat or use of force;
f. Effective cooperation among themselves.

CHAPTER II
AMITY

Article 3

In pursuance of the purpose of this Treaty the High Contracting Parties shall endeavour to develop and strengthen the traditional, cultural and historical ties of friendship, good neighbourliness and cooperation which bind them together and shall fulfill in good faith the obligations assumed under this Treaty. In order to promote closer understanding among them, the High Contracting Parties shall encourage and facilitate contact and intercourse among their peoples.

CHAPTER III
COOPERATION

Article 4

The High Contracting Parties shall promote active cooperation in the economic, social, cultural, technical, scientific and administrative fields as well as in matters of common ideals and aspiration of international peace and stability in the region and all other matters of economic interest.

Article 5

Pursuant to Article 4 the High Contracting Parties shall exert their maximum efforts multilaterally as well as bilaterally on the basis of equality, non-discrimination and mutual benefit.

Article 6

The High Contracting Parties shall collaborate for the acceleration of the economic growth in the region in order to strengthen the foundation for a prosperous and peaceful community of nations in Southeast Asia. To this end, they shall promote the greater utilization of their agriculture and industries, the expansion of their trade and the improvement of their economic infra-structure for the mutual benefit of their peoples. In this regard, they shall continue to explore all avenues for close and beneficial cooperation with other States as well as international and regional organizations outside the region.

Article 7

The High Contracting Parties, in order to achieve social justice and to raise the standards of living of the peoples of the region, shall intensify economic cooperation. For this purpose, they shall adopt appropriate regional strategies for economic development and mutual assistance.

Article 8

The High Contracting Parties shall strive to achieve the closest cooperation on the widest scale and shall seek to provide assistance to one another in the form of training and research facilities in the social, cultural, technical, scientific and administrative fields.

Article 9

The High Contracting Parties shall endeavour to foster cooperation in the furtherance of the cause of peace, harmony and stability in the region. To this end, the High Contracting Parties shall maintain regular contacts and consultations with one another on international and regional matters with a view to coordinating their views, actions and policies.

Article 10

Each High Contracting Party shall not in any manner or form participate in any activity which shall constitute a threat to the political and economic stability, sovereignty, or territorial integrity of another High Contracting Party.

Article II

The High Contracting Parties shall endeavour to strengthen their respective national resilience in their political, economic, socio-cultural as well as security fields in conformity with their respective ideals and aspirations, free from external interference as well as internal subversive activities in order to preserve their respective national identities.

Article 12

The High Contracting Parties in their efforts to achieve regional prosperity and security, shall endeavour to cooperate in all fields for the promotion of regional resilience, based on the principles of self-confidence, self-reliance, mutual respect, cooperation and solidarity which will constitute the foundation for a strong and viable community of nations in Southeast Asia.

CHAPTER IV
PACIFIC SETTLEMENT OF DISPUTES

Article 13

The High Contracting Parties shall have the determination and good faith to prevent disputes from arising. In case of disputes on matters affecting them they shall refrain from the threat or use of force and shall at all times settle such disputes among themselves through friendly negotiations.

Article 14

To settle disputes through regional processes, the High Contracting Parties shall constitute, as a continuing body, a High Council comprising a Representative at ministerial level from each of the High Contracting Parties to take cognizance of the existence of disputes or situations likely to disturb regional peace and harmony.

Article 15

In the event no solution is reached through direct negotiations, the High Council shall take cognizance of the dispute or the situation and shall recommend to the parties in dispute appropriate means of settlement such as good offices, mediation, inquiry or conciliation.

The High Council may however offer its good offices, or upon agreement of the parties in dispute, constitute itself into a committee of mediation, inquiry or conciliation. When deemed necessary, the High Council shall recommend appropriate measures for the prevention of a deterioration of the dispute or the situation.

Article 16
The foregoing provision of this Chapter shall not apply to a dispute unless all the parties to the dispute agree to their application to that dispute. However, this shall not preclude the other High Contracting Parties not party to the dispute from offering all possible assistance to settle the said dispute. Parties to the dispute should be well disposed towards such offers of assistance.

Article 17
Nothing in this Treaty shall preclude recourse to the modes of peaceful settlement contained in Article 33 (1) of the Charter of the United Nations. The High Contracting Parties which are parties to a dispute should be encouraged to take initiatives to solve it by friendly negotiations before resorting to the other procedures provided for in the Charter of the United Nations.

CHAPTER V
GENERAL PROVISIONS

Article 18
This Treaty shall be signed by the Republic of Indonesia, Malaysia, the Republic of the Philippines, the Republic of Singapore and the Kingdom of Thailand. It shall be ratified in accordance with the constitutional procedures of each signatory State.

It shall be open for accession by other States in Southeast Asia.

Article 19
This Treaty shall enter into force on the date of the deposit of the fifth instrument of ratification with the Governments of the signatory States which are designated Depositories of this Treaty and of the instruments of ratification or accession.

Article 20

This Treaty is drawn up in the official languages of the High Contracting Parties, all of which are equally authoritative. There shall be an agreed common translation of the texts in the English language. Any divergent interpretation of the common text shall be settled by negotiation.

IN FAITH THEREOF the High Contracting Parties have signed the Treaty and have hereto affixed their Seals.

Appendix B.

The Abiding Interests of the Powers in Southeast Asia

[*Note*: This paper was prepared for and delivered at a retrospective symposium on Vietnam, held in Salado, Texas, October 29–31, 1982. It is reproduced here as it was originally presented, with minor excisions indicated.]

The United States' involvement in Vietnam and Southeast Asia evidently had and has many dimensions in that region and at home: military and economic, social and political, human and moral. I tried to evoke the multiple facets of the problem in the relevant passages of my book, *The Diffusion of Power*.

I decided, however, that I could be most useful on this occasion if I focused on one important and largely neglected aspect of the subject: the strategic significance to all the relevant powers of Southeast Asia.

In their serious effort to analyze the U.S. involvement in Vietnam, Leslie Gelb and Richard Betts take as their central thesis the following proposition:

> . . . U.S. leaders considered it vital not to lose Vietnam by force to communism. They believed Vietnam to be vital, not for itself, but for what they thought its "loss" would mean internationally and domestically.[80]

George Herring's interesting historical assessment, made available to us for these sessions, contains a brief, accurate passage evoking the reasons for anxiety about Southeast Asia in Washington in the wake of the Communist takeover of China in 1949; but so far as my reading revealed, there is no further discussion of the strategic importance of Vietnam or Southeast Asia.[81]

The general view of those who opposed U.S. policy toward Southeast Asia in the 1960s is quite well captured by J. K. Galbraith's *bon mot* of April 25, 1966: "If we were not in Vietnam, all that part of the world would be enjoying the obscurity it so richly deserves."[82] Or, take the following passage from a 1968 interview with Eugene McCarthy in *The New York Times*:

> I [interviewer] asked him [McCarthy] the final question about Vietnam: "How are we going to get out?" He said "Take this down. I said that the time has come for us to say to the Vietnamese, We will take our steel out of the land of thatched huts, we will take our tanks out of the land of the water buffalo, our napalm and flame-throwers out of the land that scarcely knows the use of matches. We will give you back your small and willing women, your rice-paddies and your land." He smiled. "That's my platform. It's pretty good, isn't it?"[83]

At first glance, there would appear to be some evidence for the view that the U.S. government did not regard Vietnam of intrinsic importance; for example, neither in office nor in their memoirs did Richard Nixon or Henry Kissinger discuss Southeast Asian policy except as an inherited burden and a responsibility that had to be honored if the credibility of U.S. guarantees elsewhere were to be sustained. As I shall note later, John Kennedy and Lyndon Johnson (but not all members of their administrations) took a different view. And the fact is that over the past forty years nine successive presidents—from Franklin Roosevelt to Ronald Reagan—have made serious strategic commitments to the independence of Southeast Asia, in every case with some pain and contrary to other interests.

The story begins, in a sense, with this passage from Cordell Hull's memoirs, which is where the Pentagon Papers should have begun but didn't:

. . . Japanese troops on July 21 [1941] occupied the southern portions of Indo-China and were now in possession of the whole of France's strategic province, pointing like a pudgy thumb toward the Philippines, Malaya, and the Dutch East Indies. . . .

When Welles telephoned me, I said to him that the invasion of Southern Indo-China looked like Japan's last step before jumping off for a full-scale attack in the Southwest Pacific. . . .

On the following day the President, receiving Nomura, proposed that if the Japanese Government would withdraw its forces from French Indo-China, he would seek to obtain a solemn declaration by the United States, Britain, China, and The Netherlands to regard Indo-China as a "neutralized" country, provided Japan gave a similar commitment. Japan's explanation for occupying Indo-China having been that she wanted to defend her supplies of raw materials there, the President's proposal took the props from under this specious reasoning. A week later the President extended his proposal to include Thailand.

Indicating our reaction to Japan's latest act of imperialist aggression, the President froze Japanese assets in the United States on July 26. . . . All financial, import, and export transactions involving Japanese interests came under Government control, and thereafter trade between the United States and Japan soon dwindled to comparatively nothing. . . .

From now on our major objective with regard to Japan was to give ourselves more time to prepare our defenses. We were still ready—and eager—to do everything possible toward keeping the United States out of war; but it was our concurrent duty to concentrate on trying to make the country ready to defend itself effectively in the event of war being thrust upon us.[84]

It was, in fact, the movement by the Japanese from northern to southern Indochina in July 1941 and Roosevelt's reaction to it which made war between Japan and the United States inevitable, despite Roosevelt's deep desire to avoid a two-front conflict. The story continues down to the more familiar commitments in Southeast Asia, from Truman to Nixon, to the less well known fact that on four separate occasions the Carter administration, in the wake of the Communist take-over of South Vietnam in April 1975, reaffirmed the nation's treaty commitment to the defense of Thailand.[85] On October 6, 1981, President Reagan said this to the prime minister of Thailand on the occasion of his visit to Washington:

> I can assure you that America is ready to help you, and ASEAN, maintain your independence against communist aggression. The Manila Pact, and its clarification in our bilateral communique of 1962, is a living document. We will honor the obligations it conveys.[86]

That is where we are. With large Vietnamese forces in Kampuchea, just across the shallow Mekong from Thailand and dominating Laos as well; with the Soviet navy based in the installations we built in Cam Ranh Bay, the Soviet air force based in the airfields around Danang, and a major port in Kampuchea being enlarged for Soviet strategic purposes—just across the South China Sea from the U.S. bases in Subic Bay and Clark Field—Southeast Asia is not likely soon to disappear from the national security agenda of the United States government. I doubt, however, that there is a wide awareness in the United States of how tightly drawn the confrontation is along the Mekong and across the South China Sea. Nor do I believe there is a wide awareness of the commitments reaffirmed in the region by President Carter and President Reagan. But, for the purposes of our discussions here in Salado, my point is this: we cannot understand what we have experienced in Asia over the past two generations, nor can we formulate and sustain a viable policy in Asia, until we as a nation come to a widespread understanding of the strategic importance of Southeast Asia to our own security and to the security of the other powers concerned.

I shall begin, therefore, by trying to evoke the character of the strategic interests at work in Southeast Asia; state the linkages of Vietnam to the rest of Southeast Asia; outline tersely the strategic evolution of Southeast Asia since 1940; and reflect, finally, on the implications of the story for U.S. policy, past and future.

At some risk of oversimplification, I shall now try to define the major strategic interests of each of the principal powers concerned with Southeast Asia.

Japan. The Japanese have three abiding interests in Southeast Asia. First, a straightforward security interest that Southeast Asia (and thus the South China Sea) not be controlled by a potentially hostile power, with all that would imply for the sea approaches to the Japanese islands. Second, trading access to the countries of Southeast Asia, which have been and remain major sources of raw materials and major markets for Japanese exports, markets notably expanding in recent decades. Third, an interest that the Straits of Malacca remain reliably open for Japanese trade with the rest of the world, an interest greatly heightened by the remarkable emergence of Japan as a global trading nation and its heavy reliance on an unobstructed flow of Middle East oil.

Japan sought to achieve these objectives by creating the Greater East Asia Co-Prosperity Sphere in 1940–1945. When that effort failed, it has fallen back to reliance on the United States (and, to a degree, its own diplomacy and defense forces) to assure these vital interests.

China. China has an abiding interest that Southeast Asia not be dominated by a major, potentially hostile power. Such dominance would threaten it both over land and via the South China Sea, where Vietnamese bases could bring pressure against important coastal cities. China has pursued these interests since 1949 by contesting vigorously Soviet efforts to dominate Southeast Asian Communist parties, notably the Vietnamese; by leading the 1964–1965 effort to collapse non-Communist resistance in Southeast Asia, in association with Hanoi and Sukarno and Aidit in Indonesia; and, after the Cultural Revolution, by association with the United States and by contesting independently what the Chinese regard as Soviet efforts to encircle and isolate China.

U.S.S.R. Russia has had an abiding interest that Vladivostok remain open as a trading port and a naval base. And, since the Trans-Siberian railway went through in the 1890s, it has been a recurrent contestant for power in northeast Asia, notably vis-à-vis Japan and China. In the post-1949 period the Soviet Union moved out from this regional role to broader vistas of Asian and global power. Its contest for power developed two new dimensions: the struggle with the Chinese Communists, initially confined to contention for leadership of Asian (and other) Communist parties which, from early 1958, became a Cold War between the two countries; and the thrust, based on the radically expanded Soviet navy, to develop a string of alliances from Southeast Asia through the Indian Ocean to the Arabian Peninsula and East Africa. (I shall have more to say later about this policy, which can be formally dated from June 1969.) The Soviet air and naval bases in Indochina are, evidently, fundamental to this strategy, both to neutralize the U.S. bases at Clark Field and Subic Bay, which have hitherto dominated the South China Sea, and to guarantee Soviet access to the Indian Ocean through the Malacca Straits.

India. Aside from an Indian Ocean open freely to its commerce and not dominated by a single potentially hostile power, India's concern with Southeast Asia is that the countries of the region—Burma, above all—remain independent. It is an interest parallel, for example, to India's concern for an independent Afghanistan—a concern only recently articulated by Mrs. Gandhi.

India's interest in Southeast Asia is rarely discussed in public by its political leaders. Nevertheless, the fundamental strands of Indian policy toward the region have been consistent and deeply rooted in memories of the Japanese occupation of Burma and the possibility of a recurrence of danger on India's northeast frontier.[87] For this reason India supported Burma and Malaya against Communist guerrilla movements in the 1950s.

Australia. The abiding interests of Australia in Southeast Asia are dual: that its sea routes to the United States, Europe, and Japan (now its most important trading partner) remain open; and that Southeast Asia and, above all, Indonesia remain independent of any major power and not hostile. The Australians are not likely to forget what a close thing it was in 1942 when they were saved from Japanese invasion by the American victories in the Coral Sea and at Guadalcanal. And, unlike most Americans, they remember how close to a Communist take-over Southeast Asia was, including, especially, Indonesia in July 1965, when Johnson made his decision to introduce large U.S. forces into Vietnam.[88]

In the changing circumstances since 1965, Australian foreign and military policy has continued steadily to support the independence of Southeast Asia.

The United States. U.S. policy in Asia began, of course, with a simple concern for the maintenance of trading access in the face of special interests developed by Western powers operating in the region. From, say, the ambiguities of the Open Door notes of 1900 and Theodore Roosevelt's tilt toward the Russians in 1905 at Portsmouth, in the wake of the Russo-Japanese war, a strategic dimension to U.S. policy emerged parallel to that which emerged during the First World War in Europe; namely, a U.S. interest that a balance of power be maintained in Asia and that no single power dominate the region. A power with hegemony in Asia would command the resources to expel U.S. naval power in the Pacific, back to Hawaii at least, just as a hegemonic power in Europe could dominate the Atlantic, as German submarines twice came close to demonstrating. The U.S. has acted systematically on that principle for some eighty years when the balance of power in Asia seemed under real and present danger. At various times, that instinctive policy has brought us into confrontation in Asia with Japan, China, Russia, or their surrogates; and, at various times, it has brought us into association with Russia, China, and Japan.

As is evident from this brisk review, Southeast Asia is a critical element in the balance of power in Asia because of its relation to sea routes and the exercise of sea and air power; its resources; and its location with respect to China, India, and Japan. For the United States, Southeast Asia has a quite special meaning as an area of forward defense of the Pacific—a relationship vividly demonstrated after the loss of the Philippines to Japan in 1942. But for victory in the Battle of Midway, we might, at best, have held Hawaii.

In addition, the United States shares to a significant degree the specific interests in Southeast Asia of its allies and others whose security would be threatened by the hegemony of a single power in Asia; that is, at the moment we share to a significant degree the interests of Japan, China, India, and Australia as outlined earlier. It is, essentially, a negative interest satisfied, as all the presidents from Roosevelt to Reagan have stated, by an independent, neutral Southeast Asia.

Southeast Asia. Southeast Asia, excluding the three states of Indochina, contains some three hundred million people—a population approximating that of Latin America or Africa. They are diverse in their racial origins, historical experiences, degrees of modernization, and forms of government. History has also given them territorial and other deeply rooted conflicts to overcome. What they share is a desire to modernize their societies in their own way, true to their own cultures, traditions, and ambitions, and to be left in peace and independence by all the external powers. They do not wish to be run from Tokyo or Washington, New Delhi or Beijing, Moscow or Hanoi. They also shared an astonishing economic and social momentum in the 1960s and 1970s, including a per capita growth rate in real income averaging about 4 percent and a manufacturing growth rate of about 10 percent, as well as high rates of increase in foreign trade. They export about 83 percent of the world's natural rubber, 80 percent of its copra, palm, and coconut oil, 73 percent of its tin as well as a wide range of other agricultural products and raw materials. Their literacy rates, which ranged from 39 percent to 72 percent in 1960 now range from 60 percent to 84 percent.

Out of their several and collective experiences as objects of the strategic interests of others, strongly encouraged by Lyndon Johnson, who made Asian regionalism a major, consistent theme of his policy, and conscious that the U.S. role in Asia was likely to diminish with the passage of time, the five Southeast Asian countries (beyond Indochina) created ASEAN in 1967. It is an organization committed to economic and technical cooperation, to the peaceful settlement of its inner disputes, and, above all, "to ensure their stability and security from external interference in any form or manifestation."[89]

ASEAN moved forward slowly, building up the habit of economic cooperation and political consultation.

When the Communists took over Vietnam in April 1975, ASEAN, alarmed by the turn of events, moved forward rather than backward. At an historic, carefully prepared session of the chiefs of government at Bali in February 1976, they strongly reaffirmed a 1971 declaration calling for a Zone of Peace, Freedom, and Neutrality in Southeast Asia. And they have subsequently sought widened international support for this objective. Quite specifically, they have led the international effort to achieve the withdrawal of Vietnamese troops from Kampuchea and fostered the negotiation of a new national coalition of Kampuchean leaders committed to the authentic independence of their country. Although the countries of ASEAN command, neither individually nor collectively, the military power to deter or defeat a Vietnamese thrust into Thailand or to assure control over the critical sea lanes which surround them and link them to each other, the sturdy unity which they have managed to maintain for fifteen years makes ASEAN an element in the Asia equation of diplomacy to be reckoned with.[90]

To sum up this review of various strategic perspectives on Southeast Asia, one can assert two propositions:

—The legitimate interests of all the powers concerned with the region would be satisfied by a neutral Southeast Asia left to develop in independence, with its sea lanes and strategic straits open by international consensus.

—But the fundamental character of the various interests at stake in the region decree that the effort of any one power to achieve dominance in the region will confront serious and determined opposition from multiple directions.

Now a few words about Vietnam and Southeast Asia.

As the agenda of this conference and the bulk of the literature bearing on its themes suggest, Vietnam has tended to be discussed by Americans in isolation. None of the nine presidents caught up in the area thought in such terms, not even Nixon, who was the most reticent about articulating the importance of the region as a whole and the U.S. interest in its fate.

Rather than taking Vietnam's strategic importance for granted as part of Southeast Asia, it is worth briefly specifying both its intrinsic importance and the nature of its linkages to Southeast Asia.

A glance at the map suggests the various strategic roles of Vietnam.

First, its geography places it on the Chinese frontier; its ports and air bases make it of strategic importance with respect to both South China and the international sea lanes of the South China Sea. Thus, the Soviet naval and air bases in Cam Ranh Bay and Danang are a very serious matter, indeed, for China, Japan, and the United States, every country in non-Communist Southeast Asia, and every country with an interest in the independence of Southeast Asia.

Second, easy overland access from Vietnam to Laos and Cambodia made it likely that those with power in all of Vietnam would quickly gain control of all of Indochina. The likelihood is enhanced by the extremely difficult logistical problems for an outside power (for example, the United States or China) of bringing its forces to bear in defense of Laos or Cambodia against an overland thrust from Vietnam. Control of Cambodia by an outside power substantially enhances the capacity of that power to bring air and naval forces to bear across the air and sea lanes of the South China Sea. . . .

Third, and for American policy in the 1950s and 1960s, most important of all, a power emplaced in Vietnam, Laos, and Cambodia confronts Thailand across the long line of the shallow Mekong. The frontier is not only long and virtually indefensible against a massive attack by well-armed conventional forces but the Mekong is also a long way from the Thai ports. As I have explained at length elsewhere, this is why John Kennedy in 1961 made the decision to defend Thailand and the rest of Southeast Asia by seeking via diplomacy the neutralization of Laos and by fighting the battle for Southeast Asia in Vietnam.[91]

Thailand is, ultimately, critical to Southeast Asia because of its geographical relation to Burma, on the one hand, Malaysia and Singapore, on the other. If a single major power controls all of Indochina and Thailand, the vital interests of India, Japan, the United States, Indonesia, and Australia are in real and present danger; that is, Burma and the land route to the Indian subcontinent, control over the South China Sea, and control over the Straits of Malacca. That is why Carter and Reagan have reaffirmed the applicability of our treaty commitments to Thailand and why ASEAN's major political thrust, overwhelmingly backed by North and South in the United Nations, is to effect the withdrawal of Vietnamese forces from Kampuchea and the line of the Mekong and to create an authentically independent Kampuchean government.

As Franklin Roosevelt suggested to the Japanese ambassador in July 1941, a neutral Southeast Asia, of the kind ASEAN now proclaims, would satisfy the legitimate interests of all the powers; but he could not accept Japanese control over the region. Roosevelt's policy has, in effect, been the policy of all his successors. And the fact is that for more than forty years now a succession of powers has sought hegemony in the region and met serious resistance.

This sequence of efforts is reflected in the analysis I have thus far presented. But it may be useful briefly to specify when and the context in which each occurred.

First, of course, was the Japanese thrust of 1940–1945. Its frustration required a homeric and bloody effort by the United States, Australia, New Zealand, Great Britain, China, and India.

Second, came the systematic Communist efforts to exploit by guerrilla warfare the postwar dishevelment of the region and the confusions and conflicts of the transition from colonialism to independence. Stalin organized this campaign impelled by (to him) the surprising likelihood that the Communists would emerge victorious from the post-1945 civil war and by Truman's counterattack of Soviet aggression in Europe. The Truman Doctrine and Marshall Plan of 1947 clearly set a limit to the ample European empire Stalin acquired in the wake of the Second World War.

But with Mao evidently on his way to control over China in 1947, ambitious new Communist objectives in Asia were enunciated by Zhdanov at the founding meeting of the Cominform in September. Open guerrilla warfare began in Indochina as early as November 1946, in Burma in April 1948, in Malaya in June of that year, and in Indonesia and the Philippines in the autumn. The Indian and Japanese Communist parties, with less scope for guerrilla action, nevertheless sharply increased their militancy in 1948. As final victory was won in China in November 1949, Mao's political-military strategy was openly commended by the Cominform to the Communist parties in those areas where guerrilla operations were under way. Stalin and Mao met early in 1950 and confirmed the ambitious Asian strategy, planning its climax in the form of the North Korean invasion of South Korea, which took place at the end of June 1950.

The American and United Nations response to the invasion of South Korea, the landings at Inchon, the March to the Yalu, the Chinese Communist entrance into the war, and the successful U.N. defense against massive Chinese assault in April–May 1951 at the thirty-eighth parallel, brought this phase of military and quasi-military Communist effort throughout Asia to a gradual end. Neither Moscow nor Peking was willing to undertake all-out war or even accept the cost of a continued Korean offensive. And elsewhere the bright Communist hopes of 1946–1947 had dimmed. Nowhere in Asia was Mao's success repeated. Indonesia, Burma, and the Philippines largely overcame their guerrillas. At great cost to Britain, the Malayan guerrillas were contained and driven back. Only in Indochina, where French colonialism offered a seedbed as fruitful as postwar China, was there real Communist momentum. The settlement at Geneva in 1954 permitted an interval of four years of relative quiet in Indochina.

Although there were latent tensions between Moscow and Beijing in this phase and some contest over control and influence of the various Asian Communist parties, by and large the U.S.S.R. and PRC conducted this second effort to achieve hegemony in Asia in concert.

The third effort emerged at a meeting in November 1957 in Moscow in the wake of the Soviet launching of Sputnik in October. The chiefs of all the Communist governments assembled. They agreed the time was propitious for a concerted effort to expand Soviet power. As Mao said in Moscow:

> It is my opinion that the international situation has now reached a new turning point. There are two winds in the world today, the East wind and the West wind. There is a Chinese saying, "Either the East wind prevails over the West wind or the West wind prevails over the East wind." It is characteristic of the situation today. I believe, that the East wind is prevailing over the West wind. That is to say, the forces of socialism are overwhelmingly superior to the forces of imperialism. . . .
>
> The superiority of the anti-imperialist forces over the imperialist forces . . . has expressed itself in even more concentrated form and reached unprecedented heights with the Soviet Union's launching of the artificial satellites. . . . That is why we say that this is a new turning point in the international situation.[92]

Many enterprises followed from this assessment of "the new turning point": from Berlin to the Congo to the Caribbean. For our purposes, the most important was Soviet and Chinese agreement to permit Ho Chi Minh, under pressure from the Communists in South Vietnam, to relaunch Hanoi's effort to take over Laos and South Vietnam by guerrilla warfare after four years of relative passivity.

The spirit at Moscow was relatively harmonious between Russia and China; but by early 1958 the split, long latent, became acute over the question of the degree of control Moscow would exercise over the nuclear weapons it promised to transfer to China.[93] From that time forward the competition for influence in Hanoi between Moscow and Beijing, long a major issue, became intense.

Down to 1965 by and large the Chinese influence was predominant. Hanoi's enterprise, notably its introduction of regular North Vietnamese units into South Vietnam in 1964, was orchestrated by the Chinese, with the Indonesian confrontation with Malaysia. Sukarno left the United Nations and openly joined with the Chinese, North Vietnamese, Cambodians, and North Koreans in a new grouping of forces as Hanoi's efforts in South Vietnam moved forward toward apparent success. On January 1, 1965, the Chinese foreign minister Chen Yi proclaimed: "Thailand is next." No leader in Asia, Communist or non-Communist, doubted the potential reality of the domino theory in July 1965 when Johnson made his decision to introduce substantial U.S. forces into the region. . . .

The U.S. move was followed by the joint Communist effort, acquiesced in by Sukarno, to assassinate the Indonesian chiefs of staff and set up a Communist government. It failed. And, for related but obscure reasons, Mao's Cultural Revolution began in China a few weeks later. The Russians took over the major role in Hanoi of arms supplier and economic support, a position they still occupy.

The fourth and current thrust for hegemony in Southeast Asia is Brezhnev's, to which we have already referred. From the trough in 1965, the South Vietnamese moved forward slowly but consistently over the next two years in military, political, and economic terms. In the face of their waning position, the North Vietnamese and the Viet Cong assembled their accumulated capital and threw it into a maximum effort at Tet 1968. The result was a major military and political victory for the South Vietnamese, a major political victory for Hanoi in American public opinion.[94] With Nixon's decision for Vietnamization, based on a more confident position in Vietnam, Moscow proceeded to design and announce a new ambitious long-run policy.

The policy was explained by Brezhnev to a group of Communist leaders on June 7, 1969.[95] His plan was based explicitly on: the "vacuum" left by the British withdrawal east of Suez, the expected U.S. retraction in Asia reflected in Nixon's Guam Doctrine, and alleged Chinese efforts to expand into the vacuum. Implicitly, it was based on the greatly expanded capabilities of the Soviet Navy generated during the 1960s and planned for the future. It also constituted a response to Nixon's interest in an opening to China.

The plan called for a new Collective Security System for Asia; that is, a series of pacts with countries in Asia, the Middle East, and Africa, including Soviet bases in the periphery from the South China Sea to the western coasts of the Indian Ocean and the Persian Gulf. Over the next decade this policy, systematically pursued, included as major moves: the setting up of Soviet bases in Indochina and support for the Vietnamese invasion of Kampuchea; the 1971 Soviet pact with India; the creation of new Soviet ties to Yemen and Ethiopia; and, indeed, the Soviet occupation of Afghanistan. The policy is reflected in the number of Soviet operational ship visits in the Indian Ocean: they rise from 1 in 1968 to an average of 120 in the period 1974–1976.[96]

The outcome of Brezhnev's Soviet-led Collective Security System for Asia, in the great arc from Vladivostok to Aden and Djibouti, is, evidently, still to be determined.

Before considering the future prospects of the region and U.S. policy toward it, we might reflect a bit on the meaning of the analysis I have presented.

Perhaps the first thing to be said is that, while Americans may still debate the importance of Southeast Asia to the balance of power in Asia, as a whole, there is little ambiguity about the matter among the governments and peoples of Asia, including the Soviet Union.

As for us Americans, some may draw from the story I have sketched the simple conclusion that all nine of our presidents since 1940 have been wrong; that is, the United States has no serious legitimate interests in preventing the control of Southeast Asia by a major, potentially hostile power. In that case, they should advocate the abrogation of the network of commitments we have in the region and urge us to organize urgently to face all the profound military, diplomatic, and economic consequences that would flow from that decision.

If we assume that I have described more or less accurately the interests of all parties at stake in Southeast Asia, the sequence of events since 1940, and where the region now stands, there are a few reasonably objective observations to be made that bear on the central purpose of this conference, that is, to provide a perspective on our travail over Vietnam.

First, the nature of U.S. interest in Southeast Asia is quite complex—more so in Vietnam itself; and even when U.S. interests are less complex, we have had difficulty acting on them in a forehanded way. When the chips were down in 1917—with the German declaration of unrestricted submarine warfare in the Atlantic and the Zimmerman note promising the return of Texas to Mexico by a victorious Germany—it was not difficult for Wilson to gain congressional support for a declaration of war in a hitherto deeply divided country, five months after he was reelected on the slogans "He kept us out of war" and "Too proud to fight." But such critical circumstances were required to bring the country to act on the basis of a wide consensus. Similarly, it required Pearl Harbor to bring the United States into the Second World War after a long period dominated by an isolationism FDR couldn't break. And it took a straightforward invasion of South Korea to evoke a military response there. What Truman and Eisenhower, Kennedy and Johnson were trying to prevent in Southeast Asia was a circumstance so stark and dangerous that once again, late in the day, the American people would finally perceive vital interests were in jeopardy and be plunged into major war.

Behind their efforts was a consciousness that there has been, historically, no stable consensus in our country on the nature of our vital interest in the world. We have oscillated between isolationism, indifference, wishful thinking, and complacency, on the one hand, and, on the other, the panic-stricken retrieval of situations already advanced in dangerous deterioration. We have operated systematically on the principle enunciated by Dr. Samuel Johnson: "Depend upon it, Sir, when a man knows he is to be hanged in a fortnight, it concentrates his mind wonderfully." Right or wrong, Kennedy and Johnson did not doubt that the American people and the Congress would react to support the use of force if Communist forces were actually engulfing all of Southeast Asia; but they judged a typical, late, convulsive American reaction—a fortnight from the gallows—too dangerous in a nuclear age.[97]

Second, and quite specifically, they fought in Vietnam to prevent the situation we now confront and what may (but may not) follow from it; that is, large Vietnamese forces on the line of the Mekong backed by a major hostile power. Historians, as well as American citizens, will no doubt assess their judgment on this matter in different ways. What I am asserting here as a matter of fact is that U.S. policy in the 1960s cannot be understood without grasping this dimension in the perspectives of Kennedy and Johnson.

A third objective is that, within the American foreign-policy establishment of the 1960s—including some in the executive branch—there was a kind of geological fault line between those who regarded the balance of power in Southeast Asia as important for the United States in itself and those who, holding what I have called an Atlanticist view, regarded the maintenance of our commitments there as significant only for the viability of our commitments elsewhere, for example, in Europe and the Middle East.[98] The hypothesis of Gelb and Betts, stated at the beginning of this paper, reflects, for example, the latter view. In the early 1970s, having gathered strength for some time, a version of that view became widespread that the costs of holding the U.S. position in Southeast Asia was excessive, even though our ground forces were withdrawn by 1972 and our air and naval forces in 1973. The view was not always expressed in the colorful terms quoted earlier from Galbraith and Eugene McCarthy; but it was there.

From the perspective of the 1980s, I would only observe that the view that Southeast Asia doesn't much matter may have diminished somewhat with the emergence of ASEAN and the remarkable expansion in the economies of its members, including sophisticated trade and financial relations with the United States. They may not have yet achieved the respectability of Japan, in the eyes of Atlanticists, but they are clearly beyond the water-buffalo stage and on their way.

A fourth observation arises from the fixation in the quarter century after 1949 with China as the ultimate threat to Southeast Asia. I suspect, but cannot prove, that one element in the extraordinary performance of the American Congress toward Vietnam in the period 1973–1975 may have been the belief that, with Nixon's new opening to China, the strategic threat to Southeast Asia had been once and for all lifted and, therefore, the aid promised by Nixon to Thieu could be ruthlessly reduced. The possibility of the Soviet Union replacing China as a threat in the region, not difficult to deduce from Brezhnev's Collective Security Plan of 1969, appears not to have been envisaged by the Congress—and, perhaps, not by many in the executive branch.

So much for the complexities of interpreting the nature and extent of the nation's interest in the independence of the countries of Southeast Asia.

Now, what about the future?

From one perspective, the Soviet position in the region—and Brezhnev's 1969 plan as a whole—does not, at the moment, appear on the verge of success. The movements of Soviet naval and air forces around the region constitute a significant psychological pressure and political presence; but for the time being, one would not expect a decisive Soviet thrust to dominate the region like that of Japan in 1941 and 1942. The Soviet Union confronts a considerable array of problems which render this an apparently unpropitious time for great adventures: the costly stalemate in Afghanistan; India's taking its distance from Moscow on Afghanistan, despite the 1971 treaty; the state of Poland and all its multiple implications for the Soviet security structure; deep and degenerating problems within the Soviet economy. Similarly, the presence of the Vietnamese forces on the Thai frontier is a source of great anxiety, indeed, to all the non-Communist governments of the region and China; but Hanoi appears to have quite enough trouble in South Vietnam, in Kampuchea itself, and in trying to achieve an economic revival at home without plunging into a wider Southeast Asian war. Besides, it has been reminded forcefully that Chinese forces are on its northern frontier.

There are, no doubt, those who will say: Some but not all the dominoes have fallen; life goes on in most of Southeast Asia; what is there to worry about?

But two facts should be remembered. First, the Communists, unlike ourselves, are patient, persevering, and stubborn in pursuing their long-run strategies; and, second, there is no power capable of preventing the Soviet Union from dominating Southeast Asia—indeed, all of Asia—except the United States. Asia would promptly become a quite different place if the United States closed down Clark Field and Subic Bay, pulled the Pacific Fleet back to Hawaii, and announced that the guarantees to Thailand were no longer operative.

In short, despite the debacle of 1975, the possibility of an independent, neutral Southeast Asia—so important for so many, including the 300 million men, women, and children who live there—has not been lost. But it will not be held without a deep and steady understanding in the United States of the stakes involved—an understanding notably lacking in our nation in the intense domestic debate of the period 1965–1975 and in the subsequent literature on the subject.

As a coda to this analysis, I would only add that, beyond our time, in the next century, the peace of Asia is likely to depend on a solemn agreement between India and China that Southeast Asia should be supported by both in its desire for independence, thus creating a buffer which might avoid the two countries repeating in Asia the tragedy of France and Germany in Europe. But that is a subject for quite another paper.

Appendix C.

Vice President Johnson's Report to President Kennedy on His Trip to Asia, May 1961

[*Note:* Vice President Johnson's report to President Kennedy is to be found in Vice Presidential Security File, Box 1, "Vice President's Visit to Southeast Asia, May 9–24, 1961," folder no. 1, LBJ Library. Several paragraphs have not yet been declassified.]

MEMORANDUM

TO: The President
FROM: The Vice President
SUBJECT: Mission to Southeast Asia, India and Pakistan

The mission undertaken May 9, 1961, at your request, was informative and illuminating far beyond my expectations. Unusual candor—as well as unusual length—marked exchanges in each country. Each leader visited welcomed and sought to take full advantage of my presence as a means of transmitting to you their strongly held personal views on many matters.

The purpose of this memorandum is to convey such of my own impressions and evaluations as seem most pertinent to decisions now under your consideration. It would be unrealistic to assume that such limited visits afford a basis for detailed substantive policy judgments. It would be equally unrealistic not to recognize that the circumstances and timing of this mission elicited a depth and substance of expression not normally present in exchanges through usual channels. My purpose is to offer perspective—not, I wish to emphasize, to propose details of policy.

The Impact of Laos

There is no mistaking the deep—and long lasting—impact of recent developments in Laos.

Country to country, the degree differs but Laos has created doubt and concern about intentions of the United States throughout Southeast Asia. No amount of success at Geneva can, of itself, erase this. The independent Asians do not wish to have their own status resolved in like manner in Geneva.

The Impact of the Mission

Beyond question, your judgment about the timing of our mission was correct. [Passage deleted.] Chiang said—and all others privately concurred—that the mission had the effect of "stabilizing" the situation in the Southeast Asian nations.

What happened, I believe, was this: the leaders visited want—as long as they can—to remain as friends or allies of the United States. The public, or, more precisely, the political, reaction to Laos had drastically weakened the ability to maintain any strongly pro-US orientation. Neutralism in Thailand, collapse in Vietnam, anti-American election demagoguery in the Philippines were all developing prior to our visit. The show of strength and sincerity—partly because you had sent the Vice President and partly, to a greater extent than you may believe, because you had sent your sister—gave the friendly leaders something to "hang their hats on" for a while longer.

Our mission arrested the decline of confidence in the United States. It did not—in my judgment—restore any confidence already lost. The leaders were as explicit, as courteous and courtly as men could be in making it clear that deeds must follow words—soon.

We didn't buy any time—we were given it.

If these men I saw at your request were bankers, I would know—without bothering to ask—that there would be no further extensions on my note.

The Purpose of Joint Communiques

Starting with President Diem at Saigon, it was my conclusion that the interests of the United States would be served—and protected—by the issuance of joint communiques. My purpose was this: to attach the signature and the name of each of the leaders to a joint public statement embodying their acceptance of an agreement with the details of your letters which I delivered in your behalf. Without such statement in writing, it was clear that the United States would be victimized later by self-serving statements that you —and the Administration—had offered "nothing" or "too little," etc.

As you recognized, the joint communiques followed item by item the statements in your letters. In most instances, where substantive pledges and policies were involved, the communiques were cleared through Washington before issuance. The extensive, important and almost unprecedented communique with Nehru largely reflects the high regard the Indian Government holds for Ambassador Galbraith.

I should make these two points clear: assurances I gave were those you sent me to convey, and no commitments were asked and none were given beyond those authorized in your letters. In some instances, for various reasons, I did not express all the commitments or proposals authorized in the State position papers.

The Importance of Follow-Through
I cannot stress too strongly the extreme importance of following up this mission with other measures, other actions, and other efforts. At the moment—because of Laos—these nations are hypersensitive to the possibility of American hypocrisy toward Asia. Considering the Vienna talks with Khrushchev—which, to the Asian mind, emphasize Western rather than Asian concerns—and considering the negative line of various domestic American editorials about this mission, I strongly believe it is of first importance that this trip bear fruit immediately.

Personal Conclusions from the Mission
I took to Southeast Asia some basic convictions about the problems faced there. I have come away from the mission there—and to India and Pakistan—with many of those convictions sharpened and deepened by what I saw and learned. I have also reached certain other conclusions which I believe may be of value as guidance for those responsible in formulating policies.

These conclusions are as follows:

1. The battle against Communism must be joined in Southeast Asia with strength and determination to achieve success there—or the United States, inevitably, must surrender the Pacific and take up our defenses on our own shores. Asian Communism is compromised and contained by the maintenance of free nations on the subcontinent. Without this inhibitory influence, the island outposts—Philippines, Japan, Taiwan—have no security and the vast Pacific becomes a Red Sea.

2. The struggle is far from lost in Southeast Asia and it is by no means inevitable that it must be lost. In each country it is possible to build a sound structure capable of withstanding and turning the Communist surge. The will to resist—while now the target of subversive attack—is there. The key to what is done by Asians in defense of Southeast Asian freedom is confidence in the United States.

3. There is no alternative to United States leadership in Southeast Asia. Leadership in individual countries—or the regional leadership and cooperation so appealing to Asians—rests on the knowledge and faith in United States power, will and understanding.

4. [Paragraph deleted.]

We should consider an alliance of all the free nations of the Pacific and Asia who are willing to join forces in defense of their freedom. Such an organization should:

a) have a clear-cut command authority

b) also devote attention to measures and programs of social justice, housing, land reforms, etc.

5. Asian leaders—at this time—do not want American troops involved in Southeast Asia other than on training missions. American combat troop involvement is not only not required, it is not desirable. Possibly Americans fail to appreciate fully the subtlety that recently-colonial peoples would not look with favor upon governments which invited or accepted the return this soon of Western troops. To the extent that fear of ground troop involvement dominates our political responses to Asia in Congress or elsewhere, it seems most desirable to me to allay those paralyzing fears in confidence, on the strength of the individual statements made by leaders consulted on this trip. This does not minimize or disregard the probability that open attack would bring calls for U.S. combat troops. But the present probability of open attack seems scant, and we might

gain much needed flexibility in our policies if the spectre of combat troop commitment could be lessened domestically.

6. Any help—economic as well as military—we give less developed nations to secure and maintain their freedom must be a part of a mutual effort. These nations cannot be saved by United States help alone. To the extent the Southeast Asian nations are prepared to take the necessary measures to make our aid effective, we can be—and must be—unstinting in our assistance. It would be useful to enunciate more clearly than we have—for the guidance of these young and unsophisticated nations—what we expect or require of them.

7. In large measure, the greatest danger Southeast Asia offers to nations like the United States is not the momentary threat of Communism itself, rather the danger stems from hunger, ignorance, poverty and disease. We must—whatever strategies we evolve—keep these enemies the point of our attack, and make imaginative use of our scientific and technological capability in such enterprises.

8. Vietnam and Thailand are the immediate—and most important—trouble spots, critical to the U.S. These areas require the attention of our very best talents—under the very closest Washington direction—on matters economic, military and political.

The basic decision in Southeast Asia is here. We must decide whether to help these countries to the best of our ability or throw in the towel in the area and pull back our defenses to San Francisco and a "Fortress America" concept. More important, we would say to the world in this case that we don't live up to treaties and don't stand by our friends. This is not my concept. I recommend that we move forward promptly with a major effort to help these countries defend themselves. I consider the key here is to get our best MAAG people to control, plan, direct and exact results from our military aid program. In Vietnam and Thailand, we must move forward together.

a. In Vietnam, Diem is a complex figure beset by many problems. He has admirable qualities, but he is remote from the people, is surrounded by persons less admirable and capable than he. The country can be saved—if we move quickly and wisely. We must decide whether to support Diem—or let Vietnam fall. We must have coordination of purpose in our country team, diplomatic and military. The Saigon Embassy, USIS, MAAG and related operations leave much to be desired. They should be brought up to maximum efficiency. The most important thing is imaginative, creative, American management of our military aid program. The Vietnamese and our MAAG estimate that an additional $50 million of U.S. military and economic assistance will be needed if we decide to support Vietnam. This is the best information available to us at the present time and if it is confirmed by the best Washington military judgment it should be supported. Since you proposed and Diem agreed to a joint economic mission, it should be appointed and proceed forthwith.

b. In Thailand, the Thais and our own MAAG estimate probably as much is needed as in Vietnam—about an additional $50 million of military and economic assistance. Again, should our best military judgment concur, I believe we should support such a program. Sarit is more strongly and staunchly pro-Western than many of his people. He is and must be deeply concerned at the consequence to his country of a Communist-controlled Laos. If Sarit is to stand firm against neutralism, he must have—soon—concrete evidence to show his people of United States military and economic support. He believes that his armed forces should be increased to 150,000. His Defense Minister is coming to Washington to discuss aid matters.

9. The Republic of China on Taiwan was a pleasant surprise to me. I had been long aware of the criticism against Chiang Kai-shek and his government and cognizant of the deep emotional American feelings in some quarters against him. I know these feelings influence our US policy.

Whatever the cause, a progressive attitude is emerging there. Our conversations with Chiang and Mrs. Chiang were dominated by discussions of measures of social progress, to my unexpected but gratified surprise. As with the Republic of Germany in Western Europe, so I believe we might profitably and wisely encourage the Republic of China in Asia to export talents, skills, and resources to other Asian lands to assist in programs of progress.

10. I was assured that there were no problems for the U.S. in the Philippines. There is a great reservoir of good feeling toward America among Filipinos, with many of the usual Latin qualifications. But a widespread belief that corruption exists is sapping the effectiveness of the government. Remoteness of the leadership from the people seems a problem.

11. India could well be the subject of an entire report. Nehru,

during our visit, was clearly "neutral" in favor of the West. This Administration is highly regarded and well received in India. Only part of this flows out of hope or expectation of aid. Mainly, there is an intellectual affinity, or an affinity of spirit. This, in my judgment, should be exploited not with the hope of drawing India into our sphere—which might be as unnecessary as it would be improbable—but, chiefly, with the hope of cementing under Nehru an India-U.S. friendship which would endure beyond any transition of power in India.

12. President Ayub in Pakistan is the singularly most impressive and, in his way, responsible head of state encountered on the trip. He is seasoned as a leader where others are not; confident, straightforward and I would judge, dependable. He is frank about his belief, offensive as it is to us, that the forms of representative government would only open his country to Communist take-over at this time. Nonetheless, Ayub understands—and is in agreement with—the aims of eradicating poverty, ignorance and disease. We can have great influence and—because of his administrative organization—achieve dramatic success by supporting Pakistan's needs. Our military should see how to improve the effectiveness and achieve modernization of Pakistan's army. Ayub is wisely aware of Pakistan's strategic position, wants to make his forces more modern, and wants to resolve the Kashmir dispute to release Indian and Pakistani troops to deter the Chinese rather than each other. He spells out the fact that U.S. leadership rests on our own self-confidence and confidence we permit Asians to have in us.

To recapitulate, these are the main impressions I have brought back from my trip.

The fundamental decision required of the United States—and time is of the greatest importance—is whether we are to attempt to meet the challenge of Communist expansion now in Southeast Asia by a major effort in support of the forces of freedom in the area or throw in the towel. This decision must be made in a full realization of the very heavy and continuing costs involved in terms of money, of effort and of United States prestige. It must be made with the knowledge that at some point we may be faced with the further decision of whether we commit major United States forces to the area or cut our losses and withdraw should our efforts fail. We must remain master of this decision. What we do in Southeast Asia should be part of a rational program to meet the threat we face in the region as a whole. It should include a clear-cut pattern of specific contributions to be expected by each partner according to his ability and resources. I recommend we proceed with a clear-cut and strong program of action.

I believe that the mission—as you conceived it—was a success. I am grateful to the many who labored to make it so.

Lyndon B. Johnson

Appendix D.

Extracts from "Some Reflections on National Security Policy," Policy Planning Council, Department of State, April 1965

[*Note:* The extracts included below from this widely circulated paper of the Policy Planning Council focus on its distinctive theme: the case for regional organization in a world not yet ready for global solutions. It is to be found in the author's files to be transferred to the LBJ Library; but it is more readily accessible in the archives of the Department of State.]

SOME REFLECTIONS ON NATIONAL SECURITY POLICY
APRIL 1965

This paper was generated in the early months of 1965 as an attempt to take stock of our position on the world scene as it has unfolded since the Cuba missile crisis: a scene marked by some decline in the pressure being exerted from Moscow on the outside world; a heightening in various Communist efforts in subversion and guerrilla warfare; and a marked rise in assertive nationalism within both the Communist and non-Communist worlds.

The principal operational theme is the possible role of regionalism in the resolution of the triangular dilemma observable in many parts of the Free World; that is, the clash between simple nationalism, on the one hand, and, on the other, collective security and the requirements for collective action in the solution of welfare problems.

It goes without saying that this is an exercise of the Policy Planning Council and not an authoritative statement of United States policy.

W. W. Rostow

May 7, 1965

* * * * *

PART TWO

Regionalism and the Appropriate Degree and Character of U.S. Involvement on the World Scene

12. *Introduction.* The not unfamiliar array of tasks set out in paragraph 11 are dealt with in our government—and must largely continue to be dealt with—as more or less discrete categories of U.S. policy making. Under each heading it is possible to set out specific problems which are or ought to be systematically addressed in the months ahead. For example:

a. *Military Posture.* To maintain alertness to the possibility of a Soviet qualitative breakthrough in the nuclear arms race.

b. *Ability to Project U.S. Military Power.* To examine our overseas base structure and military technology with an eye to maintaining over the foreseeable future our ability to project our power, while economizing the burden it lays on our political relations with the rest of the world.

c. *Nuclear Proliferation.* To press on with systematic programs designed to head off the development of further national nuclear capabilities in Europe, Israel, India, and Japan, while working for international non-diffusion and non-acquisition agreements compatible with collective nuclear arrangements.

d. *Indirect Aggression.* To refine our doctrines and methods for preventing conditions from arising which lend themselves to Communist policies of political attraction or to insurrectional campaigns; for dealing with such aggression; for coping with the mounting of such aggression across international frontiers; and for maintaining effective access to vulnerable or potentially vulnerable regions.

e. *Regional Quarrels.* To gnaw away, as opportunity and our own tactful initiative may offer, at such critical and dangerous quarrels as those over Kashmir and Cyprus, as well as the Arab-Israeli dispute and the potentially lethal arms race it has triggered.

204

f. *Regional Aggression.* To develop our doctrine and refine our policies towards political leaders in the various regions who aim to dominate those regions and pursue disruptive policies to that end; e.g., Nkrumah, Ben Bella, Nasser, and Sukarno.

g. *Residual Colonialism.* To define and execute policies in Africa towards residual colonial areas which would damp the explosive playback effect of such problems on the rest of Africa.

h. *Cooperation with More Advanced Nations.* To carry forward policies with Western Europe and Japan (as well as Canada, Australia, and New Zealand) which would lead towards greater concert in the fields of nuclear, monetary, and trade policy as well as in matters of assistance and political policy towards the developing areas; German unity; Eastern Europe; East-West trade; arms control; etc.

13. This paper is not the occasion to set out detailed lines of action designed to grip such problems; although the national security planning community is, in one way or another, at work on all of them, as well as on other problems related to the tasks set out in para. 11. The purpose here is to raise a more general point. Setting concrete objectives of this type (and the broader categories in para. 10, from which they derive) against the world environment described in Part One of this paper raises the question of whether progress might not be accelerated by increased attention to the creation and strengthening of regional organizations in the Free World, within which the United States would participate over a range of issues flowing from the character of the region's dependence on the U.S. and the character of our major interests in the region. The question posed can be put simply as follows: Could regional arrangements form a path for dealing with the inherently sterile, currently dangerous, and potentially mortal national assertiveness now endemic in the Free World?

14. Specifically, the issue arises from a combination of three factors in the situation analyzed in Part One.

a. The evident desire of nations and peoples to play an enlarged role in shaping their own destiny, to reduce their dependence on the U.S., and to enhance their dignity in dealing with the U.S.

b. The inadequacy of nationalism and national states as instruments for the solution of key security, economic, and political problems.

    c. In varying degrees, the continuing reliance of the regions on U.S. power, resources, and, to a substantial extent, political leadership in the management of their security, economic, and political affairs.

Many of the smaller states in the region rely critically on our presence and leadership, not merely for protection against Communism but against the larger and more ambitious nations of their regions; e.g., Netherlands, Tunisia, Lebanon and Jordan, Korea. Moreover, even the larger states, in fact, require us for their underlying security. Nevertheless, the impulse to find ways to reconcile these conflicting considerations which enlarge the voice of local and regional authorities is quite general.

15. The concept of regionalism suggested here does not, then, aim to see emerge a group of regional organizations detached from the U.S. and the rest of the world, looking inward for the solution to their basic security, economic, and political problems. Over a narrow range it is true that certain problems can be solved wholly within a region—and are sometimes best so dealt with; for example, the Ethiopia-Somali and Algeria-Morocco disputes, and the creation of regional common markets and free trade areas (so long as they do not result in higher average levels of protection). But, in general, the military, economic, and political interdependencies of the modern world, as well as U.S. interests and responsibilities, require that the U.S. play an active role in such enterprises. The objective of regionalism in the present context is twofold:

    a. To permit nations to grip collectively problems that do not lend themselves to satisfactory solution on a national or bilateral basis.

    b. To permit nations to deal with the U.S. (and, where relevant, other industrialized powers of the Free World) on a basis of greater dignity than bilateralism permits.

16. The exercise of U.S. leadership in moving toward or strengthening effective regional organizations is inherently subtle and complex, conducted, as it must be, in an environment of increasingly assertive nationalism. Courses of conduct in each region, and on each issue, must evidently be determined on a case-by-case basis. And, indeed, in some regions the possibilities of effective organiza-

tion are not hopeful in the short run; i.e., Asia and the Middle East. We are concerned with maintaining and refining the institutions which exist; moving forward step by step, as opportunity may offer, where they do not exist; meanwhile using such devices as are open to us, bilateral and otherwise, to keep bilateral and regional problems within tolerable bounds. But these general observations may be in order:

a. We shall wish to work, insofar as possible, by encouraging the initiative and leadership of those within the regions who support the kind of collective and constructive enterprises and organization we judge likely to be effective and in our interest.

b. In many of the areas concerned, the balance between those who favor such enterprises and those who would pursue either pure nationalist solutions or exclusive regional arrangements contrary to U.S. interests, is likely to be fairly even. The object of U.S. policy must, therefore, be to strengthen the hand of leaders and groups which share our goals.

c. In pursuing this object, either dramatic U.S. pressure or U.S. passivity is apt to be counterproductive. We should define clearly the policies that we favor and be ready to play the role in negotiation and action that other leaders and governments committed to collective action wish to see us assume. Their judgment as to the U.S. role that is needed to achieve common goals will probably be a useful guide; they will not wish to be handicapped by either a U.S. presence or a U.S. passivity or withdrawal which seems excessive, in the light of the local situation.

17. The relation of these general observations on regionalism to the functional tasks set out in para. 11 is dramatized by examining briefly what is, on the whole, a rather satisfactory regional relationship; namely, that incorporated in the Inter-American System. The Rio Treaty permits us to link our nuclear and conventional military power to the defense of the region, thus constituting a persuasive deterrent. When that deterrent was directly challenged, and the whole Hemisphere fell under the shadow of nuclear blackmail, in the Cuba missile crisis, the underlying solidity of the Rio Treaty was demonstrated. Moreover, the security arrangements of Latin America with the U.S. have thus far kept the nuclear proliferation problem under control.

18. In the face of the Communist revolution in Cuba, the Rio

Treaty has been elaborated in a tolerably satisfactory way to embrace the problem of indirect aggression, permitting us access to assist in preventive measures and countermeasures. The Inter-American system has thus far kept regional quarrels within tolerable limits, providing an important and prompt damper on their escalation. We have thus far not had to face the problem of an over-ambitious Latin American country seeking regional hegemony; but we can assume that, once again, the Inter-American system is a tolerably effective check on such ambitions. Finally, the evolution of the Alliance for Progress and the enlarged role of the Latin Americans in it, symbolized by CIAP, represents an effective use of the attraction of economic development as a damper on the still potentially explosive nationalism, assertiveness, and resentment of dependence on the U.S. in Latin America. In evaluating the role of economic development as a damper in other regions, it is worth asking ourselves candidly what the state of Latin America would now be—and of our relations with it—if the Alliance for Progress did not exist.

19. Even then there is no cause for complacency in our relations with Latin America. It is passing through a revolutionary period which involves important and inevitable social and political disruption and presents to the Communists opportunities for intrusion and exploitation which they have not abandoned. The recent favorable political and economic trends are still tentative and fragile. The military are searching for a role of greater professional dignity and access to modern equipment, which may best be satisfied by an intensification of intra-Hemispheric collective ventures; e.g., a multilateral force for surveillance and ASW [anti-submarine warfare]. Moreover, there is a strong impulse in Latin America to emerge on the world scene in a role going beyond the Inter-American system. They are torn between a desire to play a role of leadership in the Afro-Asian world and a desire to emerge as serious partners in Atlantic affairs. We shall have to give continuing attention to the desire for greater dignity and stature among the Latin Americans and to help lead them into status as important partners in the Atlantic and in the maintenance of the unity of Western civilization, of which they are substantially a part. Nevertheless, the Latin American case illustrates rather dramatically, under uniquely favorable historical circumstances, how a network of regional organizations,

including a powerful concerted development effort, can permit us to cope with the functional problems posed in para. 11.

20. Something of the same can be said with respect to the more searching problems of the Atlantic community and NATO. . . .

21. With respect to Asia, no satisfactory single organizational framework exists equivalent to our elaborate Inter-American and Atlantic structures; and none is yet in sight. In a series of essentially bilateral moves, we have filled since the war the power vacuums in South Korea, Taiwan, Japan, and Indochina. Important elements of collective organization exist in SEATO, ANZUS, the Colombo Plan, and the India and Pakistan consortium arrangements. Nevertheless, we are in a position where Japan is groping to move out in a more responsible way on the Asian and world scene; there are impulses in the Philippines, Korea, Thailand, Malaya, and even Indonesia to find additional means for regional cooperation. But the possible shape of an Asian regional organization evidently awaits the outcome of the confrontation in Southeast Asia and an answer to the question of the relative power in Asia of China and the United States. Until the relevance of U.S. military power on the Asian mainland is firmly established, in the face of Communist techniques of insurrection and guerrilla warfare, the political character of Asia and its vision of long-run U.S. relations cannot be determined. In these circumstances, we must evidently move piecemeal where we can: to settle the Japanese-Korean dispute and to handle our relations with Korea in such a way as to strengthen their sense of independence and of their participation in a community which transcends the Japan-Korea relation; to encourage Japan to formulate and share with us a responsible vision of its interests and willingness to undertake commitments in Asia, beyond our narrow bilateral agenda; to cope as best we can with the surge of nationalism in Southeast Asia and elsewhere through *ad hoc* partnership arrangements in specific fields; and to work in the Indian subcontinent in ways which damp the Kashmir dispute, avoid an Indian national nuclear capability, and accelerate the critically important economic development of those vast but impoverished countries. Nevertheless, as we come to deal with and finally to settle the struggle in Viet Nam and Laos, we should begin to explore in our own minds the kinds of more substantial and extensive regional relations that might

be built up among the Asians themselves and in their relations to the U.S. The President's recent initiatives towards the regional development of Southeast Asia as well as the August discussions of the Asian Development Bank will force the pace at which we make policy in this field.

22. In the Middle East the possibilities of a systematic regional organization with a mutually acceptable relationship to the U.S. are corrupted by: the Arab-Israeli dispute; intra-regional conflicts among the Arab and Muslim nations; and by the deep commitment of Nasser to seek regional hegemony. Over the foreseeable future our objective must continue, as it has been in the past, to keep all three of these conflicts within bounds, while minimizing the power of communism within the region as a whole. If there is a conceivable regional linkage that might be generated and supported by the U.S., with the acquiescence of Nasser, it lies in the area of economic development. President Eisenhower's 1958 offer to back an Arab grouping for economic purposes, made in the context of the Lebanon-Jordan crisis, was not accepted; but some version of this offer might well be held steadily before Nasser and the Arabs, while we attempt to persuade them of the irrationality of the Arab-Israeli arms race and while regional resistances, marginally and quietly assisted by ourselves and our friends, persuade Nasser of the limits of his effective capacity to achieve hegemony in the region.

23. In Africa, as in the Middle East, it is difficult to see, in the near term, the emergence of a clear-cut and stable regional structure with which we might be systematically associated. The weakness of new and inexperienced governments is compounded by three underlying factors: the inevitably slow pace of economic development; the exacerbation of domestic politics and political emotion by the residual colonial and racial issues in Africa; and the purposeful exploitation of these facts by the Chinese Communists and the Soviet Union. Nevertheless, the OAU exists. It has served well in the Somali-Ethiopia and Algeria-Morocco disputes. If it can be kept out of the hands of extremists, it might serve an important role in bringing the Congo problem under control. And it is not impossible, with the passage of time, that the African nations will learn (as have the nations of Latin America) to accept the principle of nonintervention in each other's affairs, and develop tolerance of each other's political vagaries, while working to avoid the intervention in

Africa of outside powers. In the meanwhile, on the basis of the Economic Commission for Africa and the proposed African development bank, we might generate in this area a more systematic relation with the African governments and peoples within Western Europe and the United States in the field of development. There should be ways in which a focusing of their efforts and a heightening of our relations with them in the field of development could substantially damp—certainly not eliminate—the inherent explosive elements on the African scene: notably the colonial and racial anxieties and the frustration inherent in economic development at its present stage and level of external assistance.

The Character of U.S. Involvement on the World Scene

24. The argument here is that, broadly speaking, we face in other regions of the world, each in a context that is unique, the same kind of problem that we have already confronted and in which we have done much pioneer work in the past generation with respect to the Atlantic world and Latin America. It is further assumed that there is no region in the world to whose evolution we can be indifferent, given the character of our national interest, although our regional interests vary and are of different weight.

25. Before concluding our observations on regionalism, it is worth posing a prior question; namely, whether or not the United States is now, in some meaningful sense, overextended on the world scene.

Do our military and economic commitments on the mainland of Eurasia, as well as in Africa and Latin America, constitute an increasing or intolerable strain on our resources?

Is the potential strength of our adversaries increasing relative to our own at a rate which justifies considering a retraction of U.S. commitment?

Is there some other sense in which we are over-committed?

So far as U.S. resources are concerned, [Table D.1] makes clear that both over-all defense expenditures and foreign aid expenditures are a declining proportion of our annual output. Defense expenditures for FY 1965 are down to 7.5 percent of GNP, having fallen away from 9.5 percent a decade earlier; economic and military aid expenditures (excluding PL 480 and Export-Import Bank loans) are down to .48 percent of GNP from a figure of 1.1 percent

TABLE D-1. U.S. Defense Expenditure and Foreign Aid As Related to the U.S. Gross National Product and National Income at Factor Cost, 1946–1966

Fiscal Year	GNP ($ Bill.)	NY ($ Bill.)	Defense[a] ($ Mill.)	Defense % of GNP	Defense % of NY	Foreign Aid — Includes PL 480 & Eximbank Loans				Foreign Aid — Excludes PL 480 & Eximbank Loans				Fiscal Year
						Total ($ Mill.)	% of GNP	% of NY	Economic-Military ($ millions)	Total ($ Mill.)	% of GNP	Total ($ Mill.)	% of GNP	
1946	202.8	181.1	43,200	21.3	23.8	4,982	2.5	2.8	0					1946
1947	223.3	191.2	14,200	6.4	7.4	6,953	3.1	3.6	166					1947
1948	246.6	210.5	11,200	4.5	5.3	3,194	1.3	1.5	315					1948
1949	261.6	223.7	12,000	4.6	5.3	8,460	3.2	3.8	301	4,533	1.73	4,533	1.73	1949
1950	263.8	222.1	11,892	4.5	5.4	5,206	2.0	2.2	76	3,666	1.39	3,536	1.34	1950
1951	310.8	265.2	19,765	6.4	7.5	4,718	1.5	1.8	983	3,901	1.26	2,910	0.94	1951
1952	338.8	285.8	38,898	11.5	13.6	3,996	1.2	1.4	1,481	4,398	1.30	1,956	0.58	1952
1953	359.7	302.0	43,604	12.1	14.4	6,992	1.9	2.3	4,272	5,656	1.57	1,702	0.47	1953
1954	362.0	302.0	40,326	11.1	13.3	5,862	1.6	1.9	3,412	4,882	1.35	1,253	0.35	1954
1955	377.0	313.2	35,531	9.4	11.4	5,243	1.4	1.7	2,509	4,220	1.12	1,928	0.51	1955
1956	408.5	341.2	35,792	8.8	10.5	5,625	1.4	1.6	2,979	4,438	1.09	1,827	0.45	1956
1957	433.0	360.7	38,436	8.9	10.6	5,432	1.3	1.5	2,134	3,950	0.91	1,598	0.37	1957
1958	440.2	363.6	39,071	8.9	10.7	5,360	1.2	1.5	2,404	3,611	0.82	1,424	0.32	1958
1959	466.5	387.3	41,223	8.8	10.7	5,695	1.2	1.5	2,160	3,864	0.83	1,524	0.33	1959
1960	494.6	408.6	41,215	8.3	10.1	5,219	1.1	1.3	1,845	3,222	0.65	1,613	0.33	1960
1961	504.9	416.0	43,227	8.6	10.4	5,850	1.2	1.4	1,462	3,254	0.64	1,805	0.36	1961
1962	539.2	443.4	46,815	8.7	10.6	6,603	1.2	1.5	1,526	3,216[b]	0.60	1,826[b]	0.34	1962
1963	568.0	465.9	48,252	8.5	10.4	6,980	1.2	1.5	1,834	3,715[b]	0.65	1,994[b]	0.35	1963
1964	603.4	494.4	49,760	8.3	10.1	6,399	1.1	1.3	1,455	3,482[b]	0.58	1,997[b]	0.33	1964
1965	640[E]	525[E]	48,100[E]	7.5[E]	9.2	N.A.			N.A.	3,250[b]	0.51	2,050[b]	0.32	1965
1966										3,200[b]	0.48	2,100[b]	0.32	1966

[a] DOD expenditures; excludes atomic energy and defense-related activities (e.g. stockpiling).

[b] Excludes Social Progress Trust Fund expenditures.

E Estimate.

N.A. Not available.

in 1955. Economic assistance, at about the same absolute level as 1955 ($2 billion) has fallen from .51 percent of GNP to .32 percent of GNP. So long as the U.S. economy continues to expand at a reasonable rate there can be no serious anxiety about our capacity to sustain present military and foreign aid commitments or to expand them substantially, if necessary, without endangering the progress of our domestic life.

There is, of course, a continuing problem of assuring that outlays abroad in support of our security commitments do not endanger our balance of payments or the confidence felt in the dollar as a reserve currency. This real problem lends itself to resolution by many devices other than a retraction of defense outlays or foreign aid expenditures, notably because these expenditures are already substantially cushioned in their impact on the balance of payments and because national security should continue to enjoy a priority higher than, for example, long-term private investment in Western Europe or certain other private outlays abroad.

We could also be judged to be overextended if our potential adversaries were increasing their industrial capacity or military outlays at a rate which, if matched by us, could impose intolerable strains on our domestic life. This is, evidently, not the case. While there is no cause for complacency, with respect to the evolution of either Soviet or Chinese Communist military capabilities, they do not appear to be evolving in ways or at a pace beyond our capacity to deter within the range of recent or existing percentage allocations of our over-all resources. We are most likely to be embarrassed by qualitative, rather than quantitative, changes in the military capabilities of our major adversaries.

What, then, accounts for recent discussions of "overcommitment"?

First, the rise of national assertiveness, in forms as various as Gaullism, the burning of libraries, and Buddhist antics in Saigon, has converged with the sense of release from Soviet nuclear blackmail after the Cuba missile crisis, to make the world appear both less tractable and less dangerous than it was in, say, the period 1961–62. There is a widespread, if ill-defined, feeling that if foreigners don't like us, let's pull back, and that some pull-back would be safe.

Moreover, our painful and frustrating experience in Laos and Viet Nam makes men search for solutions and perspectives which would permit our withdrawal while believing that no grave damage would be done to vital U.S. or Free World interests.

What passes for "over-commitment" is, in this sense, simply frustration in achieving our objectives by existing means in the turbulent and assertive environment we confront, compounded by Communist methods for expanding indirectly their power and influence in that environment, combined with a correct perception that other nations are seeking ways to solve their problems which involve less brute dependence on the United States than in the past.

There is a second sense in which we are very heavily committed, if not over-committed, as compared to earlier times. Every region on the planet is now part of a sensitively interacting world community. In the immediate postwar years, major decisions could focus on the Atlantic world, Japan, and relations with Moscow. Now not only have the countries of Latin America, Africa, the Middle East and Asia entered the game but Communist China and the individual countries of Eastern Europe appear on the stage with independent or quasi-independent personalities. This proliferation of states and emerging centers of power and influence diminishes our capacity to influence or control given situations by means we have used in the past; and requires new methods and involvement of new kinds if we are to bring our residual margin of influence to bear on issues of vital interest. The number of U.S. relationships and problems capable of forcing a decision at the highest levels of the government has thus vastly multiplied. The working levels of government can be—and have been—expanded to deal with this phenomenon, at home and in the field. But we can have only one President and one Secretary of State. And here the real burden of commitment and active engagement has been enlarged.

Conclusion

26. The burden of this paper is, then, that what we confront is not a question of continuing existing policies and commitments or pulling back. What we face is the task of transforming our relations with the nations of the Free World, region by region, in such a way as to permit them an enlarged role in their own destiny while permitting us to perform the minimum security, economic, and political functions required in their interests and in ours. This concept does involve a kind of selective relaxation of presence and pressure, as we

encourage the nations themselves increasingly to take responsibility for assessing their interests and formulating responsible proposals for collective action. It does not, however, permit a significant withdrawal of U.S. security commitment and presence. And, as our experience with the OECD as opposed to the OEEC suggests, as well as our experience with CIAP, partnership in regional organizations (as opposed to dependence) tends to increase rather than to diminish the range and intimacy of contacts and common enterprise.

If all goes well, then, the present phase of rather anarchic nationalism abroad, with its counterpart in neo-isolationist impulses at home, should give way to relations of enlarging partnership in one region after the other.

That, in any case, is what the state of our environment and the character of our abiding interests appear to require. But it will not happen without a clear U.S. sense of direction, quiet leadership, and persistence. . . .

This paper began with a reference to the United Nations Charter, and it should close with an effort to relate briefly its emphasis on regionalism to the United Nations structure.

The United Nations is not a single institution, but a congeries of institutions and operations, fulfilling different functions at different levels. Nevertheless, it is clear that a strengthened United Nations must be brought about if the goal of a peaceful world community is to be attained.

It does not follow, however, that the most effective impact of the United Nations will always be on a global or universal level.

In peacekeeping, economic, and social tasks the United Nations and its varous agencies already play an important role in the regions. On the other hand, modern technology requires that we deal with some of our common tasks on a global basis; for example, the exchange of information about weather and the allocation of radio frequencies. But a healthy world community requires—and the United Nations would be strengthened by and it can contribute to—the emergence of sturdy regional enterprises which permit proud nations to cooperate with one another and with those outside in those numerous tasks which no nation in the modern world can handle on its own.

A viable world community, if and when it emerges, will evidently be a complex federal structure, marked by networks of global, functional and regional institutions, interlaced by continuing bilateral diplomacy. The argument here is, simply, that a strengthening of regionalism, at the present phase—a regionalism in which the United Nations could play a substantial role—might help resolve certain critical problems in ways which would re-enforce movement towards the larger, long-run goal.

Appendix E.

A Foreign Policy for the Johnson Administration (Memorandum by the Author, of March 29, 1965)

[*Note:* This memorandum, from the author's files to be deposited in the LBJ Library, was the culmination of various exchanges within the State Department and between the State Department and the White House.]

March 29, 1965

TO: The Secretary
THROUGH: S/S
FROM: S/P—W. W. Rostow
SUBJECT: A Foreign Policy for the Johnson Administration

The Central Theme. The position in which we now stand in the world justifies and requires a foreign policy which, while continuous with the main lines of our postwar action on the world scene, should have distinctive features which the President may wish to clarify and dramatize. This memorandum seeks to describe those distinctive features, concluding with a draft statement of a Johnson Doctrine. To anticipate a major conclusion, what emerges is this: It is our interest in each of the regions of the Free World to assist in the development of local arrangements which, while reducing their direct dependence on the United States, would leave the regions open to cooperative military, economic, and political arrangements with the U.S. This requires of us a systematic policy designed to strengthen the hand of the moderates in the regions and to reduce the power of extremists—whether those extremists are Communists or ambitious nationalists anxious to take over and dominate their regions. We are for those who, while defending legitimate national and regional interests, respect the extraordinarily intimate interdependence of the modern world and pursue policies of development and peace rather than aggrandizement.

This is the appropriate central theme of U.S. policy, transcending the distinction between developed and underdeveloped areas. It transcends to some extent, even, the distinction between the Communist and non-Communist worlds.

This central theme—the strengthening and support of moderates—has the virtue of making the President's stance at home and abroad fundamentally identical; and it conforms closely to the way we make foreign policy from day to day.

The Situation. Since the Cuba missile crisis these are the principal characteristics of the environment we have confronted:

1. With the failure of Khrushchev's campaign of nuclear blackmail (1958–1962), the Soviet Union appears less formidable in Europe and elsewhere; and it is on the defensive in many directions: with respect to the German question; in Eastern Europe; in the Communist movement generally; and in its domestic economy.

2. The deeply rooted Sino-Soviet split and the tendency towards fragmentation in the world Communist movement has worsened.

3. Frustrated in the conduct of nuclear blackmail, Communists are pursuing guerrilla warfare, subversion, programs of aid and trade and ideological attraction with a greater intensity: in Asia, the Middle East, Africa, and Latin America. The viability of these methods for indirect aggression is under critical test in Southeast Asia.

4. In the Free World, the deeply rooted tendency of nations and regions to diminish their dependence on the United States and to assert a larger role for themselves on the world scene has accelerated, partly because the decline of the threat from Moscow permits them to feel safer.

5. In each of the regions men have emerged who are pressing hard to expand their power in their respective regions, at the expense of the power and influence of the United States, using for this purpose expanded ties to the Communist world. They pursue these policies even though they are, ultimately, dependent on the United States for the protection of their independence and, in some cases,

for basic economic support. In Asia there is Sukarno; in the Middle East, Nasser; in the Magreb, Ben Bella; in West Africa, Nkrumah; in Latin America a successful Goulart would have played this role, but the mood is latent in other places—for example, in the recent statement of the Foreign Minister of Chile. De Gaulle evidently belongs on this list.

A U.S. Strategy. The United States continues to have limited but real vital interests in all of the regions of the world; namely, that they not be taken over by hostile or potentially hostile powers and that their weakness and fragmentation not tempt Communists to attempt such take over; that they not generate inter-regional conflict; that they not generate nuclear proliferation; that they remain open to a substantial degree to normal economic relations with the U.S.; that they evolve, in time, in the direction of regular economic progress and democratic political stability.

We also have an interest that the presently Communist regimes gradually evolve towards behavior as normal nation states and join in making the world environment less dangerous—including measures of effectively inspected arms control and a strengthening of the machinery of the United Nations.

The protection and advancement of these interests in the Free World requires an active U.S. military, economic, and political role on a world basis. U.S. military strength, economic resources, and political presence are still required, given local military weakness, economic problems, and political instability. But the assertiveness of Free World governments and peoples—and their desire to take a larger hand in their fate—requires that we try to operate increasingly through regional arrangements which are based on these four principles:

—The governments and peoples of the region, in cooperation with international organizations, should assume an enlarged role for their own economic, political, and security affairs.

—Given the limitations of national states in dealing with contemporary problems, such an enlarged regional role requires intensified regional cooperation.

—Given the continued potential dangers of direct Communist aggression, and the present danger of indirect Communist aggression, it is the U.S. interest, and the regional interests, to provide the cooperative security relations with the United States and, where relevant, with other external powers (notably in Asia, parts of the Middle East, and Africa).

—Regional arrangements should be democratic in character, avoiding the domination of any one state or group of states over others.

With respect to the Communist world, our policy must be to continue to contain all forms of Communist aggression, while moving as fast as changes in Communist regimes permit, to draw them towards normal pacific relations with the Free World. The possibilities here depend greatly on our success in rendering Communist indirect aggression, in Southeast Asia and elsewhere, as unattractive as we succeeded in the past in sterilizing direct conventional aggression (Korea), and nuclear blackmail (Berlin and Cuba missile crises).

Lines of Action. Lines of action to implement this strategy are already under way; but a clarification and enunciation of doctrine by the President could give them greater force and effectiveness.

Evidently, their pursuit in each region faces unique problems requiring unique solutions.

In two regions (Europe and Latin America) treaty organizations exist linking the U.S. to their defense. In Latin America (excepting Cuba) economic organizations exist or are evolving with which we can work.

In Europe, the problem of strengthening the hand of the moderates, as against a leadership which would attenuate the European tie to the U.S., is focused around the struggle with de Gaulle and Gaullism. In Latin America the problem of the orientation of regional unity is also real enough; but it is focused not around a national leader but what might be called Prebischism; that is, the notion that an integrated Latin America should play an "independent" role on the world scene, oriented in particular towards the Afro-Asian world.

In Africa, regional organizations are only now emerging. Because there is no frontier with the Communist world and no prior history of security association, like the Rio Treaty, the security links to Africa from outside tend to be bilateral. Moreover, of course, African unity is complicated by the "white redoubt" problems, on the one hand, and, on the other hand, by continuing historical ties between African states and European metropolitan nations. Nevertheless, the impulse towards regional unity, political and economic, is reflected in the OAU, the Economic Commission for Africa, and the African Development Bank. Moreover, the essence of African politics is, once again, a struggle between moderates and radical nationalists who hope to expand their influence in the regions for personal or national aggrandizement; that is, Ben Bella, Nkrumah, and Nasser.

In the Middle East, the only regional organization, aside from CENTO, is the Arab League. Its objective has been primarily to put pressure on Israel, a common interest which Nasser has tried to exploit for his own regional expansion. There, too, our problem has been to try to persuade Nasser to a more moderate course while strengthening the hand of the moderates in the Arab world; that is, Lebanon, Jordan, Tunisia, etc.

In Asia, security relations with the U.S. have been, essentially, bilateral as we sought to fill the vacuums created by the Second World War and its aftermath in Korea, Japan, Formosa, Indochina, India, and Pakistan. Regional economic organizations exist but have been weak; that is, the Colombo Plan and ECAFE. A new impulse toward economic regionalism centers around the Asian Development Bank. The Mekong development scheme is largely in abeyance due to the Laos—Viet Nam crisis. Nevertheless, there are potentialities for developing Asian regionalism in the face of the spreading desire of the Asians to take a larger hand in their fate and in the face of the common threat to Free Asia, represented by the Communist China nuclear capability. At the moment, Sukarno represents the major center of a disruptive anti-U.S. regional expansion policy; but there are elements in Pakistan policy, symbolized by Bhutto, which fall into the same pattern.

A Johnson Doctrine. In the light of this situation, what would a Johnson Doctrine look like? Here is a possible passage for a speech by the President.

> The world is entering a new phase which calls for new perspectives and new policies.
>
> The crises of 1961—62 made it clear that it was unprofitable for any country to seek to expand its power by applying nuclear pressure against others. In some ways the world is safer now than it has been at any time since the Second World War.

On the other hand, there are still Communists who believe that they may expand their power by the mounting of aggression across international frontiers, employing the illegal transit of arms and men. Our first duty is to make it clear that these efforts cannot succeed.

We cannot build a peaceful world unless nations and peoples respect international frontiers, honor international agreements, and leave their neighbors alone.

But there are other forces moving in this world of ours. On every continent men and women, having gathered confidence and strength in this first postwar generation, seek to take a larger hand in their own destiny.

They recognize that this is a highly interdependent world.

They recognize that we all need each other.

But they want to be less dependent on the United States and on other external powers.

We recognize, we understand, and we support this sentiment.

The objective of the United States since 1945 has not been to build an American empire. We dismantled our armed forces in 1945. We sought to base our policy on the United Nations. We put forward in good faith the Baruch Plan for the international control of atomic energy. We emerged—in 1947—I repeat, not to build an American empire, but to help peoples and nations maintain their independence so that they could play a constructive and dignified role in building, together with us and with others, a peaceful and prosperous world community.

This was why we supported, and we still support, a policy of European unity.

This was why we have supported, and shall continue to support, movement towards Latin American economic unity. This is why we support the Inter-American Committee on the Alliance for Progress, in which Latin Americans have assumed a major responsibility for leadership in the Alliance.

In other areas as well—in Africa, Asia, and the Middle East—we are the friends of those who wish to organize their affairs together; who wish to settle their own problems to the extent that they can; who wish to take the leadership in developing their own economies, in their own ways.

In matters of security, of course, none of us can be wholly independent. We are prepared to continue and to strengthen the instruments of collective security where nations and people feel threatened by any aggression, direct or indirect, and wish us to join in its deterrence.

In economic affairs we are, even more universally, interdependent. The United States is prepared, as it has demonstrated in Europe and Latin America, to work systematically with other regional groupings to help advance serious efforts of economic and social progress and for the expansion of trade.

We are the friends of all those who, while defending their legitimate national and regional interests, respect the intimate interdependence of all of us who live on this small planet.

We look to the development of partnerships which reach not only across the Atlantic but which would relate us to the governments and peoples of Latin America, Africa, the Middle East, and Asia in the great common task for advanced and developing nations alike—the task of building an orderly, peaceful and progressive world community.

A strengthened United Nations must, of course, be a central and vital instrument of that world community. In peacekeeping, economic, and social tasks the United Nations and its various agencies already play an important role in the regions. Moreover, modern technology requires that we deal with some of our common tasks on a global basis; for example, the exchange of information about weather and the allocation of radio frequencies. But a healthy world community requires—and the United Nations would be strengthened by—the emergence of sturdy regional enterprises which permit proud nations to cooperate with one another and with those outside in those numerous tasks which no nation in the modern world can handle on its own.

It is in this federalist spirit that we are prepared to play our part in constructing a new world order.

Appendix F.

Two Basic Documents Bearing on South Asian Regionalism

[*Note:* Following are two basic documents bearing on South Asian regionalism: the Foreign Ministers' Joint Communique and Final Declaration of August 2, 1983. The Conference Cell, Ministry of External Affairs, New Delhi, reproduced these documents at the conclusion of the conference. They also made available eighty-nine pages of previous basic SARC documents.]

SOUTH ASIAN REGIONAL COOPERATION
MEETINGS OF FOREIGN MINISTERS
New Delhi, August 1983

JOINT COMMUNIQUE

In pursuance of the recommendations of the Fourth Meeting of Foreign Secretaries held in Dhaka in March 1983, a Meeting of Foreign Ministers of Bangladesh, Bhutan, India, Maldives, Nepal, Pakistan and Sri Lanka was held in New Delhi on August 1–2 1983 preceded by a Preparatory Meeting of Foreign Secretaries of these countries at the invitation of the Government of India.

2. The Meeting of Foreign Ministers was inaugurated by Smt. Indira Gandhi, Prime Minister of India. In her inaugural address she described the Meeting of Foreign Ministers as an important step at a political level in the development of mutual relations in South Asia. She expressed the hope that cooperation among the seven countries would increase their capacity to withstand pressures, enable them to move ahead to a future of freedom, peace and prosperity

and give a strong impetus to closer friendship and greater stability in the region.

3. On behalf of the Foreign Ministers, His Excellency Mr. A. R. Shams-ud-Doha, thanked Smt. Indira Gandhi for her inspiring address. It was decided that the text of the address should form part of the final records of the Meeting.

4. Shri P. V. Narasimha Rao, Minister of External Affairs of India, was elected as Chairman by acclamation.

5. The Meeting expressed its appreciation for the valuable contributions made by the Meetings of Foreign Secretaries held in Colombo (April 21–23 1981), Kathmandu (November 2–4 1981), Islamabad (August 7–9 1982), Dhaka (March 28–30 1983) and New Delhi (July 28–29 1983).

6. At the conclusion of their Meeting, the Foreign Ministers signed the Declaration on South Asian Regional Cooperation setting out the objectives and principles of such cooperation and incorporating provisions regarding institutional and financial arrangements. They expressed their confidence that the adoption of this Declaration would promote the welfare of the peoples of South Asia, improve their quality of life and strengthen collective self-reliance among the countries of the region.

7. The Foreign Ministers Meeting noted that considerable work had been done at the technical level to identify possible areas of cooperation and prepare specific programmes in agreed areas. It also noted that the Committee of the Whole at its meeting held at Colombo and the Foreign Secretaries in their meetings held at Dhaka and New Delhi had drawn up an Integrated Programme of Acts based on the work done at the technical level. The Meeting considered the recommendations of the Foreign Secretaries and decided to launch the Integrated Programme of Action for South Asian Regional Co-operation, as recommended by them in the areas of Agriculture, Rural Development, Meteorology, Telecommunication, Scientific & Technological Co-operation, Health & Population Activities, Transport, Postal Services and Sports, Arts & Culture. The Meeting reaffirmed that it would be beneficial to continue cooperation among the National Planning Organizations and academic institutions of countries of the region.

8. The Foreign Ministers agreed to meet once a year to review the progress of South Asian Regional Co-operation. They also de-

cided to recommend to their respective Heads of States/Government that they meet at their level and agreed that the date of the Summit would be finalised at the next Meeting of Foreign Ministers.

9. The visiting Foreign Ministers expressed their deep appreciation to the Government of the Republic of India for the excellent arrangements made for the meeting and the cordial and generous hospitality extended to their delegations.

SARC FINAL DECLARATION

The Foreign Ministers of Bangladesh, Bhutan, India, Maldives, Nepal, Pakistan and Sri Lanka

Conscious of the common problems and aspirations of the peoples of South Asia and the need to accelerate their economic and social development through regional co-operation;

Convinced that regional co-operation in South Asia is beneficial, desirable and necessary and that it will help promote the welfare and improve the quality of life of the peoples of the region;

Convinced further that increased co-operation, contacts and exchange among the countries of the region will contribute to the promotion of friendship, amity and understanding among their peoples;

Recognising that each country of the region has an effective contribution to make to the promotion of collective self-reliance;

Noting that regional co-operation should be based on and in turn contribute to mutual trust, understanding and sympathetic appreciation of the national aspirations of the countries of the region;

Mindful of the Declaration on Collective Self-reliance among Non-Aligned and other developing countries adopted at the Seventh Non-Aligned Summit held at New Delhi which called upon all countries concerned to mobilise all necessary resources and deploy the requisite means in support of sub-regional, regional and inter-regional co-operation among Non-Aligned and other developing countries;

Affirming the determination of their respective governments to make joint efforts for promoting such co-operation;

Do hereby declare the collective resolve of their governments to pursue actively South Asian Regional Co-operation with the following objectives, principles, institutional and financial arrangements and to launch an Integrated Programme of Action;

And to this end have agreed as follows:

I. *OBJECTIVES AND PRINCIPLES*

A. *Objectives*

1. The objectives of South Asian Regional Co-operation shall be:

a) to promote the welfare of the peoples of South Asia and to improve their quality of life;

b) to accelerate economic growth, social progress and cultural development in the region and to provide all individuals the opportunity to live in dignity and to realise their full potential;

c) to promote and strengthen collective self-reliance among the countries of South Asia;

d) to contribute to mutual trust, understanding and appreciation of one another's problems;

e) to promote active collaboration and mutual assistance in the economic, social, cultural, technical and scientific fields;

f) to strengthen co-operation with other developing countries;

g) to strengthen co-operation among themselves in international forums on matters of common interest; and

h) to co-operate with international and regional organisations with similar aims and purposes.

B. *Principles*

2. Such co-operation shall be based on respect for the principles of sovereign equality, territorial integrity, political independence, non-interference in internal affairs of other states and mutual benefit.

3. Such co-operation shall not be a substitute for bilateral and multilateral co-operation but shall complement them.

4. Such co-operation shall not be inconsistent with bilateral and multilateral obligations.

II. *INSTITUTIONAL ARRANGEMENTS*

A. *Technical Committees*

5. A Technical Committee, open to participation of all countries of the region, shall be responsible for the implementation, coordination and monitoring of the programme in each area of co-operation, with the following terms of reference:

a) determination of the potential and the scope of regional cooperation in agreed areas;

b) formulation of programmes of action and preparation of projects;

c) determination of financial implications of the sectoral Programme of Action;

d) formulation of recommendations regarding the appointment of costs;

e) implementation and co-ordination of sectoral Programmes of Action; and

f) monitoring of progress of implementation.

6. The Technical Committees shall submit periodic reports to the Standing Committee.

7. The Chairmanship of the Technical Committees shall rotate among the countries of the region in alphabetical order, every two years.

8. The Technical Committees may, inter-alia, use the following mechanisms and modalities, if and when considered necessary;

a) Meetings of Heads of National Technical agencies;

b) Meetings of experts in specific fields;

c) Contacts amongst recognised centres of excellence in the region. These centres may be reinforced and extended as considered feasible and desirable for the optimal use of the resources of the region for meeting the requirements of the co-operation programme.

B. *Action Committees*

9. In the case of projects involving more than two countries but not all the countries of the region, Action Committees comprising the countries concerned may be set up for their implementation, with the prior approval of the Standing Committee.

C. *Standing Committee*

10. A Standing Committee shall be established at the level of Foreign Secretaries for the co-ordination and monitoring of South Asian Regional Co-operation with the following terms of reference:

a) approval of projects and programmes, and the modalities of their financing;

b) determination of inter-sectoral priorities and overall co-ordination of Programmes of Action;

c) mobilisation of regional and external resources; and

d) identification of new areas of co-operation based on appropriate studies.

11. The Standing Committee shall meet as often as is deemed necessary but at least once a year.

12. The Standing Committee shall make a reference, as and when necessary, to the Foreign Ministers for decisions on policy guidelines, both in respect of the approval of projects/programmes as well as the authorisation of modalities for financing. The Standing Committee shall provide necessary support services for meetings of Ministers.

D. *General Provisions*

13. Decisions at all levels shall be taken on the basis of unanimity.

14. Bilateral and contentious issues shall be excluded from the deliberations.

III. *FINANCIAL ARRANGEMENTS*

15. The participation of each country in the financial costs of the Programmes of Co-operation shall be voluntary.

16. Each Technical Committee shall make recommendations for the apportionment of the costs for implementing the programmes proposed by it, taking into account inter-alia the following guidelines:

a) Except to the extent otherwise agreed, the cost of travel and subsistence for participants in seminars, workshops and training and other programmes shall be met by their respective governments and the cost of organising seminars, workshops and training and other programmes may be met by the host country or apportioned among participants in proportion to the facilities availed of or financed from external sources;

b) Except to the extent otherwise agreed, the cost of subsistence for experts shall be met by the receiving countries and the cost of travel and/or salary of the experts may be paid for by the sending countries, or shared among participating countries or financed from external sources;

c) Other costs, including the costs of preparation of studies, shall be shared on a mutually agreed basis; and

d) In the case of long term projects, the Technical Committee concerned shall estimate the costs involved and shall submit recommendations to the Standing Committee on the modalities for meeting the costs.

17. In the case of projects and programmes for which sufficient

financial resources cannot be mobilised within the region, recourse may be had to external assistance from appropriate sources, with the approval of the Standing Committee.

Done in New Delhi on the Second Day of August in the year Nineteen Hundred and Eighty-three.

Notes

1. The process by which Johnson arrived at his decision to dispatch U.S. forces to Vietnam has been widely reviewed and analyzed. The story as seen by Johnson is presented in detail in his *The Vantage Point* (New York: Holt, Rinehart and Winston, 1971), pp. 112–153. An even more detailed historian's account is Larry Berman's *Planning a Tragedy: The Americanization of the War in Vietnam* (New York: W. W. Norton, 1982). Although Berman's analysis of the background to Johnson's decision announced on July 28, 1965, is incomplete and his interpretation of it and subsequent events debatable, his book contains a great deal of documentary material on the process by which the July 1965 decision was reached.
2. Howard Beale, *This Inch of Time* (Melbourne: Melbourne University Press, 1977), pp. 168–169.
3. *Public Papers of the Presidents: Lyndon B. Johnson, 1965* (*LBJ Public Papers*), vol. I (Washington, D.C.: Government Printing Office, 1966), pp. 396–397.
4. On the origins of the ADB, see, notably, Eugene R. Black, *Alternative in Southeast Asia* (New York: Praeger, 1969), especially pp. 96–105; and John White, *Regional Development Banks* (New York: Praeger, 1972), especially pp. 33–51. The Annual Report of the ADB for 1967 also contains a useful account of its origins, organization, and early operations (pp. 4–27). The memoirs of the first president of the ADB, Takeshi Watanabe, are also illuminating (*Towards a New Asia* [Singapore: Asian Development Bank, 1977], especially pp. 1–45).
5. *LBJ Public Papers, 1966*, II, 720–721.

6. Johnson, *The Vantage Point*, p. 599.

7. *LBJ Public Papers, 1966*, II, 1235.

8. Charles J. V. Murphy, *Fortune*, December 1966, p. 136. In London, *The Economist* carried a strongly supportive lead article in the edition of October 29, 1966, entitled "The Pacific Consensus." It began: "The Johnson doctrine for Asia is starting to pay off." *The Economist* article was the most detailed current analysis of the potential meaning of Asian regionalism.

9. Lee Kuan Yew's statement was made at the close of a speech at the University of Singapore Democratic Socialist Club.

10. A special place in history ought to be reserved for those political leaders who settle old quarrels. President Park of South Korea put it well in a conversation with me in 1965: "I haven't been in politics long, but I have already learned it is easier to keep a quarrel alive than to settle it. . . . But tell President Johnson that despite the opposition, I shall normalize relations with Japan." This he proceeded to do. The leaders of Malaysia and Indonesia in 1967 belong in the select club of those who made the choice Park did in 1965.

11. *LBJ Public Papers, 1967*, I, 13.

12. Ibid., *1968–1969*, I, 26.

13. Ibid., II, 1268.

14. The origins of this initiative are traced out in my *Division of Europe after World War II: 1946* (Austin: University of Texas Press, 1981), especially pp. 70–75.

15. White, *Regional Development Banks*, p. 34.

16. Black, *Alternative in Southeast Asia*, p. 95.

17. Sir Percy Spender, *Exercises in Diplomacy* (New York: New York University Press, 1969), p. 195. Part Two of Spender's memoir (pp. 193–282) is a detailed account of the origins and early days of the Colombo Plan.

18. Antonin Bosch, "The Colombo Plan: A Case of Regional Economic Cooperation," *International Organization* 9, no. 1 (February 1955): 1.

19. Address of Secretary General, November 20, 1980, in *Proceedings and Conclusions of the Twenty-Eighth Consultative Committee Meeting, Jakarta, Indonesia*, p. 110.

20. *LBJ Public Papers, 1966*, II, 1220–1221.

21. LBJ Library, Vice Presidential Papers.

22. In this reaction Lyndon Johnson was not unique among American presidents. Dwight Eisenhower's 1960 visit to India and other Asian countries appeared to have crystallized his rather abstract and equivocal support for development assistance influencing the large increase in the foreign-aid budget he recommended to the Congress in his final budget submission to the Congress. Still earlier, John Kennedy's 1951 trip to Asia and the Middle East radically transformed his perception of the world, the role of the developing regions within it, and the appropriate priorities for American foreign policy.

23. *The Pentagon Papers*, as published by the *New York Times* (New York and Chicago: Quadrangle Books, 1971), pp. 432–433.

24. I made two talks on regionalism in this period reflecting the views emerging in the government: "The Role of Emerging Nations in World Politics," *Department of State Bulletin* 52, no. 1345 (April 5, 1965): 492–497; and "Regional Organization: A Planner's Perspective," ibid., no. 1356 (June 21, 1965): 994–1000.

25. Following are hasty, undated, but evidently contemporary and authoritative notes by Jack Valenti on the writing of the Johns Hopkins speech from the LBJ Library speech file.

> The Johns Hopkins speech
>
> President gave orders to prepare such a speech two weeks before. Mac Bundy did the original draft.
>
> On _____ Goodwin was ordered to take Bundy's draft and recompose it.
>
> The draft was completed on Friday and sent to Camp David on Saturday.
>
> Meanwhile Pres has asked Tex Goldschmidt to come down. Goldschmidt spent two nights at the White House. Conferred with Goodwin and Valenti on the Mekong River project.
>
> Goodwin had inserted: a proposal to send immediately a team of distinguished Americans to work out a food program in Viet Nam. Suggested Sol Linowitz to head it.
>
> Also an economic plan for the Mekong—with a billion dollar contribution from U.S.

Speech was read by the President (leaving out the specifics of the money) to a 1:00 meeting with 25 ADA members headed by Joe Rauh and John Roche. The President read it aloud to the people, who received it with enthusiasm. Even kept the Security Council waiting for a half hour.

When they left, Pres said to bring in Security Council, "it would be good for them to rub shoulders with the ADA."

Friday at 6:00 Pres went to Camp David with Valenti and Busby—Marianne Means and John Chancellor.

Bundy was speaking at Johns Hopkins on Monday and Pres told Bundy he would take over that slot. We were prepared to make the speech on Monday night.

PM Pearson made speech in Philly at Temple Univ in which he "gave advice" to Pres. on Viet Nam—suggested a cease fire, a "pause" . . . Pres incensed. He was ready to call off the meeting. Was surly with Bundy.

Pearson came in with Ritchie, Canadian ambassador. Pres then called off speech for Monday and left open its time of delivery.

Bundy and Valenti suggested calling in all ambassadors and giving the speech to them.

On Monday, Pres. decided [*sic*] to go to Johns Hopkins on Wednesday and this was announced on Monday.

Val called in Phil Potter who made a suggested change in the speech—a paragraph that Potter composed about our responsibility in SE Asia—same as our resp. in Europe after WW II.

Also called in Jack Horner of the STAR. He read it and thought it fine except said that the "unconditional talks" left ambiguous whether and what the Prs. meant. Suggested that George Reedy background press as to whether this meant a cease fire, or any other terms.

Then Pres. came in late Tuesday night with Charlie Mohr, Muriel Dobbins, Doug Cornell and unidentified pressman. He read them speech. I was there. I had put in the "billion dollar" specifics after State dept in his re-draft had left it out (they said it was too specific and we didn't have a plan for using it) Pres read it with billion dollar in—and said: I see you put this back in—that's good.

I wrote in at his request a piece about his going to bed at night wondering if he had done everything he could—as well as a piece . . .

State did not react well to the bold proposals of the Pres.

Bundy and I worked with Pres on Wednesday afternoon—we were to put out the speech at 4:00 pm. At noon, Bundy and I conferred with Pres. He—at my suggestion—wanted to beef up the specifics since we were still not immediate with anything. He thought of Gene Black to head a team to move on the problem now. Bundy agreed this was fine and would neutralize Fulbright.

Bundy called Black right there and Pres. talked to him. "We'll give you a doctor and a nurse and a 707 but we need you now." Okay with Black.

With that we put speech to bed. I edited it more—got it down to about 2700 words, but told the Pres it was only 2400 words.

Potter worked in my office. Goodwin took out Potter's revisions, but we put them back in. Horner and I worked in Pres small outer office.

26. Goldschmidt deserves a special word. He had known Johnson since the latter's NYA days in Texas. In the 1960s he was a member of the United Nations secretariat deeply involved in Asian economic affairs, notably the effort to develop the Mekong Valley, of which Johnson became aware on his 1961 trip to Asia. Johnson consulted Goldschmidt before the Baltimore speech and subsequently, contacts reported vividly in an oral history interview (with contrapuntal comments from Mrs. Goldschmidt) of June 3, 1969, pp. 53–67. The interview, filed at the Lyndon B. Johnson Library, was conducted by Paige Mulhollan. C. V. Narasimhan, the Indian civil servant, then Chef de Cabinet to U Thant, also played a significant role at the United Nations, notably in dealings with Eugene Black in April 1965, in the wake of the Johns Hopkins speech. It was almost certainly in the course of these discussions at the United Nations that the central focus of Johnson's initiative shifted from

the Mekong Committee to the Asian Development Bank. See, especially, R. Krishnamurti, *ADB—The Seeding Days* (Manila: Asian Development Bank, 1977), p. 23.

27. For some those positive purposes, pursued amidst an ugly war, had deep personal meaning. David Lilienthal captures it vividly in this passage from his memoirs reflecting on his acceptance of an assignment from Johnson to work with the Vietnamese on a postwar economic plan.

So many of my friends and well-wishers say what a "distinction" it is to be asked by the President of the U.S. and the Prime Minister of Vietnam (both world figures in a world-shaking struggle) to help design a future for that country, even while war and violence continue to rage. But more of them say, "Poor Dave," and even those who don't actually say it quite evidently feel sorry for my getting into such a "mess."

What I'm about to say, before the work actually begins, may be "famous last words"; that is, after wrestling with this task for two weeks or two months or two years, I may have to swallow my present longe-range viewpoint. But anyway, here it is:

First of all, the issue isn't limited to the ugly war in South Vietnam. The issue I'm bound to face, in charting a future for that little country, is the shape of things to come in Eastern Asia, indeed in all that vast part of the world that borders on the Pacific seas.

This future will require *several decades* completely to unfold. But I firmly believe the coming *new balance of history* lies in those lands of the Pacific.

That this is true is as difficult to see in our present-day agonies in Vietnam—the cost in lives and treasure, the corruption, disorganization, all the things that so disturb all of us—as it would have been difficult to see the real importance of the war of 1776 when the puny upstart American colonies defied and defeated the British (with the "intervention" in *that* civil war, it should be remembered, of the French).

A new world balance of thinking, of influence, of trade, of civilization began with the emergence of the American continent three hundred years ago. But the significance of the emergence of Southeast Asia is even more difficult to see and comprehend, for Asia for many centuries was powerful and mature, and died away; until almost yesterday Japan was literally closed to the modern world.

Now, for David Lilienthal, by a freakish set of accidents, to have a ringside seat, and some influence on the beginnings of this Asian emergence, not as a scholar or writer but as a participant with extraordinary freedom to speak and even to act on the beginnings of this emergence, this new balance, and public recognition of it, is surely a stroke of infinite good fortune for a guy who has always relished great experiences, however tough. (*The Journals of David E. Lilienthal*, vol. 6, *Creativity and Conflict, 1964–1967* [New York: Harper & Row, 1976], p. 364.)

28. Johnson, *The Vantage Point*, p. 347.
29. Ibid., pp. 347–348.
30. *LBJ Public Papers, 1968*, II, 783–784.
31. *LBJ Public Papers, 1966*, I, 556–560.
32. *Firing Line*, taped November 1, 1972, telecast November 12, 1972, Public Broadcasting System. The questioner was Helene Middleweek.
33. Henry Kissinger, *White House Years* (Boston: Little, Brown, 1979), pp. 222–225.
34. Ibid., p. 224.
35. Ibid.
36. Quoted ibid., pp. 224–225.
37. Nixon had clearly foreshadowed his stance toward China in "Asia after Vietnam," *Foreign Affairs* 46, no. 1 (October 1967): 111–125. Movement toward the opening of a serious U.S.-PRC dialogue began late in 1967, with the abatement of the Cultural Revolution (see, for example, my *The Diffusion of Power*, [New York: Macmillan, 1972], pp 432–434).
38. Kissinger, *White House Years*, p. 1470.
39. President Ford's description of the circumstances underlying the North Vietnamese victory is, essentially, in the same terms:

In January 1973, the U.S. finally negotiated a settlement that made it possible for us to remove our combat forces and bring home our prisoners of war. If necessary, we agreed at the time, the U.S. would back up the terms of the Paris accords, and we would continue to provide adequate military and economic assistance to South Vietnam. The North Vietnamese, however, never considered the Paris peace accords as the end of the conflict. They had an estimated 160,000 troops in South Vietnam at the time, and they violated the agreement flagrantly by sending an additional 300,000 men into the south. They also sent in massive amounts of modern equipment and launched offensive military operations.

In the face of this situation, the U.S. failed to respond. Watergate had so weakened the President that he was not about to take a major military action, such as renewed bombings. Moreover, by November, Congress had succeeded in passing the War Powers Act of 1973, which severely limited his ability to enforce the peace agreement. North Vietnam could violate the accords with impunity. Next, Congress reduced our economic and military assistance to the Saigon regime. Finally, Congress signaled an increasing desire to cut off all support. Unsure of any more help, President Nguyen Van Thieu ordered a quick withdrawal to more defensible positions. This maneuver, decided upon without consulting us, was executed poorly and hampered by floods of refugees. Predictably, panic ensued, making the situation worse. (Gerald R. Ford, *A Time to Heal* [New York: Harper & Row, 1979], pp. 249–250.)

40. One of the first historians to try to deal systematically with this episode is P. Edward Haley in *Congress and the Fall of South Vietnam and Cambodia* (Rutherford, N.J.: Fairleigh Dickinson University Press, 1982). See also George C. Herring, *America's Longest War: The United States and Vietnam, 1950–1975* (New York: John Wiley, 1979), pp. 252–272.

41. For a useful, factual account of the evolution of ASEAN in these years, see Association of Southeast Asian Nations, *10 Years ASEAN*, 1978, especially pp. 6–78. The volume was written

and its documents assembled by the ASEAN secretariat under the direction of and with a prefatory message by the secretary-general, Umarjadi Njotowijono. Lawrence B. Krause provides a brief account of the evolution of ASEAN's economic policies down to 1982 in his *U.S. Economic Policy toward the Association of Southeast Asian Nations: Meeting the Japanese Challenge* (Washington, D.C.: The Brookings Institution, 1982), pp. 5–16.

42. Keynote address by [H. E.] Tan Sri M. Ghazali Shafie, "ASEAN—Today and Tomorrow," at the Fletcher School of Law and Diplomacy, Boston, Mass., November 11, 1981, pp. 14–15.

43. John Wong, *ASEAN Economies in Perspective* (Philadelphia: Institute for the Study of Human Issues, 1979), p. 194.

44. Brezhnev's proposal was presented in a single sentence within a speech of some 15,000 words delivered on June 7, 1969, at an international conference in Moscow of representatives of seventy-five Communist parties: "We think the course of events also places on the agenda the task of creating a system of collective security in Asia" (*Current Digest of the Soviet Press* 21, No. 23 (July 2, 1969), p. 16). When later questioned about Brezhnev's enunciation of a collective security system for Asia, Soviet officials referred inquiries to Matveyev's article. See, especially, Bernard Gwertzman's despatch in the *New York Times*, June 14, 1969, pp. 1 and 5. Matveyev's article, as summarized in the *Current Digest of the Soviet Press* 21, no. 22 (June 18, 1969): 14, follows:

> Commentator's Opinion: A FILLED "VACUUM." (By. V. V. Matveyev, *Izvestia*, May 29, p. 3. 650 words. Condensed text:)
>
> According to plans announced by the British Labor government, the British troops, air force and navy are to be evacuated from their present bases in the Persian Gulf area, the Far East and the Indian Ocean by the end of 1971. Foreign policy commentators do not rule out the possibility that the timetable formulated in London will be substantially changed either by the Labor leaders or by a Conservative government, if one comes to power in the event of certain internal "surprises." But this is a separate subject.

This question has been raised here because the plans drafted in London for the evacuation of the British armed forces from the Far East and the Indian Ocean have provoked in certain circles what at first glance seems to be a rather strange reaction. It has found reflection in a number of foreign newspapers. Much has been said and written to the effect that the measures planned by the Laborites will lead to the formation of some sort of "vacuum" in the areas and countries where the British armed forces are now stationed. The London Conservative press has been writing in this vein. Veteran commentators in the U.S.A. are given to similar reflections. Recently even the Peking press has added its voice to the chorus of such statements. In its pages too one sees cant about the "vacuum" that might be formed in the aforementioned areas.

A vacuum is an empty space. The application of this term to our planet is altogether inappropriate today. There are hardly any "white spots," i.e., areas without independent, autonomous states.

India, Pakistan, Afghanistan, Burma, Cambodia, Singapore and other Asian countries are making efforts to consolidate their sovereignty and strengthen their economic autonomy. It cannot be to their interest for foreign powers to interfere in their internal affairs. The question of foreign military bases can therefore be regarded only from one standpoint by these and other countries seeking to protect their national interests from the machinations of the imperialist, expansionist forces: The freer the expanses of the Asian continent are from such bases, the better!

We know that it is not Britain alone that maintains military forces on the territories of several countries in this vast region. American military bases are located at many spots in the Far East and Southeast Asia. The government of Australia, prodded by Washington, has recently been seeking the role of unbidden patron of the peoples of the Asian countries. Some people in Japan would not be averse to establishing themselves on Asian soil in the same fashion. Judging from articles in the Peking press, Mao Tsetung and his associates have quite definite designs on several countries in the area while supporting the notorious "vacuum" thesis. Peking propaganda has solemnly declared that there is not a single Chinese soldier outside the Chinese People's Republic. But what is the situation in northern Burma? Peking has not denied the reports that armed detachments from the C.P.R. are in this area. But the main point here is that Mao Tse-tung forces are making intensive use of the numerous Chinese communities in several Asian countries for purposes having nothing in common with the sovereignty of these countries. This leads to complications and incidents. . . .

45. *New York Times*, June 14, 1969, p. 5.
46. This table is drawn from Ngandani, "ASEAN and the Security of Southeast Asia: A Study of Regional Resilience," (doctoral dissertation draft, University of Southern California, 1982), p. 146. *Naval War College Review* 38, 1, 307 (Jan.–Feb. 1985) contains four useful articles on strategy in the arc from Vladivostok to Djibouti: Edward A. Olsen, "Security in Northeast Asia: A Trilateral Alternative," pp. 15–24; Thomas B. Modly, "The Rhetoric and Realities of Japan's 1,000-Mile Sea-Lane Defense Policy," pp. 25–36; Kenneth G. Weiss, "The Naval Dimension of the Sino-Soviet Rivalry," pp. 37–52; and Howard M. Hensel, "Superpower Interests and Naval Missions in the Indian Ocean," pp. 53–74.
47. Kissinger, *White House Years*, p. 866.
48. Shafie, "ASEAN: Today and Tomorrow," pp. 2–4, captures this linkage well:

> You may remember that following the Communist Party Congress in Moscow in 1969 the rift between the Soviet Union and China was no longer repairable. Both parties went in earnest to compete for the allegiance and support of the local communist parties. In many parts of the world, particularly in Asia and Africa, solidarity movements were being pushed forward hand in hand with widening peace offensives.
> In Southeast Asia there were immediately two very important fallouts of the Sino-Soviet rivalry. First, there was

a change in the attitude of China towards Hanoi and the Vietnamese leadership in the communist struggle in Indochina. The People's Republic of China was no longer willing to allow free passage of military hardware and supplies from the Soviet Union into North Vietnam. This change is extremely useful to the understanding of Chinese policy in Southeast Asia today.

The second fallout of the rivalry was the galvanisation by China of the Afro-Asian solidarity movement which was first harnessed at the Bandung Conference in 1955, and which by 1960 had reached a high pitch in Southeast Asia culminating into the so-called "new emerging forces" or NEFO. At the fore-front of this movement was the Partai Komunis Indonesia (PKI), under the leadership of D. N. Aidit who was pushing the late President Sukarno into a state of "confrontation" against the proposal to form a Federation of Malaysia. . . .

Malaysia spent almost three painful years in a state of belligerence under "Konfrontasi" which was spearheaded by D. N. Aidit. During that period China was devising ways of beating the Soviet Union to the seat of power in Indonesia. You may recall also that for years the Soviet Union had been assisting in the development of the Indonesian Armed Forces and the execution of economic projects, such as the Krakatoa Steel Complex in West Java, and the Asahan Dam. But "Konfrontasi" proved to be too costly to Indonesia. The nation was showing signs of breaking at the seams; and well before Colonel Untung of the G-30s Movement struck at the Generals in Jakarta, Malaysian and Indonesian officials were already making clandestine contacts to bring "Konfrontasi" to an end.

The final breakthrough was made when the Commander of KOSTRAD General Suharto (now President of the Republic of Indonesia) sent a team led by his intelligence officer, General Ali Moertopo, presently Indonesian Minister of Information. He was assisted by General Benny Moerdani, an officer of very high calibre who is now serving in the Indonesian Defence Ministry. On the Malaysian side, I was leading the team; and I had the assistance of Tan Sri Zainal Abidin Sulong, a diplomat of exceptional ability, who is presently Malaysia's Permanent Representative to the United Nations. . . .

Ali Moertopo and I, and our assistants, drew the same lessons from our common historical past, i.e.: that Indonesia and Malaysia were the kingpin to peace and stability in Southeast Asia. This was a very important conclusion which led us to work relentlessly together to create the "entente cordial" between our two peoples regardless of the temporary abrasions of "Konfrontasi." Perhaps I could underscore this crucial point as it is extremely important to the understanding of ASEAN—a development out of the pains of "Konfrontasi."

49. Ibid., p. 221.
50. U.S. Congress, Senate Committee on Foreign Relations, Subcommittee on East Asian and Pacific Affairs, *U.S. Policy Objectives in Southeast Asia*, 97th Cong., 1st sess., July 15, 21, and 22, 1981 (Washington, D.C.: Government Printing Office, 1981), pp. 36–37.
51. Ngandani, "ASEAN and the Security of Southeast Asia," p. 2. In his opening statement at Bali on February 23, 1976, President Soeharto of Indonesia made the point succinctly: "Our concept of security is inward-looking, namely to establish an orderly, peaceful and stable condition within each individual territory, free from any subversive elements and infiltrations, wherever from their origins might be." (ASEAN, *10 Years ASEAN*, p. 88.)
52. In his opening statement at Bali on February 23, 1976, Lee Kuan Yew articulated the doctrine as follows:

The countries of ASEAN have not been ravaged by war. We have, for the present, the greater capacity to forge ahead. Our economies are in various stages of dynamic growth. If we are able to combine our individual forte's, whether it is national resilience in Indonesia, Rukunnegara of Malaysia, the New Society of the Philippines, the traditions of monarchy and Buddhism of Thailand, or Singapore's matter of fact habit of facing up to the realities of life, together, we can do what we individually cannot do as well. (ASEAN, *10 Years ASEAN*, p. 100.)

53. *Public Papers of the Presidents: Gerald R. Ford, 1975*, vol. II (Washington, D.C.: Government Printing Office, 1977), pp. 1950–1955.

54. Ibid., pp. 1953–1954.

55. For a discussion of these developments, see, especially, Krause, *U.S. Economic Policy*, pp. 11–15.

56. The best single bibliography on the Pacific Basin is The JCIE Papers: *The Pacific Community Concept: A Select Annotated Bibliography* (Tokyo: The Japan Center for International Exchange, April 1982). The notes and author and subject indexes are particularly helpful. A useful chronological bibliography of the Pacific Community concept is to be found in Sir John Crawford, ed., and Greg Seow, asst., *Pacific Economic Co-operation: Suggestions for Action* (Petaling Jaya, Selangor, Malaysia: Heinemann, 1981), pp. 235–240.

57. Lawrence B. Krause and Sueo Sekiguchi, eds., *Economic Interaction in the Pacific Basin* (Washington, D.C.: The Brookings Institution, 1980), p. 18.

58. Ibid., p. 17.

59. Miyokei Shinohara, *Industrial Growth, Trade, and Dynamic Patterns in the Japanese Economy* (Tokyo: University of Tokyo Press, 1982), especially Ch. 6.

60. ASEAN's anxieties about a Pacific Basin organization are lucidly set out in Zakaria Haji Ahmad, "ASEAN and the Pacific Basin: Centripetal or Centrifugal?" in *Forum on the Pacific Basin: Growth, Security, and Community*, report of a conference sponsored by the Asia and World Forum (Taipei), the Center for the Study of Security Issues (Tokyo), the Foreign Policy Research Institute (Philadelphia), and the Institute of International Studies (Seoul), May 28–30, 1980, Taipei, pp. 47–54. See also Rhonda M. Nicholas, "ASEAN and the Pacific Community Debate: Much Ado About Something?" in *Asian Survey* 21, no. 12 (December 1981): 1197–1210.

61. The statements in the text which seek to summarize attitudes toward the Pacific Basin as perceived in July–October 1983

are inevitably generalized. Attitudes in each country have distinctive characteristics; and even these are difficult to summarize because the Pacific Basin has been nowhere a major political issue and neither the leadership nor citizens have been forced to take firm positions. It may, nevertheless, be useful as a supplement to the text to set down a few impressions about attitudes toward the Pacific Basin in individual countries.

New Zealand. As a rather isolated and somewhat lonely country facing a long-term racial transformation, New Zealand would find a Pacific Basin organization congenial. It would insist, however, that the problems confronted in the small Pacific islands be taken seriously by such an organization. New Zealand not only bears responsibility for the development of five of these islands (or island groups), with a population of about 266,000, but some 58,000 Polynesians have migrated from them to New Zealand—the equivalent of more than 5 million immigrants into the United States. Quite aside from the domestic problems caused by this flow, the development problems confronted on the islands themselves are subtle and baffling. Having provided the islanders with an education and some knowledge of the world outside, how does one render the islands viable in ways which respect the cultures of the peoples? The population of the individual islands is generally small. Most of them lack natural resources to develop. Communication among them is generally poor. To a degree, tourism is an answer; although, as in the Caribbean, it poses problems as well. The New Zealanders argue that unless a concerted effort is made to find answers to the problems of development by those who bear responsibility (the French, Australians, Americans, and themselves) the islands will become tropical slums, living on welfare, generating increasingly corrosive political and social problems, vulnerable to subversion; for the Russians are already fishing in these lovely but troubled waters. In their view small central Pacific islands belong high on the agenda of any Pacific Basin organization.

Australia. Australia is increasingly conscious that its future is tied up not only with the Pacific Basin in general but with the ASEAN countries in particular. That perception has been heightened as the rate of increase of Japanese production in the older industrial sectors slows down and with that slow-down comes reduced demand for Australian raw-material exports. The newer industrial countries, including those of ASEAN, become increasingly important potential export markets. Strategically, Indonesia—and Australian-Indonesian relations—are moving toward the center of the stage. Indonesia is not only the largest of the ASEAN countries, but Australia confronted major strategic crises involving Indonesia in 1942 and 1965. These are not forgotten, and memories are heightened by the uneasy situation in New Guinea, where both governments bear responsibilities. In the face of its problems and changing external environment Australia is comforted to a degree by the notion of a possible Pacific Basin organization, which would institutionalize its links with its neighbors on the western side of the Pacific and with the United States; but there is also a good deal of scepticism about its likely real benefits and some (well-justified) concern that it might require of Australia, as one of the more affluent members of a regional North-South club, some increase in allocations to foreign aid.

Malaysia. Kuala Lumpur is a major center of anxiety that a Pacific Basin organization might involve increased power and influence in Southeast Asia by Japan and the United States. It is quite comfortable with ASEAN as it has evolved and with the series of bilateral meetings that now regularly take place between the five members of ASEAN acting collectively and ASEAN's major trading partners and friends. On the other hand, there is not only some sense in Malaysia that a Pacific Basin organization is inevitable but also great interest in any possible activity of such an organization that might be helpful to narrow Malaysian interests. The lack of a single, clear concept of what a Pacific Basin organization might do is a strongly felt weakness in discussions with Malaysians.

Singapore. As a high-income, sophisticated, world-class financial, trading, and manufacturing center, Singapore has no anxiety about joining a Pacific Basin club and considerable positive interest in it. On the other hand, its strategic, political, and economic ties to Southeast Asia enjoy and will continue to enjoy overriding priority. It will move on the Pacific Basin only when ASEAN as a whole is prepared to move.

Indonesia. Domestic problems virtually dominate political life in all the countries of the region. This is perhaps a bit more true of Indonesia because of its size and relatively early stage of economic development. Nevertheless, in sophisticated circles, which have rapidly widened from the exceedingly narrow base left by the Dutch, there is a good deal of practical if skeptical thought about a future Pacific Basin organization. As in Kuala Lumpur, one gets the impression in Djakarta that Indonesia would join a Pacific Basin organization which promised clear net benefits in terms of conventional national interests; and there is a pervasive sense that, soon or late, a Pacific Basin organization in inevitable.

Thailand. Thailand's economy is enjoying a momentum, based on internal development, better insulated than its neighbors from the vicissitudes of the world economy. On the other hand, its problems on the borders of Kampuchea are real from day to day and potentially dangerous. They are, naturally, the focus of Thai diplomacy yielding priority for ASEAN, which supports the cause of an independent Kampuchea in the United Nations with considerable skill; for relations with China, which constitutes a major check on Vietnamese behavior; and for relations with the United States, still the ultimate guarantor of Thai independence, despite vivid memories in Bangkok of U.S. behavior toward South Vietnam in 1973–1975. The Pacific Basin is not, then, an immediate-priority item in Thai diplomacy. The leading role of Thanat Khoman in trying to bring a Pacific Basin organization to life could be influential; but the Thai government is most unlikely to move unless it moves in step with its fellow members of ASEAN.

Hong Kong. There is some interest in Hong Kong as to where the colony might stand if a Pacific Basin organization were set up; but thought is overwhelmingly concentrated on the future of Hong Kong itself in relation to the PRC. Like Singapore, Hong Kong has no difficulty envisaging itself as a thriving center in an effective organization of the Pacific Basin.

The Philippines. Domestic political and economic crises dominate Philippine thought as of the autumn of 1983; but one senses less resistance to the concept of a Pacific Basin organization than in Kuala Lumpur or Djakarta, less concern that

ASEAN might be diluted, and a positive interest if the ADB in Manila were to play a major role in a Pacific Basin organization.

Japan. The Japanese interest in a Pacific Basin organization remains positive for abiding economic and political reasons. Having found its initial strong, explicit advocacy counter-productive, Japan awaits the emergence of a consensus, playing its own role in the process modestly and with circumspection.

South Korea. For Seoul the Pacific Basin is viewed not as a trap likely to enhance dependence, but as a route to diluting what is judged to be current excessive reliance on the United States and Japan. On the other hand Korea is not a member of ASEAN and, for reasons outlined in the text (see above, pp. 23–24), it continues to seek the kind of wide, diversified regional associations it hoped ASPAC might provide. It is now an unabashed and vigorous advocate of a Pacific Basin organization, quite confident that it can deal with Japan and the United States without losing its dignity. The government has, however, concluded that advocacy of a Pacific Basin summit was unwise as well as premature; and it now looks to less-dramatic devices to bring the organization to life, notably the tripartite group.

PRC. Given the undulations in Chinese politics it is difficult to come to confident conclusions about Beijing's view of a possible Pacific Basin organization. I can only report a few informal impressions as of the late summer of 1983. I would guess that the PRC has not come to a firm view of its interests, if any, in a Pacific Basin economic organization; it is following developments related to it closely; it does not exclude an active role for the PRC; it recognizes the pragmatic legitimacy of Taiwan's participation in such an organization, and it is prepared to consider, at least, the possibility of a formula like that used in international sporting events in which teams from both the PRC and "Taiwan, China" appear. The formula is based on the agreement of the two governments across the Taiwan Straits that Taiwan is a province of China.

62. *Far Eastern Economic Review*, October 30, 1981, quoted in Hadi Soesastro, "ASEAN and the Political Economy of Pacific Cooperation," *Asian Survey*, 23, no. 2 (December 1983): 1259.

63. The origins and background papers for the first meeting flowing from the decision of the two prime ministers are incorporated in Crawford, ed., and Seow, asst., *Pacific Economic Co-operation.*

64. Ibid., p. 23.

65. The formulation is that of Peter Drysdale and Hugh Patrick, "Evaluation of a Proposed Asian-Pacific Regional Economic Organization," in *An Asian-Pacific Regional Economic Organization: An Exploratory Concept Paper*, prepared for the Committee on Foreign Relations, United States Senate, by Congressional Research Service, Library of Congress (Washington, D.C.: Government Printing Office, 1979).

66. *Hemispheric Cooperation and Integral Development* (Washington, D.C.: Organization of American States, August 6, 1980).

67. I have argued extensively elsewhere and shall not repeat here the case for regarding the world economy as caught up in the fifth protracted phase of relatively expensive basic commodities. See particularly *The World Economy: History and Prospect* (1978), especially Pts. 3 and 6; *Why the Poor Get Richer and the Rich Slow Down* (1980), Chs. 1 and 2; *The Barbaric Counter-Revolution: Cause and Cure* (1983), Chs. 2 and 5. These books were all published in Austin by the University of Texas Press. Each of the previous phases of rising or high relative prices for basic commodities, which can be associated with the upswings of the cycles identified but not explained by Nicolai Kondratieff, required for its correction a large-scale shift in the direction of investment toward resource-related sectors. As I have noted on a number of occasions, it is still to be seen whether the mid-1980s' relative softening of basic commodity prices is the start of a new protracted trend or a transient deviation from an upward trend that will resume.

68. Hahn-Been Lee, "Generating Momentum toward a Pacific Community" (paper presented at the seminar entitled The Pacific Basin Community: America's Failure to Meet the Challenge, the Wilson Center, December 4, 1982), pp. 19–20. Mimeograph.

69. Jean Monnet, *Memoirs* (Garden City, N.Y.: Doubleday, 1978), p. 109.

70. Soesastro, "ASEAN and the Political Economy," p. 1269. Soe-

sastro notes that he owes the paradigm to a suggestion of Narongchai Akrasanee.

71. For a brief but useful discussion of the possible role of energy on the agenda of the Pacific Basin, see Richard E. Bissell, "Asian-Pacific Regional Cooperation: The Energy Dimension," *Forum on the Pacific Basin*, pp. 113–120.

72. Krause and Sekiguchi, eds., *Economic Interaction*, especially pp. 259–262.

73. I shall not burden the reader with the elements of legitimacy and oversimplification involved in grouping the new technologies as the Fourth Industrial Revolution. For discussion, see my *Barbaric Counter-Revolution*, especially pp. 55–62 and 89–94.

74. Tarlok Singh, "Co-operation and Complementarity in South Asia," Commerce Annual Number, November 1981, p. 13. Singh is a former member of the Indian Planning Commission and a major figure in the research now going forward in support of SARC.

75. For the evolution of this subregional development research effort, see, especially, CSCD, "Scheme of Studies and Review, 1978–1983," Information Note, August 1983.

76. White House Central Files, Box 182, "Remarks of the President on TV to the American Alumni Council, July 12, 1966," folder, LBJ Library.

77. Boston: Little, Brown, 1890.

78. Australia is one of several countries of Asia and the Pacific where the East Asia-South Asia nexus is widely understood. (Malaysia, Singapore, and Indonesia are others.) Outside Australia it is sometimes forgotten that Perth is not only closer to Singapore than it is to Sydney but it is also on the Indian Ocean. Australian consciousness of this fact is reflected, for example, in an editorial of August 12, 1983, in the conservative newspaper the *Australian* entitled "A New Sense of Realism in Defense Thinking." It praises Labor Foreign Minister Hayden for urging an Australian naval presence in the Indian Ocean not only to symbolize a degree of independence vis-à-vis the U.S. naval forces in the area but also because Australia carries responsibility for a series of Indian Ocean islands. The editorial goes on:

To many Australians the recent presence of a powerful modern Soviet naval task force South of the Cocos Islands—in our own front yard and near the scene of Australian naval engagements in both world wars—has had disturbing connotations. While the Soviet force was ostensibly engaged on a space mission, its very presence indicated clearly the capability of that nation to project its power into our region.

79. Chapter 9 in *Forum on the Pacific Basin*, pp. 97–109.
80. Leslie H. Gelb with Richard K. Betts, *The Irony of Vietnam: The System Worked* (Washington, D.C.: The Brookings Institution, 1979), p. 25.
81. George C. Herring, *America's Longest War: The United States and Vietnam, 1950–1975* (New York: John Wiley, 1979), pp. 10–12. The heart of this passage is the following:

The loss of an area so large and populous would tip the balance of power against the United States. Recent Communist triumphs had already aroused nervousness in Europe, and another major victory might tempt the Europeans to reach an accommodation with the Soviet Union. The economic consequences could be equally profound. The United States and its European allies would be denied access to important markets. Southeast Asia was the world's largest producer of natural rubber and was an important source of oil, tin, tungsten, and other strategic commodities. Should control of these vital raw materials suddenly change hands, the Soviet bloc would be enormously strengthened at the expense of the West.

American policymakers also feared that the loss of Southeast Asia would irreparably damage the nation's strategic position in the Far East. Control of the off-shore island chain extending from Japan to the Philippines, America's first line of defense in the Pacific, would be endangered. Air and sea routes between Australia and the Middle East and the United States and India could be cut, severely hampering military operations in the event of war. Japan, India, and Australia, those nations where the West retained predominant influence, would be cut off from each other and left vulnerable. The impact on Japan, America's major Far Eastern ally, could be disastrous. Denied access to the raw materials, rice, and markets upon which their economy depended, the Japanese might see no choice but to come to terms with the enemy.

American officials agreed that Indochina, and especially Vietnam, was the key to the defense of Southeast Asia.

82. Compiled by William G. Efros, *Quotations Vietnam: 1945– 1970*, (New York: Random House, 1979), p. 51.
83. *New York Times Book Review*, August 4, 1968, p. 24.
84. *The Memoirs of Cordell Hull*, vol. II (New York: Macmillan, 1948), pp. 1013–1014.
85. In the Carter administration those reaffimations were made in May 1978 in Bangkok by Vice President Mondale; in February 1979 in Washington by President Carter; in July 1979 in Bali by Secretary Vance; in June 1980 in Washington by Secretary Muskie.
86. The reference to the "bilateral clarification" is to the Rusk-Thanat communique of March 6, 1962, which stated that the United States' obligation in the event of aggression against Thailand "does not depend on the prior agreement of all other Parties" to the Manila Pact.
87. India's policy toward Southeast Asia is traced down to 1960 in Ton That Thien, *India and Southeast Asia, 1947–1960* (Geneva: Librairie Droz, 1963). India's concern was brought home starkly to me when I was sent to India and Pakistan by Kennedy and Rusk, April 1–7, 1963, to assess the likelihood of a settlement of the Kashmir question then under negotiation. At the insistence of the U.S. ambassador to India (J. K. Galbraith), I spent several hours at his residence with the Indian Army Chief of Staff General Chaudhuri. He underlined the critical importance to India and Pakistan of the continued independence of Burma, which depended, in turn, on the independence of Thailand. He described Burma as "India's Ardennes." Therefore, he wished me to know and to report in Washington India's concern for the continued independence of Laos and South Vietnam, which were buffers for Thailand and Burma.

I later asked Prime Minister Nehru if this was a correct inter-pretation of India's view of its interests. He affirmed that it was. In Dacca I reported this view to President Ayub, who said that this was, of course, a view common to the military of both countries. Ayub went on to say it was one major reason for the urgency of settling the Kashmir issue. Such a settlement would permit joint staff talks and planning with respect to the sub-continent's northeast frontier which, he said, would not be dif-ficult, since the officers on both sides had been trained to-gether and shared a strategic view.

88. See above, n. 2.
89. See ASEAN, *10 Years ASEAN*, p. 14.
90. See above, pp. 85–87, and nn. 42 and 48.
91. Rostow, *Diffusion of Power*, pp. 265–272.
92. Quoted in John Gittings, *Survey of the Sino-Soviet Dispute, 1963–1967* (London: Oxford University Press, 1968), p. 82.
93. For analysis of this critical turning point in modern history, see my *Diffusion of Power*, pp. 29–35.
94. For a detailed analysis of this episode, see my *Diffusion of Power*, pp. 438–503.
95. See above, n. 44.
96. Richard B. Remnek, "Soviet Policy in the Horn of Africa: The Decision to Intervene," in Robert H. Donaldson, ed., *The Soviet Union in the Third World: Successes and Failures* (Boulder, Colo.: Westview Press, 1981), p. 130.
97. Here is Kennedy's articulation of the prospect which led him to make his critical 1961 decisions on Southeast Asia:

> Before deciding American power and influence had to be used to save Southeast Asia, Kennedy asked himself, and put sharply to others, the question: What would happen if we let Southeast Asia go? Kennedy's working style was to probe and question a great many people while keeping his own counsel and making the specific decisions the day re-quired. Only this one time do I recall his articulating the ultimate reasoning behind the positions at which he ar-rived. It was after the Taylor mission, shortly before I left the White House for the State Department.

He began with domestic political life. He said if we walked away from Southeast Asia, the communist takeover would produce a debate in the United States more acute than that over the loss of China. Unlike Truman with China or Eisenhower in 1954, he would be violating a treaty commitment to the area. The upshot would be a rise and convergence of left- and right-wing isolationism that would affect commitments in Europe as well as in Asia. Loss of confidence in the United States would be worldwide. Under these circumstances, Khrushchev and Mao could not refrain from acting to exploit the apparent shift in the balance of power. If Burma fell, Chinese power would be on the Indian frontier: the stability of all of Asia, not merely Southeast Asia, was involved. When the communist leaders had moved—after they were committed—the United States would then react. We would come plunging back to retrieve the situation. And a much more dangerous crisis would result, quite possibly a nuclear crisis. (Rostow, *Diffusion of Power*, p. 270.)

Johnson stated a similar proposition in an address at San Antonio on September 29, 1967:

I cannot tell you tonight as your President—with certainty—that a Communist conquest of South Vietnam would be followed by a Communist conquest of Southeast Asia. But I do know there are North Vietnamese troops in Laos. I do know that there are North Vietnamese trained guerrillas tonight in northeast Thailand. I do know that there are Communist-supported guerrilla forces operating in Burma. And a Communist coup was barely averted in Indonesia, the fifth largest nation in the world.

"So your American President cannot tell you—with certainty—that a Southeast Asia dominated by Communist power would bring a third world war much closer to terrible reality. One could hope that this would not be so.

But all that we have learned in this tragic century suggests to me that it would be so. As President of the United

States, I am not prepared to gamble on the chance that it is not so. (*LBJ Public Papers, 1968,* p. 488.)

And, retrospectively:

> . . . knowing what I did of the policies and actions of Moscow and Peking, I was as sure as a man could be that if we did not live up to our commitment in Southeast Asia and elsewhere, they would move to exploit the disarray in the United States and in the alliances of the Free World. They might move independently or they might move together. But move they would—whether through nuclear blackmail, through subversion, with regular armed forces, or in some other manner. As nearly as one can be certain of anything, I knew they could not resist the opportunity to expand their control into the vacuum of power we would leave behind us.
>
> Finally, as we faced the implications of what we had done as a nation, I was sure the United States would not then passively submit to the consequences. With Moscow and Peking and perhaps others moving forward, we would return to a world role to prevent their full takeover of Europe, Asia, and the Middle East—*after* they had committed themselves.
>
> I was too young at the time to be aware of the change in American mood and policy between the election of Woodrow Wilson in November 1916 ("He kept us out of war") and our reaction to unrestricted German submarine warfare in the Atlantic in April 1917. But I knew the story well. My generation had lived through the change from American isolationism to collective security in 1940–1941. I had watched firsthand in Congress as we swerved in 1946–1947 from the unilateral dismantling of our armed forces to President Truman's effort to protect Western Europe. I could never forget the withdrawal of our forces from South Korea and then our immediate reaction to the Communist aggression of June 1950.
>
> As I looked ahead, I could see us repeating the same sharp reversal once again in Asia, or elsewhere—but this

time in a nuclear world with all the dangers and possible horrors that go with it. Above all else, I did not want to lead this nation and the world into nuclear war or even the risk of such a war.

This was the private estimate that brought me to the hard decision of July 1965. (Johnson, *The Vantage Point*, pp. 152–153.)

98. For an analysis of this difference in perspective, see, for example, Rostow, *Diffusion of Power*, pp. 492–497.

Index

dochina policy of, 85–86; internal trade in, 18; and Japan, 83; and Japan's 1977 initiative, 92–93; 1976 summit of, 76, 84–85; 1977 summit of, 85; 1984 meeting of, 117; and Pacific Basin security, 128–129; permanent committees formed, 67; potential for subversion in, 87–88; and raw materials, 123; reassured by international situation, 91–92; secretariat established, 84; and Sino-Soviet rivalry, 84; and Thailand, 154; Vietnamese threat to, 87

Australia, 12, 13; and assistance to South Vietnam, 4–5; coal from, 122; and LBJ, 31; linked to Asia, 21–22; and Pacific Basin consensus, 105–106; supports Pacific Basin organization, 95, 245; and Pacific Basin security, 127–128, 250–251; and regionalism, 25

balance of power, 151
Bali summit, 76, 84–85
Bangladesh, 81, 131, 137
Bangraen, 15
Barbaric Counter-Revolution: Cause and Cure, The, 145
Beale, Howard, 4–5
Beijing. *See* People's Republic of China
Belgrade conference, 6
Berlin, 34
Berman, Larry, 231
Bhutan, 131, 133
biomass energy, 122
Black, Edwin F., 155–157
Black, Eugene, 18, 53; cited, 20–21, and creation of the ADB, 8–9

Bolivar, Simon, 45
Borneo, 4
brain drain, 127
Brandt Commission, 109
Brezhnev doctrine, 77–78, 239; problems of, 82–83
Bundy, McGeorge, 4, 39–41
Burma, 131; and India, 27–28
Burns, Jack, 32
Busby, Horace, 41

Cambodia, 27, 65, 81. *See also* Kampuchea
Cam Ranh Bay, 66, 81
Canada, 127–128
Canberra. *See* Australia
Carretera Marginal, 46
Carter, Jimmy, 90–91
Central American Common Market, 47
China. *See* People's Republic of China
Churchill, Winston, 23
Colombo Plan, 21–22
COMECON, 81
Committee on Studies for Cooperation in Development in South Asia (CSCD), 131
Congress: and Paris Accords, 63, 65; balks LBJ, 46; and U.S. guarantee to Thailand, 91
Council for Mutual Economic Assistance (COMECON), 81
CSCD, 131
Cuba missile crisis, 35–36
Cultural Revolution (in PRC), 10
Cyprus, 36
Czechoslovakia, 52

Danang, 66, 81
Daud, Mohammed, 82
Declaration of ASEAN Concord, 84
de Gaulle, Charles, 52
détente, 49–52

Diem, Ngo Dinh, 3
Diffusion of Power, The, 26
Division of Europe: 1946, The,
34
Djakarta. *See* Indonesia
Djakarta initiative, 117–118
DMCs (Developing Member
Countries of ADB), 120
domino theory, 4–5

Eastern Europe, 50–51
East-West Center, 12, 31, 34
ECAFE, 16, 19–21
ECE. *See* Economic Commission
for Europe
economic advantage, 55
Economic Commission for Asia
and the Far East (ECAFE),
16, 19–21
Economic Commission for Europe (ECE), 19, 34–35
ECOSOC, 19
education, 133
EEC, 30
Eisenhower, Dwight, 233
energy: as basis for Pacific Basin
organization, 109–110,
119–123; future require-
ments for, 110–111
environment, 112
ESCAP, 19, 21, 29
Ethiopia, 82
EURATOM, 123
European Atomic Community
(EURATOM), 123
European Economic Commu-
nity (EEC), 30
external investment: in agriculture, 111; in energy, 110–
111; in the environment,
112; general need for, 113;
motives for, 114–115; in raw
materials, 111–112

Ford, Gerald: cited, 237–238;
and the *Mayaguez* incident,

65; and a new Pacific doctrine, 89–90
forests, 123
Fortune, 14
Fourth Industrial Revolution,
124–125, 127
free trade area, 95
Fukuda, Takeo, 93

genetic engineering, 118
Germany, 52; and Mahan's doc-
trine, 149; as model for PRC
and India, 159; and U.S. strat-
egy, 151
Gilstrap, Sam, 31
Goldschmidt, Arthur, 41,
235–236
Goodwin, Richard, 41
Great Britain, 149
Great Society, 44
Guam Doctrine. *See* Nixon
Doctrine

Harmel, Pierre, 52
Hawaii, 31–32
Hayakawa, Samuel, 87
Herrera Commission, 110–124
Hong Kong, 247
Horner, Jack, 41
Howland, Richard, 81
human resource development,
117–118

IADB. *See* Inter-American Development Bank
IEA, 121
Illia, Arturo, 46
India, 10, 131; and Burma, 27–
28; economic character of,
136–137; education in, 133;
future role of, 158–161; and
Pakistan and USSR, 132–133;
and SARC, 138–139; science
and engineering in, 127; and
South Asian security, 157;
and Southeast Asia, 252–

253; and USSR, 80−81
Indian Ocean, 28, 78
Indochina: and SEATO, 23; and
　USSR, 81
Indonesia, 4−5, 27, 84; at-
　tempted coup in, 10; and
　emergence of ASEAN, 15−
　16; favors regionalism, 25;
　oil from, 122; and a Pacific
　Basin organization, 247; and
　the PRC, 26; resists subver-
　sion, 88
*Industrialization and Foreign
　Trade*, 92
*Influence of Sea Power upon
　History, 1660−1783, The*,
　147
information gap, 125−127
Inter-American Bank (IAB),
　46−47
Inter-American Development
　Bank (IADB), 9, 111
International Energy Agency
　(IEA), 121
Iran, 131−132

Japan: ASEAN initiative of, 92−
　93; and ASPAC, 9; favors re-
　gionalism, 24; fear of, 104−
　106; and forming of ASEAN,
　142; and Mahan's doctrine,
　149; and Malacca Straits, 28;
　and Pacific Basin consensus,
　95, 105; and a Pacific Basin
　organization, 115−116, 248;
　and Pacific Basin security,
　127−129; and USSR and
　PRC, 83; and U.S. strategy,
　151
Johns Hopkins speech, 3, 6−8,
　41−42, 233−235
Johnson, Lyndon B., 66; and Af-
　rica, 48−49; and Asian coop-
　eration, 10−12; and Asian
　regionalism, 140−141; and
　China problem, 26; East-

West Center speech of, 31−
　32; and concepts of region-
　alism, 31−55 passim; foreign
　policy principles of, 51; im-
　pact of, assessed, 52−53; and
　importance of Asia, 34; Johns
　Hopkins speech of, 3, 6−8,
　41−42, 233−235; and Kash-
　mir question, 157; and Ma-
　nila Conference, 12−13; and
　1961 report on Asia, 32−33;
　and Punta del Este meeting,
　46−47; supports region-
　alism, 16−17, 42−48; and
　Vietnam, 4, 231; and WWR,
　38−39, 44

Kampuchea, 90, 154; and
　ASEAN, A5−86; invasion of,
　81. *See also* Cambodia
Kashmir, 132−133, 253; and
　SARC proposals, 139
Kennedy, John F., 38, 233
Khoman, Thanat, 107, 115, 143
Kissinger, Henry, 58n; and
　Brezhnev doctrine, 78; cited,
　59; on Paris Accords, 62−63
Kojima, Kiyoshi, 95
Korea. *See* North Korea; South
　Korea
Korean War, 31
Korry, Edward, 48
Kriangsak, 90
Kusumaatmadja, Mochtar, 117

Laos, 15
lasers, 118
Latin America: economic ineffi-
　ciencies in, 45−46; energy
　needs of, 111; LBJ boosts
　regionalism in, 44−48; re-
　gional economic commission
　for, 19
Lea, Homer, 155−157
Lee, Hahn-Been, 116
Lee Kuan Yew, 5, 14; on ASEAN

Pol Pot, 85
Potter, Philip, 41
PRC. *See* People's Republic of China
Prek Thnot, 9
Prince of Wales (ship), 81
private sector collaboration, 93
Punta del Este meeting, 46–47
Pyongyang. *See* North Korea

Qui Nhon, 3

Rahman, Tunku Abdul, 143
Rahman, Ziaur, 131
raw materials, 111–112
Razak, Tun Abdul, 15
Reagan, Ronald, 91, 110
Regional English Language Center, 16
regionalism, 9, 232; and American ideals, 42; in Asia, elusiveness of, 18–20; and environmental issues, 112; forces favoring, 24–28, 141–143; in Johns Hopkins speech, 3, 6–8; and a Johnson doctrine, 40–41; and LBJ, 10–14; and LBJ in Africa, 48–49; and LBJ in Latin America, 44–48; LBJ's approach to, 140–141; LBJ's rationale for, 42–44; and the Nixon Doctrine, 56–75; observations on initiatives in, 29–30; and a Pacific Basin Organization, 108; as a pragmatic approach, 124; recommended as policy, 36–38; problems and prospects of, to 1964, 54–55; slighted by press, 113–114; and security, 55; in State of the Union Message, 43–44; and WWR, 34–36
Republic of Korea. *See* South Korea

Repulse (ship), 81
robots, 118
Roosevelt, Franklin D., 151
Roosevelt, Theodore, 147
Rostow, Walt W.: boosts regional concept, 39–41; and early focus on regionalism, 34–36; and fall of SVN, 89; as foreign policy advisor, 38–39, 44; and a Johnson doctrine, 40–41; and LBJ speech on Asia, 33; and NATO, 48–52; on a Pacific organization, 96, 103–106; on South Asian co-operation, 132–139
Rusk, Dean, 38, 40, 44

San Andres, 47
San Salvador, 47
SARC, 130–139
SEA. *See* Southeast Asia
sea lanes, 129
SEAMEC, 16
SEATO. *See* Southeast Asia Treaty Organization
security: in ASEAN, 144; as a factor in regionalism, 55
Senate Subcommittee on East Asian and Pacific Affairs, 86–87
Seventh Non-Aligned Summit, 132
Shafie, Tan Sri M. Ghazalie, 68–69
SHAPE, 151
Shinohara, Miyokei, 103
Singapore, 25, 246
Sitthi, 91
Soesastro, Hadi, 117
"Some Reflections on National Security Policy," 35–38
South Asia: and East Asia and the Pacific, proposed organization of, 96; economic pathology of, 136; economies of, 133–138; obstacles to or-

157–158; historic interest of, in SEA, 28; and Mahan doctrine, 147–150; and nationalism in developing nations, 36; and a Pacific Basin organization, 115–116; and Pacific Basin security, 127–130; Pacific security arrangements of, 151–152; and perceptions of East and South Asia, 155; policy of, since 1975, 88–92; preparedness increase in, 91; role of, in Southeast Asia, 26; and Thailand, 152–154; and trade with East Asia, 96–97

UNRRA, 142

U Nyun, 8

U.S. News and World Report, 14

USSR, 66; and Afghanistan, 82; ambitions of, 76–83; and ASEAN summit, 83–84; and Ethiopia, 82; and India, 80–81; and India and Pakistan, 133; and Indochina bases, 81; declining influence of, 53–54; international problems of, 92; and Japan, 83; and NATO, 50–51; and Nixon Doctrine, 58; and Pol Pot, 85; and PRC, 28, 84; and security in the Pacific Basin, 127, 129; and South Asia, 132, 157–158; and South Yemen, 82; and U.S. military policy, 152–153

Valenti, Jack, 39, 41, 233

Vance, Cyrus, 91

Van Tien Dung, 63–64

Viet Cong, 60

Vietnam, Democratic Republic of, 128; and present U.S. policy, 152; problems of, 92; as a threat to Thailand, 90; and the USSR, 127. *See also* North Vietnam

Vietnamization, 57–59

warfare: and regionalism, 26–27; underlying reasons for, in SEA, 27

War Powers Act, 90

Watergate, 62; effect of, on Paris Accords, 63–65

White, John, 19–20

World Bank, 29, 48, 112, 136; and future energy investments, 120–121, 123; opposes ADB, 8

WWR. *See* Rostow, Walt W.

Zone of Peace, Freedom, and Neutrality (ZOPFAN), 84–85, 159